HIMALAYAN HOUSEHOLDS

HIMALAYAN HOUSEHOLDS
Tamang Demography and
Domestic Processes

Thomas E. Fricke

BOOK FAITH INDIA

Published by:
BOOK FAITH INDIA
416, Express Tower
Azadpur Commercial Complex
Delhi-110 033

© 1993
ALL RIGHTS RESERVED

ISBN: 81-7303-010-3

Paragon Book Gallery
1507 S. Michigan Ave.
Chicago, IL 60605
www.paragonbook.com

Printed at:
Rama Printograph
Delhi-110 051

Contents

List of Figures   *vii*

List of Tables   *ix*

Acknowledgments   *xiii*

Introduction   *1*

1 Issues in the Study of a Mountain Adaptation: Toward an Anthropological Framework for Population Research   *7*
    Population Studies in Search of a Framework
    An Anthropological Framework
    Timling: Population and the Analysis of a Mountain Adaptation
    Summary

2 Timling: A Mountain Village in Nepal   *29*
    Timling: The Physical Setting
    The Village
    The Tamang House in Timling
    Clans and the History of Timling
    Religious Life
    Administration in Timling
    Age-Sex Distribution

3 Data and Methods   *53*
    Formal Survey Instruments and Procedures
    Informal Methods

4 The Subsistence Economy   *61*
    Resources
    Ways of Working in Timling

vi   Contents

5   Demographic Processes I: Fertility   85
    Issues in Fertility Analysis in Small Populations
    The Experience of Women of Completed Fertility
    Fertility Performance over Time: Measures of Period Fertility
    Proximate Determinants of Fertility in Timling

6   Demographic Processes II: Mortality and the Tamang Life Table   111
    Mortality
    A Tamang Life Table

7   Transitions: The Tamang Life Course and the Household Developmental Cycle in Timling   129
    Talking about the Household
    Individual Time: Ethnographic Notes on the Life Course
    The Household Developmental Cycle in Timling

8   Variations in the Working of the Domestic Economy   157
    Distribution of Wealth
    Organizing Work and Exchange in Timling
    Household Time and the Expansion of the Domestic Economy
    Lineage Expansion: The Ghale of Ganglememe
    Another Way of Getting Rich: A Damrong Family History
    Households in Decline: Another Damrong Lineage
    The Struggle to Break Even: Chamdi Ghale
    Overview of Household Processes in Timling

9   Timling in a Changing World: Implications for Theory   187
    Timling's Adaptations: Spatial and Economic
    Decision-Making, Adaptive Strategies, Adaptive Processes
    Implications for Theory
    Timling's Future

Appendix 1: Inventory of Tamang Material Goods   201

Appendix 2: Household Inventory for 30 Sample Households in Timling   205

Glossary   207

Bibliography   209

Index   223

List of Figures

2.1. Map of Nepal Showing Relationship between Kathmandu and Timling   *33*

2.2. Map of Timling and Its Daughter Villages   *35*

2.3. A View of Timling from the Southwest Ridge   *36*

2.4. Tamang Kinship Chart for Timling   *40*

2.5. Tamang Lama Administering Final Death Ritual   *43*

2.6. Grazing Cattle on Household Plots   *45*

2.7. Household Goats Grazing above Lapdung   *45*

2.8. Members of Ghale Clan   *47*

2.9. A Tamang Mother and Two Daughters   *47*

2.10. Timling's Age-Sex Pyramid, 1981   *51*

5.1. Age-Specific Fertility for Timling and Three Regions of Nepal Compared   *90*

5.2. Cumulative Fertility for Five-Year Periods—Synthetic Cohorts   *96*

5.3. Mean Age at Childbearing for Most Recent Five-Year Period and for Five-Year Cohorts   *98*

5.4. Age-Specific Fertility for 152 Tamang Women and for Women Younger than 45 and Older than or Equal to 45 Separately   *99*

viii   List of Figures

5.5.   Age-Specific Fertility and Age-Specific
       Marital Fertility for 152 Tamang Women   105

5.6.   Cumulative Fertility for 152 Tamang Women
       under Different Exposure Assumptions   107

6.1.   Survivorship of Male and Female Children
       Born to 150 Tamang Women   122

6.2.   Survivorship of Female Children with Three
       Survivorship Curves from Coale-Demeny
       Female West Models   124

6.3.   Survivorship of Male Children with Three
       Survivorship Curves from Coale-Demeny
       Male West Models   127

7.1.   Sequence and Timing of Life Cycle Events
       in Timling   150

7.2.   Tamang Household Growth Assuming No Children
       Die and Event Occurrences at Average Ages for
       Timling's Population   151

7.3.   Tamang Household Growth Assuming One Male
       Child Dies and Event Occurrences at Average
       Ages for Timling's Population   153

8.1.   Lorenz Curve for Distribution of Wealth
       in Timling and Thak Compared   162

8.2.   Ganglememe Lineage History   175

8.3.   Embi Damrong's Lineage History   178

8.4.   Norgay Damrong's Lineage History   180

List of Tables

2.1. Timling's Age and Sex Structure   49

3.1. Tamang 12-Year Calendrical Cycle with Tibetan and English Equivalents   54

4.1. Total Livestock Owned in Sample Households   72

4.2. Household Livestock in Three Villages   72

4.3. Rupee Value for Livestock, Timling 1981   72

4.4. Household Capital in Timling and Thak   73

4.5. Timling's Agro-Pastoral Calendar   75

4.6. Ritual Holidays in Timling   76

4.7. Domesticated Plants in the Upper Ankhu Khola   79

4.8. Labor Inputs (Person-Days) per Land Unit and Percent of Labor by Crop   81

5.1. Parity Distributions for Five-Year Cohorts of Women 45 Years Old and Older   87

5.2. Age-Specific Fertility Rates for Women 45 Years Old and Older   88

5.3. Cumulative Fertility for Timling and Selected Nepali Populations   91

List of Tables

5.4. Average Age at First and Last Birth and Length of Reproductive Span for Women 45+   92

5.5. Timling's Age-Specific Fertility Rates for All Women by Period   94

5.6. Age-Specific Fertility for 152 Tamang Women   100

5.7. Age-Specific Fertility, Age-Specific Marital Fertility, and Woman-Years of Exposure for All Tamang Women   104

5.8 Years of Exposure and Proportions of Total Woman-Years Exposed under Differing Assumptions about Marriage and Death   106

6.1. Reported Causes of Death for Children of Surveyed Tamang Women   115

6.2. Mortality Measures on Ever-Born Children of Surveyed Tamang Women   116

6.3. Infant Mortality Rates for Timling and Nepal   118

6.4. Mortality Measures on Ever-Born Children by Sex   120

6.5. Estimates of Demographic Measures under Different Female Mortality Assumptions   125

6.6. Comparison of Empirical Case with Different Stable Population Model Parameters at Given Rates of Population Growth and Mortality Level   126

7.1. Distribution of Ages at First Marriage and First Cohabitation for 149 Tamang Women   138

7.2. Comparison of Means for Selected Marriage Variables (Tamang Women)   140

7.3. Average Age at Inheritance for Tamang Men   142

7.4. Household Structure in Timling and Two Gurung Villages   149

7.5. Production and Consumption Units in the Life of a Tamang Household Using Two Assumptions of Developmental Cycle   *155*

8.1. Distribution of Total Wealth for 30 Timling Households   *160*

8.2. Value of Household Investment by Category (in Rupees)   *161*

8.3. Gini Indices for Timling and Selected Groups   *164*

8.4. Pearson's r for the Relationship between HH Size Variables and Value of Investment   *171*

8.5. Average Consumer/Worker Ratio throughout Household Cycle, Chayanov and Timling   *184*

Acknowledgments

It is nearly impossible to do anthropological research today without incurring debts to people throughout the world. This project has been no exception. I need first to acknowledge His Majesty's Government of Nepal, the Research Division of Tribhuvan University, and the Center for Nepal and Asian Studies at Kirtipur for permission to conduct fieldwork in Nepal. The fieldwork was supported by a Fulbright-Hays Doctoral Dissertation Research Award, and support for analysis and writing was provided at the East-West Population Institute in Hawaii.

The real work of turning my interest to the Himalaya occurred during my graduate training in anthropology at the University of Wisconsin in Madison. I especially thank John T. Hitchcock for channeling my cultural ecological leanings toward Nepal and for providing the exemplary warmth, humanity, and articulate expression that kept me in anthropology. My earliest training in demographic methods fell to Robert D. Mare in the Center for Demography and Ecology, while Krishna Bhai Pradhan taught me the Nepali language in the Department of South Asian Studies. Comments by Arnold Strickon, Doris P. Slesinger, Ann L. Stoler, and Robert A. Brightman have helped to strengthen earlier versions of this manuscript. I extend my thanks to all of them and exonerate them from the responsibility of my errors.

In Kathmandu, I was fortunate to have the gracious help of Robert Cardinalli and Krishna P. Rimal, who first suggested the walk up the Ankhu Khola. Dilli R. Dahal, whom I met at the East-West Center and who is now a member of the Center for Nepal and Asian Studies, was very helpful in matters of research clearance. He has also commented on much of the manuscript in an earlier form.

In Nepal, I thank most of all the people of Timling—strong, curious, and full of good humor in a hostile world. In particular, I extend my gratitude to Lama Mingmar Ghale, Gompo Lama of Timling, for the many moments of shared food and beer and quiet conversations in the shadow of prayer flags and on the trail; Shelthapa Damrong Tamang, my near constant companion in the village; Meme Norjang Ghale for long talks on my porch in the village and later in Kathmandu; Sirman Ghale for help during trips to the high pastures and Timling's daughter settlements; Anteri Ghalsheni for generous meals of *makai*, *teme*, and *polo* and her insights on being a woman in Timling; Lama Larjon Ghale for late night *rakshi;* and the many kids who sat on my porch cadging smokes and tea.

Others who read and commented on portions of the manuscript include Fred Arnold, who helped with the demography, and Peter C. Smith, who provided insights on the household. Earlier versions of some chapters were presented at the weekly East-West Population Institute seminars and benefited from the comments of those attending. Alfred Pach, David Zurick, Tony McCall, Tlaloc Tokuda, and Christopher Deegan all sparked changes in earlier versions of chapters and I extend my thanks to them.

Finally, I thank my parents, Neil and Joan Fricke, for encouraging me to finish something they weren't always sure of, and my wife, Christine Stier, who read the many drafts more times than she cares to think about. This would not have been written without each of these people, and I extend my gratitude to all of them.

Introduction

And there is this: the chunk sound of stone against stone, the smell of moss and mud in the fog. Clusters of people scattered across the hillside, smoking and talking, keening or staring. A woman has died in Lapdung and she has been brought to this place above the goths and below the forest, a place between two worlds, to be burned and sent to another. The rain and mist are steady and cold and the slope is alive with people huddled under umbrellas or bamboo shelters. They talk in low tones, an occasional laugh drifting from some odd corner, the shaman whose mother is to be burned wailing rhythmically and calling out, "Ama!" by his mother's body, wrapped in red cloth and sheltered by the canopy of red, blue, white, and yellow.

The lamas have finished consecrating the ground and an old pyre is being dismantled and rebuilt on the ground they have marked—that sound of stone again, the grunting of men as they lift heavy rock. Another shaman stands downhill, a stare silhouetted against the mist—wool shepherds' cloak and water beading on it, the matted dreadlocks of his long shaman's hair wet against his shoulders and a face without expression.

The weeping. Confined to the ground around the body and to the family sitting there. Its sound rises and falls in waves and sobs. The lamas have moved to a narrow level spot up the hill. Kanchalama stands with two dorje— lightning bolts—in his hands and the chanting begins. "Om mane padme hung" is the refrain; the whole crowd joins in here mournfully, a ghost song that goes before the smoke from the body waiting to be placed on the pyre.

I am standing by the men building the pyre—watching the faces and hearing the sounds, stone, chanting, drum, bell, stone, low talking. The sound is the thing. Muffled by the damp and by the mist and joining with the scents. This place becomes old to me, older than my time or the time of that woman of 90 years waiting for the fire where it all ends. There is something here that is out of time—in the repetition of events. How many people have died to be burned on this hill? How many times have the grinding of rock and the archival smell of moss or smokey woolen shepherds' cloaks mingled with the sour scents of human bodies and old ghee? I am spelled in the rain.

And I look up to the lamas. Wooden flasks of barley beer are being passed their way. Kanchalama holds six by a cord, his gold tooth flashing in his smile. The Gompo Lama motions for me to join them, to chant and drink beer. The spell is broken. I climb the hill to where they sit and drink beer being passed our way and eat the corn that comes by and chant the refrain to prayers in the rain.

—Timling Field Notes, 19 August 1981

I open this study with this somewhat personal invocation from my field journals to convey two ideas and to frame this study of the demography and household processes that characterize an agro-pastoral people of north central Nepal. My first point is an obvious one, even if it is not often made explicit: in spite of the abstractions and frequent recourse to quantitative methods that readers will find in this study, I hope they will remember that it is rooted in an encounter that was often intensely private. I will describe the methods used to allow me to objectify my findings; nevertheless, this personal component of ethnographic research must be thought of as a constant background to all that follows.

Second, I want to use this funereal image to suggest that this study is, in part, elegy. This is a complex point, not meant to imply that the Tamang I describe are actually dying; rather, the study of a people's way of life must finally be a study of process. The patterns of behavior by which people extract a living from their environments are movements that persist in broad outline for many years. Change comes from a combination of intervening external events and processes over which a population has no control and through the consequences of behaviors designed to work in a particular environment but which must paradoxically alter the very environment to which they are adapted. John Berger, in *Pig Earth,* has written of peasants everywhere that they are a class of survivors. He means by this that their lifeway is one committed to survival and at the same time one that has survived the coming of capitalist and socialist states. It is also one that is being radically transformed throughout the world.

While the people of Timling are not strictly peasants, having retained control over their primary productive resources at least until the time of my fieldwork, they can also be thought of as survivors and as a group whose way of life is poised at the threshold of great transformation. To some extent this has always been their situation. From time to time in the past, the Tamang as a people have modified their lifeways to accommodate new conditions. Until the present, these changes have taken the form of new additions or emphases in the local subsistence regime—opening new land to agriculture, including potatoes in the diet, or pasturing yak in the high country. The threshold at which they now stand, however, differs from the rest in that the people of Timling are for the first time faced with the inability of their local environment to supply the vast weight of their subsistence needs. More important, the options for taking care of those needs outside of the village put them in a clearly subordinate position relative to other groups in Nepal. While in the past they bargained from a postion of equality because they traded grain desired by Tibetans for the salt that they required, they are becoming increasingly involved in an economy that requires them to sell their labor in unequal exchange and in competition with others who must do the same. The Tamang, then, are a specific case of a people overwhelmingly organized for local self-sufficiency confronted with a new need to look elsewhere to satisfy their subsistence requirements. I argue that the most important cause of this change is their expanding population and that this follows from the organization of their economy itself.

This book is an attempt to describe and place into context the processes that encourage population expansion in a Nepali mountain community. I will look most closely at the adaptive strategies employed by the people of Timling and show how those strategies intersect with demographic and household processes. The perspective is that of cultural ecology, specifically that version presented by John Bennett. Thus, the intent of this study is to show how particular strategies of making a living have implications for household structure and the organization of the village. In the course of describing these connections, I will also show how anthropological research can gain from demographic methodology while simultaneously making its own contribution to the fuller understanding of demographic processes themselves. Three major processes will be shown to intersect in Timling's adaptation: the annual subsistence cycle, demographic processes of fertility and population expansion, and the household developmental cycle.

My original motivation for this project derived from an interest in the cultural ecology of Julian Steward and a perception that the interaction of culture, behavior, and environment would be most easily examined in those marginal environments where human labor was still the most important means of extracting a living from the local ecology. Although this broad net includes a range of peoples throughout the world, John Hitchcock very quickly directed my studies to the Nepal Himalaya and encouraged me to learn Nepali and read the literature on mountain adaptation in the three years I spent in Madison before going into the field. The obvious stresses imposed on the Himalayan environment by increasing population caused me to take up coursework in demographic methods and to direct my research interests into the relationships between human fertility and adaptation.

I arrived in Kathmandu in January of 1981 armed with a Fulbright-Hays Dissertation Research Grant, an ability to speak Nepali, and a set of questionnaires developed while on grant at the East-West Population Institute in Honolulu. The initial site of my research was to have been a Kham Magar village in northwest Nepal, some eight days' walk from a remote airstrip near Jajarkot, but a combination of events—including the disappearance of a Peace Corps volunteer the previous fall and the consequences of that—convinced me after a six-week stay in that village that I would have to choose a new location.

Thus it was that I set out at the end of May on a walk from Trisuli Bazaar and up the Ankhu Khola in search of a village that retained most of the important characteristics of the earlier village and in which I would be allowed to conduct my fieldwork. After a week of walking through Tamang country with two porters, I arrived in Timling, a village of 132 households in the rugged country of Ganesh Himal. The requirements for my research were amply satisfied in Timling: its people were warmly receptive to my staying; its size allowed the possibility of doing reliable demographic analysis without being too large for a single researcher; the economy was geared to agro-pastoral subsistence within the local environment.

While in the village, I stayed with a Majhi (a member of the ferryman caste from southeast of Kathmandu) cook in the upper story of a newly constructed house. My landlord lived below. I made it a policy to welcome anybody who stopped by for tea and cigarettes on the porch and operated a minor health clinic, dispensing aspirin and attending to the frequent cuts and gashes that people acquired on the slippery mountain trails during the monsoon. This guaranteed me a steady stream of visitors even after the first weeks when my novelty diminished. As much as possible, I ate the food grown in the village area—potatoes, corn meal, a garnish made from boiled stinging nettles (thus removing the sting), and occasional meat from a cow that had fallen off the trail and died—but the harvest was unusually poor that year and I was forced to pack in most of my own food. I was sick often and had a shaman blow mantra over me. I suffered from leech bites. I had head lice. The fleas and rats were maddening. I could not have been more pleased with any other field site.

Most Tamang men over the age of 15 spoke some Nepali, and I was able to begin fieldwork in that language immediately. Unfortunately, nobody in the village could read and write Nepali well enough to administer the questionnaires I had developed. I had to do that work myself, accompanied by Shelthapa Damrong Tamang, my 27-year-old assistant and friend. Shelthapa helped to translate my apparently absurd questions into Tamang when it was necessary, made people feel comfortable by vouching for my character if he had to, and helped me to figure out if answers were outright lies or close to the truth. At the beginning of my stay nearly all children under five cried and fled from the sight of me, and old women would rub my skin and touch my blonde hair, asking why I made it that color. But the people of Timling soon became used to my erratic comings and goings, and I could move anywhere without creating a disturbance. Interviews became long sessions of conversation around bowls of beer and a shared pot of boiled potatoes.

After I had set up my household, my first step was to sit on the ridge above the village and draw a rough sketch map of Timling, numbering the households so that I could later match different sets of questionnaires with one another. Next I censused the entire village by visiting each household and getting information on age, sex, clan, literacy, marital status, and relation to household head. Marriage and fertility questionnaires were then administered to all ever-married women. The nature of work in the village made this a time-consuming process since it was difficult to pin people down for interviews during the day and I could not simply assign the process to an assistant. To prevent myself from becoming little more than a survey researcher, I selected a random sample of 30 households that I could focus on for the economic, life history, and value of children portions of my survey forms. This worked a little better, but I still found that I could not get everybody for each round of questions. The people of Timling are amazingly mobile even within the bounds of their local mountain environment, and tracking down the person to be interviewed can take days, with no guarantee in the end that the person will have time to answer questions. Or he may be very happy to talk and smoke but find that there are a lot more things to talk about than bizarre questions on the number of children he wants.

The economic survey includes each of the sample households; as I carried out the others, I changed my strategy from the time-intensive one of searching for each designated respondent to one of focusing on the sample when I could but taking information from anybody who was available. Thus, while I can claim on statistical grounds that the economic data are representative, information based on the timing of events in life histories or on questions from the value of children survey needs to be argued from other grounds.

In order to protect the privacy of the people of Timling, individuals have been given pseudonyms for the purposes of this book. Their clan affiliations, however, are accurately portrayed. The village identity has also been protected. While it is known as Timling by its inhabitants, its name is rendered differently on maps.

I conducted research with the Tamang from June 1981 to January 1982, a short time by anthropological standards. Nearly the whole period was spent in Timling, with one trip to Kathmandu in September 1981 to resupply and collect my mail. After my return to Kathmandu in December I continued working with people from Timling who came to the valley in search of wage labor. The short period of fieldwork places obvious constraints on the things I can say about the Tamang (for more detailed cultural information on the Tamang of this area, see András Höfer [1969, 1981], David Holmberg [1983, 1984], and Kathryn March [1983]); much of this study is necessarily confined to the level of quantifiable facts. Nevertheless, I hope that some of the spirit of these gentle, helpful people comes through. I dedicate this study to them.

1

Issues in the Study of a Mountain Adaptation: Toward an Anthropological Framework for Population Research

The life of the village, as distinct from its physical and geographical attributes, is perhaps the sum of all the social and personal relationships existing within it, plus the social and economic relations—usually oppressive—which link the village to the rest of the world. But one could say something similar about the life of a large town. What distinguishes the life of a village is that it is also a living portrait of itself: a communal portrait, in that everybody is portrayed and everybody portrays. As with the carvings of the capitols in a Romanesque church, there is an identity of spirit between what is shown and how it is shown—as if the portrayed were also the carvers. Every village's portrait of itself is constructed, however, not out of stone, but out of words, spoken and remembered: out of opinions, stories, eye-witness reports, legends, comments and hearsay. And it is a communal portrait; work on it never stops.
—John Berger, *Pig Earth*

... to convey a sense of the essence of fieldwork—that tension between sensuous reality, especially as expressed in the uniqueness of individuals and events, and those abstractions with which we try to capture it and give it order.
—John Hitchcock, *The Magars of Banyan Hill*

The anthropologist, crouching near a peasant's cooking fire and sharing corn beer, lives in a world of imposing immediacy. In a village of a hundred or so households, those events that are swallowed up by the grand scale of an urban or national context take on an enlarged, often passionate significance. One night there is laughter and joking with a father-to-be about the paternity of his child. Another day there is the intrusion of sudden death when a hunter loses his footing on a rain-soaked trail. The anthropologist observes, or hears about, these happenings as they occur and gives them a kind of permanency by writing them down.

Events overlap on other events and before long the processes of which they are a part take shape. New marriages, even those as subtle as the quiet regrouping of households, are talked about and noted—as are the moments when an arranged marriage breaks down and a delegation of angry clan brothers must mount the trail to the next village to negotiate restitution; or the times when a son demands his inheritance to form a household set apart from his father's. The anthropologist records the events in hopes of exposing the order beneath them.

Surprisingly, anthropologists working among small groups of relatively self-contained people, exactly those societies where small changes in number must reverberate throughout the whole, expressed only minimal interest in demographic work until very recently (Macfarlane 1968:519). As Alan Macfarlane notes, in a work in which he himself takes up the challenge of anthropological demography, the reason was largely "the blinding effects of a theoretical system" (1976:2) that separated anthropology and demography:

> The first problem is the basic assumption, implicit in most anthropological work, that population growth is unimportant as a variable. The second is the basic difference between the disciplines of anthropology and demography; one is characteristically static and the other dynamic. Thirdly, anthropology tends to be qualitative and demography quantitative. Fourthly, there is a technical difficulty of establishing ages in many non-literate societies. (1976:5)

That anthropology stands to benefit from demographic techniques is hardly at issue. Contributions to ecological anthropology, in particular, make frequent reference to population variables such as measures of density and carrying capacity (cf. Steward 1938:46-49; Geertz 1963). Rappaport, in attempting to clarify the connection between Tsembaga Maring ritual and ecosystem stability, inevitably discusses these issues (1968:88-96); yet his treatment of Tsembaga demography (1968:14-17) is no more than an abbreviated description of the population structure. Left unexamined are important processual variables such as birth spacing or the rate of natural increase. Conversely, Lee's contribution (1972) to a collection specifically addressed to the anthropological implications of population growth (Spooner 1972) shows how the use of demographic measures can add depth to an analysis of changing settlement patterns among the !Kung San. The addition of demographic methods has transformed other disciplines, notably history (cf. Wrigley 1969; Laslett 1972), by expanding the range of questions that can be addressed; this suggests the possibility of similar depth in anthropological inquiry.

Anthropology is also in a strong position to make its own contribution to population studies, although this needs to be fleshed out. A narrow view of anthropology's potential would confine it to merely proliferating village demographic studies in "primitive" or "peasant" societies. From this view Howell's excellent monograph (1979) on the Dobe !Kung might be considered the model for anthropology's contribution. But this begs the question of whether anthropology can only give empirical breadth rather than theoretical depth to the study of population.

Mamdani's critique of problem-oriented family planning programs indicates another direction:

> The political and scientific reasons for the emphasis on overpopulation are, in fact, two sides of the same coin. One follows the other and the two sustain each other in a symbiotic relationship. If population control is to be a substitute for fundamental social change, then the theorist must look at the population "problem" *independently* of other aspects of social relations. It also follows that he must look at motivation as individual motivation, independent of the individual's social existence. (1972:9)

Although Mamdani's conclusions are part of a debate on the definition of the population problem and the sociopolitical implications of family planning programs (cf. Kleinman 1980; Gorz 1980; Lappé et al. 1980), the process by which he arrived at them is patently anthropological. For Mamdani, a society's demographic regime is a manifestation of a whole range of other variables; the context is social and economic.

Anthropology's potential contribution is rooted in its traditional holism, in which all aspects of human behavior are fair game as variables in explaining one another. At a time when the discipline suffers from struggles over the extent to which particular research strategies must dominate it (cf. Harris 1979; Johnson 1982; E. Ross 1982), we must remember that some of the most important contributions may come from the tension between anthropology's humanistic and scientific origins (Bennett 1969:21-22). For an anthropologist, the discussion of mortality must be grounded in the scrape of stone on stone and the cooperation of clan members at the building of the funeral pyre.

This chapter will give context to the arguments that follow by first, and somewhat artificially, discussing contributions to population theory from the point of view of other disciplines and then from that of anthropology. The separation of disciplinary approaches is more a historical accident than a theoretical necessity (Godelier 1977:25-27). Nevertheless, I will argue that the writings of anthropologists offer a productive approach to population issues. After discussing the perspective of this analysis, the chapter will move on to a narrower look at this special case: the Tamang village of Timling in Nepal.

Population Studies in Search of a Framework

Research interest in population took off in the 1960s when development workers from western countries identified a population problem in the less developed, nonwestern world. The problem's source appeared self-evident when, using gross measures of national income and per capita GNP in conjunction with the new wealth of demographic statistics, analysts could document the far more rapid growth of population than of national wealth. Population growth was seen as the most serious inhibitor of development (Jackson 1977:3-4), and early work concentrated on family planning programs in spite of the absence of any well-articulated theory (Freedman 1975:4). Since then, research has always moved in tandem with the needs of administration and policy. It was exactly this early emphasis on intervention without regard for the social matrix of high fertility that Mamdani later attacked.

The best candidate for a theory of fertility change existed in the Demographic Transition Theory, which was based on an oversimplified view of the western experience, a view since altered by historical work (Population Council 1981:314; Freedman 1979:1-2; Berelson 1976:230). Caldwell's (1976) discussion of the theory exposes some of its early assumptions while suggesting modifications.

The onset of "modernization and industrialization" is generally associated with lower fertility (Berelson 1976:230), although the growing number of empirical studies has never clearly established why this should be so (Population Council 1981:315). Demographic transition theory begins with the presumed change in European societies from high fertility, family-centered households to low fertility, individualized lifestyles more congruent with urban or industrialized society:

> The mainstream arguments of the theory are that fertility is high in poor, traditional societies because of high mortality, the lack of opportunities for individual advancement, and the economic value of children. All of these things change with modernization or urban industrialism, and individuals, once their viewpoints become reoriented to the changes that have taken place, can make use of the new opportunities. (Caldwell 1976:324)

Caldwell goes on to criticize the implicit ethnocentrism in early versions of the theory, quoting a number of writers who contrast the irrational, superstition-laden traditional societies with the rational, calculating modern societies (1976:325). The connection with the organic, developmental analogy that has been the mainstream of western social thought since the Greeks (Nisbet 1968) and which has been criticized by more recent writers on social change (Greenfield and Strickon 1981) is apparent.

Demographic Transition Theory is more observation than explanation; the rise or fall of a particular explanatory scheme affects only the extent to which it can be used as a template for the experience of all societies. Rather than a mold into which we hammer all experience, we need a theory that can explain a whole range of transitions (McNicoll 1980:441; Freedman 1975:5). Since earlier versions of the theory proved unsatisfactory, the most important new insight has been that people everywhere behave rationally (Caldwell 1976:326). Even this narrowing of first principles, however, leaves room for a range of complementary and antagonistic emphases.

For example, the micro-economic approaches of Becker (1960) and Easterlin (1978), although motivated by similar faith in economic models, have only recently converged (Sanderson 1976). Easterlin has tended to give room to such variables as changing tastes and a generally wider range of sociological variables. Yet NcNicoll (1978:684) suggests that all such approaches are weak in their handling of institutions and the power structure within a decision-making environment.

National-level analysis has tended to be based on these more economic approaches, and the divergent views of Mueller (1976), who worked at this level, and Nag (1978:8), an anthropologist more concerned with village experience, may stem from their orientation to different research environments. Neither Easterlin's nor Becker's approach may be entirely appropriate to the village setting.

Approaches much more applicable to the community include the work of Caldwell and his students (Caldwell 1976, 1978; Ware 1978), Cain (1981, 1982), and the value of children studies sponsored by the East-West Population Institute (Fawcett 1972; Arnold et al. 1975; Bulatao 1979). These approaches all inform one another and have much in common with those that come more directly from the anthropological tradition. Caldwell and Cain, in particular, make much use of the anthropological literature, while the value of children literature is hardly confined to a single discipline. Fawcett's (1972) collection includes contributions from anthropology, psychology, and economics, for example. In addition, McNicoll's (1980) theoretical suggestions are grounded in the same complex social matrix that motivates the anthropological perspective.

Caldwell's Approach

Caldwell's perspective derives from his efforts to explain the demographic transition from high to low fertility in the Yoruba community of Nigeria. He uses his first major theoretical statement to criticize the failure of earlier explanations of this transition on the basis of their ethnocentrism, assumptions that industrialization and urbanization must necessarily precede development, and confusion about the overlap between modernization and westernization (1976:325-28). The first step toward an explanation, Caldwell argues, is to assume that high fertility is rational in certain settings (1976:326). From there, it is only necessary to work from actual observation of a high fertility society in the transition process to determine the components of this rationality.

Caldwell's supporting arguments are complex and difficult to summarize, but he makes use of the literature from all the social sciences to arrive at his propositions. A basic point is that the family—defined as those groups of close relatives who share economic activities and obligations, whether or not they are co-resident—is the basic context of fertility decision-making. Rationality must be defined in terms of relationships within the family.

Second, based on a fertility and family focus, two types of society exist:

> one of stable high fertility, where there would be no net economic gain accruing to the family (or to those dominant within it) from lower fertility levels, and the other in which economic rationality alone would dictate zero reproduction. The former is characterized by "net wealth flows" from younger to older generations, and the latter by flows in the opposite direction. These flows are defined to embrace all economic benefits both present and anticipated over a lifetime. (1978:553)

Within the first type, Caldwell identifies "primitive" and "traditional" components, apparently to distinguish more pristine from more changed Yoruba groups, since their organizational and structural supports for high fertility are virtually identical (1976:338-42). The values of children within this high fertility society are not confined to their economic contribution but ramify throughout the society into politics, lineage status, and psychological well-being:

> such disaggregation is a product of external observation or, even more significantly, of hindsight. In relatively unchanging societies no one sees these separate bonuses conferred by fertility. The society is made by a seamless cloth. . . . Indeed, the respondent's ability to see clearly the separate aspects of children's value shows that the old system is already crumbling and that children's roles are not as certain as before. (1976:343)

For Caldwell, the context of high fertility is a whole way of living, in which the familial mode of production includes the integration of ideology, the extended family, and economic relations.

A third proposition is that pre-transition societies are characterized by sex and age hierarchies in which older males dominate the economic decision-making environment. This translates into fertility decision-making, as well, through control of such intermediate fertility variables as the age of marriage and the practice of contraception before and after marriage (1978:557). From the point of view of older males in a society where intergenerational wealth flows in their direction, there is no disadvantage to high fertility. Indeed, there are a great many benefits.

Finally, the transition from high to low fertility is attributed to the familial mode of production giving way to capitalist production. This is not to say that industrialization must precede the change:

> It is not the factories and the steel mills that count in the reduction of fertility; it is the replacement of a system in which material advantage accruing from production and reproduction flows to people who can control or influence reproduction by a system in which those with economic power either gain no advantage from reproduction or cannot control it. This usually occurs only with the collapse of familial production, although it can follow fundamental changes in the balance of material advantage and decision-making within the family. (1978:568)

Caldwell identifies this change in mode of production and the ideology of high fertility as westernization, a process that he stresses is rooted in the overwhelming power of the west rather than in any inherent behavioral superiority (1976:356; 1978:571). The peasant familial mode of production is no longer stable according to Caldwell; among the contributors to the transitional environment are increasing opportunities for wage labor, expanding educational opportunity, and the lure of household consumption goods (1978:571).

Reaction to Caldwell

In addition to spurring new research into the structural supports for high fertility (T. Hull 1975; V. Hull 1980; Ware 1978), Caldwell's work has provoked a number of critiques (Cain 1982, 1981; Thadani 1978). Although he must be credited with a major impact on the way people think about fertility in the developing world, problems with the specifics of his hypotheses have been brought to light. Cain (1982:159-60), for example, makes the point that too much hinges on the Yoruba experience to make for safe generalization. Indeed, Caldwell argues that his model is applicable to at least sub-Saharan Africa and the arc of countries from Morocco to Bangladesh (1978:554).

Cain finds four other problems with the model (1982:160) in addition to Caldwell's overstatement. First, where Caldwell emphasizes the extended family network in pre-transitional societies, Cain feels that the relative independence of the nuclear unit is an empirical problem to be settled anew in each instance. Secondly, Caldwell lays great stress on intergenerational hierarchy and antagonistic interests within the family. While there may be some truth to this, Cain submits that the importance of factors advantageous to the whole nuclear unit is ignored. Thirdly, although Cain and Caldwell agree that sexual stratification within the family supports high fertility, they disagree on how the mechanism operates. Caldwell tends to emphasize the control of intermediate fertility variables by older males while Cain stresses that female dependence encourages them to bear children as security against the possible loss of a husband. Lastly, Cain suggests that an alternative consequence of the extended family network is that it could just as well lower fertility by de-emphasizing the need for children as social security.

Cain's approach is to be more situation-specific than Caldwell by suggesting that each case be evaluated before determining the operable constraints on fertility within the familial mode of production.

> The value of children as a source of insurance will be highest in poor settings with a harsh environment of risk, where more effective forms of insurance do not exist. If the possible consequences of inadequate insurance in such settings include loss of all assets or death from starvation, children may indeed be "priceless." If, however, the environmental risk is more benign, the need for insurance in any form will be smaller; and if reliable alternative sources of insurance exist, the security value of children is also likely to be lower. (1982:167)

These environments of risk are determined by a combination of natural factors that threaten the subsistence economy and socio-political factors such as threats of war or lawlessness from minimal administrative development. Caldwell is given credit for mentioning the insurance aspects of children (security in old age, etc.), but he is criticized for stressing the opportunities (immediate economic advantages) provided by them instead (Cain 1982:166).

Thadani provides a complementary criticism: putting the argument into a theoretical perspective, she argues that Caldwell relies ultimately on a diffusion model to explain the acceptance of western family ideology. This leaves unanswered the question of just how the mechanism of acceptance works. Thadani is also uncomfortable with the weight that Caldwell gives to the normative factors in his analysis (Thadani 1978:478-81). Thus Caldwell fails to come up with an adequate explanation in Thadani's view because he misses the interplay between infrastructure and superstructure (1978:492) and relies too heavily on the fertility transition in Europe as a model for developing societies (1978:489). Finally, Thadani criticizes all approaches that fail to pay explicit attention to social organization, especially lateral connections between households, in each setting (1980).

McNicoll's work also stands as an implicit criticism of Caldwell. For example, McNicoll is able to write that population studies are still without a theory of fertility—"a coherent body of analyses linking a characterization of society and economy, aggregate or local, to individual fertility decisions and outcomes, able to withstand scrutiny against the empirical record" (1980:441). The timing of this statement, after Caldwell's two most programmatic expositions, suggests that something more than a reworking of transition theory is needed.

McNicoll wishes to retain the complexity of fertility decision-making while giving it order through explanation. Consumer demand theorists who simply link fertility decisions to a few variables are far too reductionist from his point of view (1980:442). Like Caldwell and his critics, McNicoll is interested in the social matrix of fertility, and like Cain, he is interested in explaining the important decision-making variables as they exist in each setting (1980:442-43). His solution is to look at rationality as a process of bounded decision-making in which institutions constrain the alternatives that individuals may choose from:

> These constraints enter not (or not alone) as direct costs of the search for information nor, at least in the conventional elusive meaning of the term, as psychic costs, but as an outcome of the structuring of the decision environment facing individuals set up by the surrounding institutional forms and cultural patterns. The immediate institutional setting in which fertility decisions are made hence comes directly into play. (1980:442-43)

This concern with the decision-making environment is consistent with earlier statements (1975, 1978) in which McNicoll posited the value of community-level policy and criticized simple cost-benefit analysis. Thus fertility is a process, parts of which are involuntary or by-products of other decisions, parts of which are normative, and parts of which are up to the individual (1978:684; 1980:443). These components need to be separated in any explanation.

Value of Children (VOC)

While it is true that all perspectives starting from the assumption of rationality must have a value of children component to their reasoning, the most explicit attempt to get at the psychological basis is the Value of Children project sponsored by the East-West Population Institute (Fawcett 1972; Arnold et al. 1975). The VOC project begins with the recognition that some part of this process must include the filter of individual perceptions. Fawcett (1980:x) writes that the motive behind the project was to gather information on the relationships between these perceptions, family size preferences, and actual fertility. At the time of the 1972 conference on the value of children, little attention had been paid to these relationships.

The VOC project provided a large body of data on perceived child values within a cross-national sample. Some important points were made. First, the psychological aspects of fertility decision-making are conceived as a component of the explanation of fertility, "an important link in the chain of events through which general social and economic changes are related to fertility changes" (Arnold et al. 1975:1). These aspects are part of the mechanism by which other factors influence actual fertility (Bulatao 1980:17); as a part of the larger explanation of fertility behavior, there is no presumption that ideational factors have precedence in the fertility transition. Second, some of the results of the study support the assumption that fertility decision-making in peasant populations is rational. For example, in all countries the expectations of economic benefits or help from children were higher in the rural than in urban populations (Arnold et al. 1975:42). Lastly, the VOC study shows important correlations between psychological variables and fertility and family planning indices (Arnold et al. 1975:137). Even without proof of direct causal relationships, these findings underline McNicoll's point about the complexity of the process.

An Anthropological Framework

Asserting that anthropology has a contribution to make is not to suppose that it possesses a coherent theoretical package on the order of a Kuhnian paradigm (Kuhn 1962). Anthropology has been characterized as "preparadigmatic" by a number of writers (cf. Stocking 1968:7-10; Martin 1972; Leone 1972), and some of the fiercest theoretical battles have been waged by those who consider this a disciplinary weakness (Harris 1979; E. Ross 1982). This study proceeds from a different perspective, one that considers the competing approaches in anthropology as a source of strength. Thus the questions that will be answered here fall into the domain of cultural ecology, one tradition among many that coexist in anthropology (Johnson 1982:418). The kinds of questions that will be asked stem from a concern with process; before getting into these, I will briefly review some of the main trends in anthropological thinking on population.

Trends in Anthropological Demography

Early anthropological writing treated population variables as another aspect of human culture, something to be described as a part of the background in which aspects of more direct concern were embedded. The first work to see fertility as a part of the causal matrix was a part of the functionalist tradition. Early reviews of fertility (Carr-Saunders 1922; Ford 1945) are noteworthy for their emphasis on population limitation in pre-industrial societies. Lorimer (1954:19) later criticized the implicit equilibrium approach of these earlier studies and suggested that research into the functional relationships among social institutions would be more valuable than the focus on social factors and economic adaptation in environments. Yet Lorimer's hypotheses (1954:247-48) fail to explore the operating mechanisms that would associate social organization with high or low fertility.

An important work from outside of anthropology (Davis and Blake 1956) suggested a framework for looking at the causes of a particular fertility regime and has been used by anthropologists from Moni Nag (1962) to more recent work (Macfarlane 1976; J. Ross 1981). Nag's attempt was the first systematically to relate intermediate fertility variables and social structure to actual fertility, and it brought anthropology closer to a causal explanation of fertility. He demonstrated the considerable variation in pre-industrial fertility (1962:142) and implied that the most significant factors affecting fertility may not be consciously connected to the desire to have or limit births (1962:149). In spite of its advance over earlier studies, Nag's analysis was seriously limited by the lack of detailed data.

Anthropological demography began to expand in earnest only after 1970 with the convergence of three trends. One of these was the growth of methodological sophistication motivated by the needs of physical anthropologists and archaeologists. In particular, the work of Weiss (1972, 1973, 1975, 1976) and Weiss and Smouse (1976) has provided theoretical justification for applying stable population models to small populations. Nancy Howell's work with the Dobe !Kung, in addition to supporting the possibility of demographic fieldwork (1974, 1976a), also contributed to the development of field methods for data collection (1976b, 1979). Work in other village and band societies has also contributed to this expansion of techniques (Lauro 1979; Fix 1977; Roth 1981; Wood et al. 1985).

A second trend includes the criticisms of family planning programs already mentioned, coupled with the awareness of their inadequacy by funding agencies themselves (Population Council 1978:79). Mamdani's (1972) work was one of the earlier anthropological critiques, but other examples include the work of Polgar (1975b, 1972) and other writings in a collection he edited (1975a). Ben White's research in Java (1976) challenges the assumptions of classic Demographic Transition Theory by showing that colonial contact and capitalization of indigenous populations can actually accelerate population growth by increasing the demand for children.

The third trend, ecological anthropology, possessed a longstanding interest in population that became activated with these other developments. Ecological analysis has always focused on subsistence behavior within an environmental context, and demographic variables were always seen as a part of the relationship. Steward writes that ecological analysis:

> requires consideration of the density and distribution of the population, of the role of the sexes, the family and communal groups in hunting, fishing, and seed gathering, of the territory covered and the time required for different economic pursuits, and of the size, distribution, and degree of permanency of villages. (1938:2)

He later even more explicitly stated that cultural ecology needed to determine how much exploitive behavior influenced other aspects of culture, including "demography, settlement pattern, kinship structures, land tenure," and land use (1955:41-42).

This focus on production began to take on more explicit demographic trappings after Boserup's thesis (1965) that population growth gave rise to agricultural intensification. The lively debate on the role of population variables in social change was joined by anthropologists and archaeologists and continues to the present (Spooner and Netting 1972; Spooner 1972; Polgar 1975b, Cohen 1977; Netting and Elias 1980).

Cultural ecology has long possessed the potential for contributing to population studies because of its general perspective on all human behavior. Where Caldwell initiated research into the sociocultural matrix of fertility behavior in population studies, anthropology has carried the theoretical justification for such study within its ecological tradition. The interest awaited the development of methods to become manifest.

In spite of this, no well-articulated theory of population exists for ready transfer to population studies. Nor does this imply that the perspectives of Caldwell, Cain, and McNicoll are without value for anthropology. Even within ecological anthropology a number of viewpoints vie for prominence (Keesing 1974). I am suggesting here that the ecological tradition espoused by Bennett (1969, 1976a, 1976b) and elaborated by others (Barlett 1980; Orlove 1980) provides a useful framework for tying population variables into the study of village society.

The Adaptive Context

Cultural ecology directs our attention to the problem of human survival within specific environments. Where earlier studies of the relationship conceived of the environment merely as a limiting factor in human cultural expression (Kroeber 1939), Steward opened the door to more dynamic analyses (Netting 1977:6) in which the interaction between environment and human behavior became important. Nevertheless, there was a tendency to stress the equilibrium aspect of cultural adaptation to environments, as with Rappaport's (1968) study of Tsembaga Maring ritual. This was criticized by Friedman (1975) and Salisbury (1975). Non-equilibrium studies of sociocultural change arose out of the interests of archaeologists in describing the move from simple to complex forms of social organization (cf. Sanders and Price 1968; Flannery 1972) and in explaining the transition from hunting and gathering to agriculture (Cohen 1977). These archaeological studies usefully employed the concept of adaptation to explain large-scale changes in social organization and modes of subsistence through time. But a fuller understanding of social process requires concepts that can explain both the apparent existence of societies in balanced relationships with their environments and the changing behavior observed in the historical and archaeological record.

What was needed was a transformation akin to the change from "typological" to "population" thinking identified by Ernst Mayr to explain the impact of Darwin on the biological sciences (1959:2-3; 1970:3-5). Typological thinking concentrates on defining classes and assigning individuals to a particular category on the basis of how closely they approach the ideal, while population thinking stresses variation and the individuals that make up a population—a collective description of individuals must be statistical (1959:2).

Mainstream social thought in the west has tended to be typological (Nisbet 1968; Richerson 1977; Greenfield and Strickon 1981), pursuing the analogy of a developing organism to explain social change. Thus, within the society, considered as analogous to an individual, there was no place for variation. One outcome was to attribute goal-directed behavior to whole societies (cf. White 1949) in discussions of cultural change. Richerson (1977) has pointed out the teleological fallacy of assigning such behavior to entities above the decision-making unit itself. While it is possible to speak abstractly of societies in adaptation with their environments, it is more accurate to relate the individual strategies of people seeking to attain specific ends.

Adaptation as an ordering principle must incorporate variation and differential selection (Kirch 1980; Dunnell 1980). Not only are equilibrium models of adaptation unrealistic (Vayda and McCay 1975), but the anthropological use of such models has tended to slight goal-directed and problem-solving aspects of behavior (Bennett 1976a; Jochim 1981:13-31).

In this study, I will be using adaptation to refer to the process "by which behavior is fashioned in such a way as to attain certain ends" (Brush 1977:xii). This parallels Bennett's use (1969:14). Like Bennett, I will distinguish between adaptive strategies, those patterns formed by the many separate adjustments of people to obtain and use resources, and adaptive processes, the long-term changes that result from these choices.

At the level of decision-making, individual adjustments can be thought of as strategic behavior (Bennett 1976b:272) or individual coping to achieve immediate ends. At this level, the decision-making approach of Barth (1967) is appropriate. As Barlett (1980:549) writes, the adaptive framework allows us to integrate concerns with institutions and processes with the emphasis on individual choice and strategic behavior. Institutionalized behavior is, in part, a set of proven solutions to past problems. Its continued existence depends on its continued success.

Adaptation at any level does not occur in a vacuum. Choices can be made only where alternatives exist. The advantage of one particular strategy over another strengthens the chance that others will use it. Codified patterns of behavior must continue to offer advantages to individuals in their social context. The process is analogous to natural selection in biological evolution; and, as in natural selection, it is not necessarily the case that the best or only solution to a problem is the observed pattern (cf. Greenfield and Strickon 1981). As Barlett observes (1980:549), the existence of a particular adaptation implies only that enough positive features allow a complex to exist even when negative features may also be present.

To return to the decision-making level, a person makes choices among alternatives constrained by the intersection of natural and sociocultural environments and his or her own goals. Adaptation is not a cyclical or seasonal process but a continuous one rooted in actors who must constantly decide and act. Change is possible at the level of population because repetitive patterns of behavior may shift with the changing constellation of choices made by individuals.

Such a model can accommodate a number of reasons for social change. The factors influencing a person's decisions can originate in any level of social organization. Thus, this perspective does not exclude the possibility that national or international events may not have a local effect. Power relationships that have encouraged a change in population trends in Java are not inconsistent with this model. Nor are the cases where population growth is itself the independent variable responsible for major social change. Since the description of process is not wedded to any special primary cause, the model can also show how earlier choices can have consequences that are maladaptive in the long run. Large family size can, for example, be a reasonable solution to particular problems of survival at one time. Yet the population expansion that this solution generates must eventually force new changes in behavior when the limits of resource availability are reached.

Modern cultural ecology is distinguished from past analyses by its focus on process. It is a reaction and advance from previous neofunctionalist and neoevolutionist schools represented by Rappaport, Steward, and White, although it incorporates many of the same issues of human and environmental interaction. Orlove has summarized the advantages of this approach:

> Adopting an historical time frame rather than examining synchronic homeostatic equilibria or the many millenia of human history, permits a closer focus on mechanisms of change. By studying units other than the local population on which the neofunctionalists concentrated, studies have been carried out of larger units (political economy) and smaller ones (actor-based models). The elimination of functionalist assumptions has had several consequences: (a) a focus on the mechanisms which link environment and behavior; (b) an ability to incorporate conflict as well as cooperation by recognizing that not all goals are population-wide; (c) more precise studies of productive activities, settlement patterns, and the like without assumptions about equilibrium maintenance. (1980:261)

This study is processual in the sense that it seeks to discuss the conditions of change in a single setting while not assuming that this village is without important links to the outside world. In the context of Timling, "adaptation" cannot be taken to imply long-term equilibrium since that would imply either no limits to the resources on which the population depends or a steady state model in which no system grows at the expense of another. Since population is increasing with obvious consequences for traditional production, the focus must be on change. Thus "rationality" is not taken here as the perception by actors that they need to take the limits of their resources into account in having children. It is taken, instead, to refer to the internal consistency of their decisions and the logic of their behavior in achieving the perceived goals of survival. Thus the focus here is on the perspective of the actors themselves, while the changes that occur are the result of these entirely rational courses of action.

Timling: Population and the Analysis of a Mountain Adaptation

The adaptive perspective is an advance from the various theories mentioned earlier because it integrates demographic change into a general theory of society and social change (cf. Caldwell 1982:269-72), provides a mechanism that can both generate new behavior and retain past behaviors, and is not wedded to any unicausal theory of change. Some of the defects of other theories of fertility transition arise from a confusion of general trends with the empirical forms they take. The adaptive model avoids this problem by, for example, not insisting on directional change as demographic transition theories do. The focus is on process and its constituents.

From the ecological perspective, the primary analytic concern is the process of procuring a living in the local environment. Demographic processes become important in this analysis to the extent that they constrain and offer opportunities to people in search of their livelihood. Thus the logic of ecological analysis is to begin with the subsistence economy, moving outward to the most directly connected systems impinging on it (cf. Barlett 1980:549). This suggests looking at the organization of production and the relationship between population processes and those levels of organization most important to subsistence.

Certain features of the setting make Timling an especially interesting case for study. The village lies at an extremely rugged corner of the Himalaya and holds a number of traits in common with mountain populations throughout the world. (On mountain cultural ecology, see Peattie 1936; Pant 1935; Brush 1976a, 1976b, 1977; Pawson and Jest 1978; Messerschmidt 1974, 1976a; Rhoades and Thompson 1975; Guillet 1983; Orlove and Guillet 1985.) In these marginal or extreme environments, the range of solutions to the problems of survival is relatively narrow compared to that of more generous environments. Steward's point (1938:1) that cultural ecological analysis will be most successful where the level of social organization is relatively simple and institutions more closely patterned by the requirements of subsistence pertains here.

The chief feature of these environments is their great variability within small areas (Peattie 1936:79; Brush 1976a:126). Among the factors to which human adaptation must respond are five:

> These are relatively high degrees of: 1) environmental heterogeneity and 2) unpredictability, 3) low primary productivity spread over wide regions, and 4) high environmental fragility accompanied by a 5) downslope flow of materials. (Thomas 1979:147)

Mountain adaptations, of which Timling is an example, have been approached from a number of perspectives: in general terms (Hitchcock 1966, 1973, 1980;

Messerschmidt 1974; Brush 1976a, 1976b), in terms of land tenure and inheritance systems (Weinberg 1972; Netting 1972; Wiegendt 1977; Guillet 1981; McGuire and Netting 1982), in terms of population variables (Macfarlane 1976; Goldstein 1976, 1977; Netting and Elias 1980), and in terms of long-range process and recent change (Hitchcock 1963, 1977; Messerschmidt 1976; Sacherer 1977; Netting 1981). This study seeks to incorporate all of these issues into a single look at Timling's adaptation. The key topics will relate to the interaction of population, social organization, and the working of the economy; analysis is directed toward a commentary on general population issues.

Population as a Determined Variable

Timling's value for population analysis stems from its unique position relative to other studies. Where past analyses have largely focused on societies already affected by western contact or the integrating efforts of national programs, Timling is in many ways an extreme case. It is a natural fertility population—its people practice no birth control and express no desire to do so. More importantly, they are not subject to any active family planning campaign. To use Nardi's (1981:49) continuum from more or less determined to self-regulated fertility, Timling lies at the determined end of the spectrum. In Timling, we are able to examine the effects of social practices not consciously directed to population control or family building. And we are able to do so in a setting where the economy is only now poised at the threshold of major change.

At one level, population will be examined as a dependent variable whose expression is determined by the interaction of biological and social factors. Models for this analysis have been developed following the work of Davis and Blake (1956), Leridon (1977), and Bongaarts (1975, 1976). Leridon isolates the following components of reproductive physiology:

1) fecundability—the monthly probability of conception;
2) intrauterine mortality—conceptions not resulting in a live birth;
3) nonsusceptible period—period when conception is not possible, from the moment of fertilization to the resumption of the ovulatory cycle or intercourse, whichever is later;
4) sterility—interruption or end of the fecund period. (1977:16)

None of these components is independent of the others or of the more behavioral factors. For example, fecundability and sterility are closely related; one way of thinking of sterility is as an extreme form of low fecundability. The close relationship between physiological and behavioral components is best illustrated by the length of the nonsusceptible period, which is partially dependent on the resumption of intercourse.

Measures for these variables were not obtained in Timling, but the general characteristics of each component suggest that women should bear about 12 children throughout their reproductive careers in the absence of other intervening factors. (For a discussion of the effects of sterility, see Leridon 1977:103 and Bongaarts 1975:293. Bongaarts [1975:294] also discusses average times added to birth intervals by intrauterine mortality and the nonsusceptible period.) This is not the case in Timling, where the average completed family is far smaller; the question of how other factors impinge on fertility thus becomes important. Davis and Blake summarized the behavioral determinants of fertility in their classic statement of the interaction of social structure and reproduction. Bongaarts improves the model by attempting to standardize measures for the effects of the separate variables. He modifies the Davis and Blake model by organizing it along a scale ranging from the purely sociological influences to the more physiological, while collapsing Davis and Blake's eleven factors into eight:

1) proportion married
2) contraception
3) induced abortion
4) lactational infecundability
5) frequency of intercourse
6) sterility
7) spontaneous intrauterine mortality
8) duration of the fertile period. (1978: 107)

By examining the components of fertility for which we have data, we will be able to answer the important question of why Timling's fertility is so low. When this is coupled with an understanding of the rest of Timling's demographic regime—mortality, in particular—we will be in a position to show how these variables intersect with the problem of survival in the local environment.

Social Organization and the Economy

Understanding how demography affects subsistence requires a look at Timling's social organization. The village economy will be seen to share a number of characteristics with peasant organization as it is generally defined. (See Geertz 1961; Silverman 1979; Shanin 1973; Mintz 1973; Orlove 1977; Halperin 1977; Macfarlane 1979.) The most important features of peasant society for this analysis are that the units of reproduction, production, and consumption largely overlap (cf. Scott 1976:13; Macfarlane 1978a:105) and that peasant production is more closely constrained by natural ecosystems than are other types of production (Halperin 1977:11-13). Peasants are considered to be more dominated by outsiders than has been the case in Timling (cf. Shanin 1973:4), but the focus on production makes much of this literature useful for comparison. As Greenwood (1974:1) notes, peasants share similar structural positions within national systems but a variety of adaptations define each case.

Nearly all of the features that Macfarlane includes in his definition of the peasantry (1979:18-32) apply to some extent in Timling, yet it is possible to argue

Issues in the Study of a Mountain Adaptation 23

that the people of this village are not strictly peasants. Macfarlane's definition is based almost entirely on earlier discussions of eastern European village society and includes the following characteristics:

1) non-individualized ownership of land; heirs are co-owners and not able to be alienated;
2) the unit of ownership is also the unit of production; growth of a labor market signals peasantry's demise;
3) there is a striking material and symbolic attachment to land; mobility is curtailed, and a person's entire life cycle occurs in a restricted setting;
4) the authority structure within the household tends to inhere in adult males;
5) ages at marriage tend to be young, and marriages are usually arranged because of the strong economic component;
6) these features combine to create little social differentiation within the village;
7) yet there is substantial inequality relative to relations with the outside.

This collection of traits has been criticized on the grounds that it fails to incorporate the role of landlords in addition to ignoring the operation of the economy (Faith 1980). From a broader point of view, the definition's failings may stem from its being too contingent on a limited example. Further, it tends to be overly typological and static, so that Macfarlane is forced to acknowledge that a particular case could deviate from all these conditions and still be considered a peasant society (1979:32). If these limitations are abandoned, the definition then becomes a discussion of a particular kind of economic organization in which the household, or domestic group, is the focus of production and consumption. We are then left with a definition approaching Sahlins' Domestic Mode of Production (1972) and a logical unit within which to analyze the interaction of demographic and economic variables: the household. Orlove's (1977) contention that we do away with attempts at definition to focus on process is then upheld, and the extent to which all aspects of Timling's adaptation approach the classic definition of peasantry becomes a secondary issue.

In terms of process, the important issue is how demography and social organization define the household's development through time. Pioneering work along these lines began with Fortes (1958) and has been expanded in the recent explorations of Hareven (1977, 1978) and Foster (1978). Again, we need not be vitally concerned with problems of definition except to begin with those overlapping functions and to describe the culturally specific unit that fulfills them (Yanagisako 1979). The questions to be examined include the extent to which population variables influence the developmental cycle and the economic context of this process.

Berkner (1972) has demonstrated that cross-sectional analysis can obscure the real significance of household types in a society. Simply noting the predominance of nuclear family households, for example, will not expose the underlying formation systems and rules. A majority of nuclear households is compatible with a system in which each household passes through a stem family stage. Since the processes that impinge on household structure and composition include individual and family cycles (Elder 1981; Hareven 1974, 1978), it is necessary to explore the culturally defined life course along with the demographic determinants of family building. Foster (1978, 1981) shows the strong correlation between population processes and household formation and suggests that changes in the cross-sectional distribution of household types can be a consequence of changes in either of these systems. Meanwhile, household composition, as it changes through time, can be an important determinant of economic status (Cain 1978).

This has implications for the way we look at children in Timling. It is reasonable to assume that if large families were a disadvantage, people would find a way to limit their number. While recent studies of the value of children (Nag et al. 1978) have looked at their economic contributions and have tied fertility directly to the economy (Odell 1982), the Tamang do not closely quantify each child's potential input into the household. I suggest that the value of children can also be sought in the role they play in the organization of village economy centered around the household. In Timling, children are a way of exploiting the diverse environment. The more children born to a family, the greater the number of economic frontiers that can be efficiently exploited by a household—including expansion into the new wage economy.

This household-centered economy, coupled with the reliance on children, suggests that households move through identifiable changes in economic potential with the different stages of the developmental cycle. The fortunes of a particular household are a function of complex factors involving the timing of births, marriages, and the separation of children into household units of their own. The primary decisions affecting family size in Timling have to do with the timing of marriage and inheritance and not with having children. Thus there is a combination of random events resulting in the expression of fertility with the outcomes of actual decisions that affect the demographic profile of the village and are embedded in the logic of the economy.

Population and Long-Term Process

These issues relate to the present adaptation in Timling. In Bennett's terms, they define the adaptive strategies of the Tamang. Population is also involved in the long-term adaptive processes that have characterized Timling's history. This brings up the question of how far population growth can be considered a primary cause in economic change.

One school in the criticism of population policy has emphasized the degree to which fertility is an expression of economic organization. White's already cited work in Java and Mamdani's monograph on village India are good examples of this. Indeed the last section is predicated on the interaction between population and economy. At the level of immediate strategies, there seems to be a strong correspondence between family size and household success in economies organized along the lines of the domestic mode of production. When we think of historical processes, however, it becomes legitimate to ask how processes that are rational within the context of the immediate economy may themselves lead to changes in the adaptive context. Cohen (1977) and Boserup (1965) have shown how changes in economy can be motivated by population growth. The important variables here are the subsistence environment and the minimal requirements of economic units. An adaptation, taken as a collection of behaviors, will be stable only as long as the major constraints and opportunities remain constant. In the Himalaya, the crucial variable maintaining community social structure has been land (Macfarlane 1976:199; Hitchcock 1966:105; the literature tying land to social stability in Nepal is invariably linked to the issue of ecological deterioration as in Eckholm 1976; Calkins 1981; Hoffpauir 1978).

Thus the important question of adaptive process in Timling will be answered by showing how the logic of the household economy and its effect on population contribute to the changing subsistence context through the opening of new economic frontiers. The monetization of peasant economies and their growing links with the world economy (cf. Gudeman 1978) are processes affecting large portions of the world today. For Timling, the immediate impetus for this change is rooted in population pressure (cf. Dahal 1983 for another example from Nepal).

Summary

In order to get at the interaction of these factors, I examine three broad categories of Tamang life: demography, the organization of subsistence, and the household. Chapter 2 establishes the historical and ethnographic setting for the study so that we can know the people of Timling and their place in the larger national context. Chapter 4 lays out the general adaptation of the Tamang in their particular environment and establishes the requirements of subsistence. In chapters 5 and 6, I examine the demography of the Tamang, showing how social practices (intermediate variables) affect fertility and establishing the mortality regime of the village. Chapter 7 brings in the household. I will show how the developmental cycle in Timling is a function of the timing of life course events, especially birth and marriage. Here the demographic regime becomes an independent variable constraining the economic potential of households. Some of the opportunities and constraints that must be weighed in the major life course decisions of marriage and the timing of inheritance will also be presented here. Once the broad pattern of household development has been established, chapter 8 brings in the variations that can occur even in a fairly homogeneous society such as Timling's. I use case histories here to show how the fortunes of households can rise and fall through a combination of chance and choice. In this chapter I also begin to consider some of the implications of these patterns for longer term processes of change.

The final chapter summarizes the argument and shows how the pursuit of discrete adaptive strategies can have long-range implications that force the village as a whole to change its adaptation. What were tenable solutions to the problems of survival in the past are shown themselves to create new problems that alter the nature of the decision-making environment. This examination of long-term processes shows how an economy organized for self-sufficiency can begin to shift to capitalization and what the consequences of this shift are for decision-making. I suggest that some of these consequences involve radical changes in institutionalized solutions to the problem of survival.

The limiting factor throughout this process is the relation between population and locally available resources. A secondary factor is the level of organization of outside groups. In the past, Timling dealt with these people on the basis of essential equality as trading partners; they no longer do so because the outside world no longer needs what Timling can offer, even as the villagers become more dependent on the wage economy outside.

In describing the processes that define Timling's adaptation, I move between two levels of analysis (Brush 1977:19). The first of these concerns itself with the general patterns that typify the village, while the second concerns the experience of individual households. Thus a picture of adaptation that incorporates the inherent variability of populations is presented.

This study of demography and household process in a village adaptation is geared in anthropological fashion toward the intensive description of a particular case. Although it hovers at the descriptive level, its points bear on more general theory. A number of relationships will be illustrated.

First, the examination of Timling's fertility will show that, in spite of the absence of conscious family planning, Tamang fertility is drastically reduced from a potential of 14.3 births to only about 5.4 per woman. The two factors having the largest effect on this reduction are the pattern of marriage and cohabitation and the pattern of breastfeeding. Second, Timling's productive economy is organized to take advantage of a special kind of environment. The two elements of greatest importance here are a high degree of diversification and a precise meshing of various productive cycles. Because the economy is organized at the household level, the importance of children is related to their diversifying, security potential. The third point follows from this: a natural fertility population organized into such an economy means that household fortunes are largely the fortuitous result of household recruitment and retention of new members. The alternative strategies of later age at marriage or inheritance are ways of coping with the demographic hand dealt to a family. Thus the household's economic potential closely follows its developmental cycle.

This describes Timling's adaptation in the presence of relatively equal access to productive resources. But my fourth point is that Timling's egalitarian structure and the close correspondence between household development and economic standing rests on the availability of land. Timling's population growth at a doubling time of roughly 60 years has brought land into short supply. The consequences include smaller inheritances, less chance of acquiring new land by the simple input of labor, greater reliance on the monetized economy, and a destabilization of the mode of production. Threatened are the stability of cooperative kin links, rules of property transmission across generations, and the relatively classless nature of

Tamang society. I argue that this process has been fueled by population increase in a production regime constrained by land availability; that population growth is a necessary by-product of a household-centered economy in a rigorously diversified production environment; and that class formation begins at that point where monetization threatens the utility of kin links. A secondary argument is that relationships transformed from essential equality to subordination to peoples outside of the Ankhu Khola region hasten the process by creating new statuses. When land was plentiful, the most rational course for a livelihood was to identify with the family and the village. A new set of rewards in a land-scarce environment requires new kinds of status based on values from outside of the village.

Finally, this study provides an example from the earliest extreme of the demographic transition. It suggests that Caldwell's perspective is correct—that supports for high fertility are built into the familial mode of production and that the system begins to change with the collapse of this mode of production. Collapse begins with the denial of equal household access to the fundamental resources, and fertility change lags behind economic transformation.

2

Timling: A Mountain Village in Nepal

> ... hair of head copious and straight; of the face and body deficient; stature rather low, but muscular and strong. Character phlegmatic, and slow in intellect, but good-humoured, cheerful and tractable, though somewhat impatient of continuous toil. Polyandry yet exists partially, but is falling out of use. Female chastity is little heeded before marriage, and drunkenness and dirtiness are much more frequent than in the plains. Crime is much rarer, however, and truth more regarded, and the character on the whole is amiable.
> —Brian Hodgson, *Essays on the Languages, Literature, and Religion of Nepal and Tibet*

> In the more rude and mountainous parts of Nepal Proper, the chief population consisted of these Murmis, who are by many considered as a branch of the Bhotiyas, or the people of Thibet. . . . The doctrine of the Lamas is so obnoxious to the Gorkhalese, that, under pretence of their being thieves, no Murmi is permitted to enter the valley where Kathmandu stands, and by way of ridicule, they are called Siyena Bhotiyas, or Bhotiyas who eat carrion; for these people have such an appetite for beef, that they cannot abstain from the oxen that die a natural death, as they are not now permitted to murder the sacred animal. They have, therefore, since the conquest, retired as much as possible into places very difficult of access. . . . They never seem to have had any share in the government, nor to have been addicted to arms, but always followed the profession of agriculture, or carried loads for the Newars, being a people uncommonly robust.
> —Francis Buchanan, *An Account of the Kingdom of Nepal*

In A.D. 640 the armies of Songtsen Gampo, the first Tibetan king to embrace Buddhism, moved south and occupied parts of present-day Nepal, including the Kathmandu Valley and the mountainous country to the north. These armies remained for a number of years and some attribute the beginnings of Tamang (also called Lama or Murmi) history in Nepal to those who remained behind (Shakabpa 1967:37; Norboo 1981). Whatever the timing of their arrival in Nepal, the Tamang are clearly a people of Tibetan origin. Physically, linguistically, and culturally they bear strong affinities with their northern neighbors. Not only do their own traditions have them coming from Tibet via Kyerong, but to the more Hinduized people of the hills the Tamang are still *Bhote,* the word used to describe the Tibetan peoples of the plateau.

Today, the main Tamang territory extends in a broad arc to the west, north, and east of the Kathmandu Valley, although Tamang settlements can be found to the south and far to the east in Sikkim. To the west, the Buri Gandaki forms the effective boundary to Tamang country; the Gurung, another people of Tibetan origin with much in common with the Tamang, are dominant beyond that. To the north, Tamang villages stretch all the way from the outskirts of Kathmandu to the Tibetan plateau. And to the east, the main territory of the Tamang is bordered by that of the Sherpa and the Rai.

Within this extensive network of villages, ranging in altitude from about 4,000 to a little above 9,000 ft., a variety of cultural strategies manifest themselves, and often the best indicator of whether a group is Tamang is whether they call themselves by that name. A significant difference exists between dialects of the eastern and western groups (cf. Taylor et al. 1972; Mazaudon 1973), with many words in their vocabularies not being mutually intelligible. This is only an exaggeration of the condition that may exist between villages from one valley to the next in the same region. The different axes along which variation may run between Tamang settlements include: proximity to Kathmandu or a major bazaar town; proximity to a motorable road or a major trail; altitude; and the ethnic make-up of the surrounding population.

For example, the Tamang settlements of the Kathmandu Valley show far more integration into the national culture of Nepal than do the isolated villages several days' walk from a road. In these villages, the Kathmandu Valley is still called "Nepal" or known by the Tibetan word *Yambu.* Certain features of the local economy may differ from region to region within Tamang country although most Tamang pursue some kind of mix of agriculture and pastoralism. Those Tamang who happen to be from villages close to the source of wage income often work as porters—the "Sherpa" porters who cater to the trekking groups from wealthy western countries are more likely to be Tamang than Sherpa—and some of the high quality *thankgka* painted in the Kathmandu Valley are by Tamang artists.

In spite of all the possible variations in cultural style within the Tamang territory, a number of features bind the people into a single ethnic identity. Linguistically, differences in dialect are not an insurmountable barrier to understanding. Other, more important similarities include their religion, social organization, and, perhaps most important, a kind of stereotyped image that other groups hold of them.

The Tamang practice a form of Buddhism that closely resembles that of the Gurung to the west (Pignede 1966) as well as that of the Sherpa to the east (Furer-Haimendorf 1964), having a common source in Tibet. Tamang *lamas,* although generally not able to study at their own monasteries, often receive training in those of the Sherpa or Tibetans. Otherwise, they learn to perform their rites and to read the woodblock print books from other *lamas* in the village who, like themselves, combine their role as *lama* with other roles as farmer and family head. A Tamang village of any size nearly always has at least one *stupa* (Tm. *mani*) in a conspicuous place and a *gompa* for the performance of Buddhist ritual.

Tamang religion is a complex mixture of Tibetan Buddhist, Hindu, and shamanic elements. Other than the *lama,* a second important ritual practitioner is the *bompo* (Tm.), or shaman, who deals with many of the illnesses that afflict the people and is especially important for dealing with local deities. Although the *bompo* role is of slightly lower status than that of the *lama,* it is an indispensable feature of Tamang ritual life even where they have been most exposed to Hindu and urban influences (Peters 1978, 1981, 1982). (On Tamang religion, see Holmberg 1983, 1984 and Höfer 1981. March's 1983 discussion of gender and metaphor is also relevant.)

The Tamang are organized into a large number of exogamous patrilineal clans called *rui* (Tm.) (Macdonald 1969:138; Lama 1981). Each clan has its own place of origin and deity. Although clan names may differ from east to west, the Tamang recognize equivalencies between certain differently named clans. The Tamang practice cross-cousin marriage with no preference for either the mother's or father's side in choice of spouse. Fürer-Haimendorf (1956:167) writes of a horizontal division into two groups of clans in Tamang society, an organization parallel to that of the Gurung (Macfarlane 1976:17; Messerschmidt 1976b). This hierarchical arrangement is apparently not practiced by the western Tamang as a group (cf. Höfer 1969) and is not found in Timling. On the whole, the Tamang are an extraordinarily egalitarian group with no institutionalized basis for distinguishing among the status of clans.

Historically, the Tamang have had the mixed blessing of sharing part of their territory with organizationally more complex peoples, especially in the Kathmandu Valley. There, the Newar city-states were followed by the unified power of Prithvi Narayn Shah's national capital after 1769. Their less complex level of social organization, coupled with their proximity to centers of power in Nepal, made the Tamang a natural population for exploitation as laborers for those made wealthy by trade and conquest. Fürer-Haimendorf found

> particularly in the hills surrounding the Nepal Valley, that the Tamangs have sunk to the position of tenant-farmers, daily laborers and carriers. Unable to support themselves on the produce of the marginal lands alone left to them, they furnish the greater part of the porter-force required for the movement of trade-goods along the mountainous paths permitting of no other means of transport. . . .
> In these areas of mixed populations the Tamangs are gradually assuming the character of a caste of low economic and ritual status, and it is only in the regions where they form a majority of the population that they meet the members of other ethnic groups on equal terms and even retain the political leadership on village-level. (1956:177)

This process goes back far into the history of Nepal. Northey (1937:14) writes that although the Tamang serve in the British army, they are relegated to only the more menial positions in the Nepali army. Landon calls them: "the hewers of wood and the drawers of water, coolies by heritage and ready to merge their individuality in almost any adjacent tribe. . . . The Murmis do most of the menial work in the Valley of Katmandu" (1928:246). Again, Wright (1877:27) notes that the Tamang, whom he calls Bhotiyas, are noted for carrying loads; Buchanan, in the long quote at the head of this chapter, notes their clear subservience.

Höfer (1978) reports that the Tamang have been able to challenge some of these patterns of dominance in the western part of their territory. In part, this process was due to the return of Tamang who had served in the British and Indian armies during World War II and after. Also important was the return of the monarchy to power and the subsequent cultivation of a national rather than an ethnic polity in Nepal. In the remoter valleys such as Timling's, however, the Tamang are often the only ethnic group, with the exception of small settlements of low-caste metalworkers, called Kami.

These areas have been unable to command the attention of government officials, and they are overlooked in the administration of government functions to varying degrees. For example, Timling has yet to be visited by a government school inspector even though one is required to certify the village school each year. This school, already three years old, managed only in the fall of 1981 to acquire a teacher who showed signs of staying longer than a few weeks. The explanation given by the people of Timling is, "These Brahmans down in the district center don't see us or hear us. We are only Tamang and live far away."

Timling: The Physical Setting

The Ankhu Khola (Ankhu River), with its headwaters in the Ganesh Himal northwest of Kathmandu, joins the Buri Gandaki from a northeasterly direction. In the short distance of about 20 miles, it passes through ecozones ranging from the alpine to the tropic, from an altitude of over 24,000 ft. to one of slightly over 2,500 (Toffin 1976a:34). The traveler headed north in this almost unbelievably rugged country must endure the constant rise and fall of trails as they cross side-ridges and tributary valleys to the Ankhu Khola. This valley is the home of one of the northwesternmost groups of Tamang, and the northern portion has been called the original home of this group in Nepal (Hagen 1961:66). In the southern parts they share the hillsides with scattered Brahman and Chetri households along the lower slopes; in the upper reaches, they are alone except for the Kami settlements, some Gurung who moved in after the Tamang, and a few Newar shopkeepers who moved to the village of Sertang to deal in tobacco and cloth at the invitation of an early chieftain of that village. (See Toffin 1976a for a description of Ankhu Khola Valley peoples focusing on Sertang.)

Timling lies off the Bhabil Khola, northeasternmost tributary of the Ankhu Khola, at an elevation of about 6,500 ft. Although presently a part of Sertang Gaon Panchayat, Timling was historically an independent chiefdom equal in status to

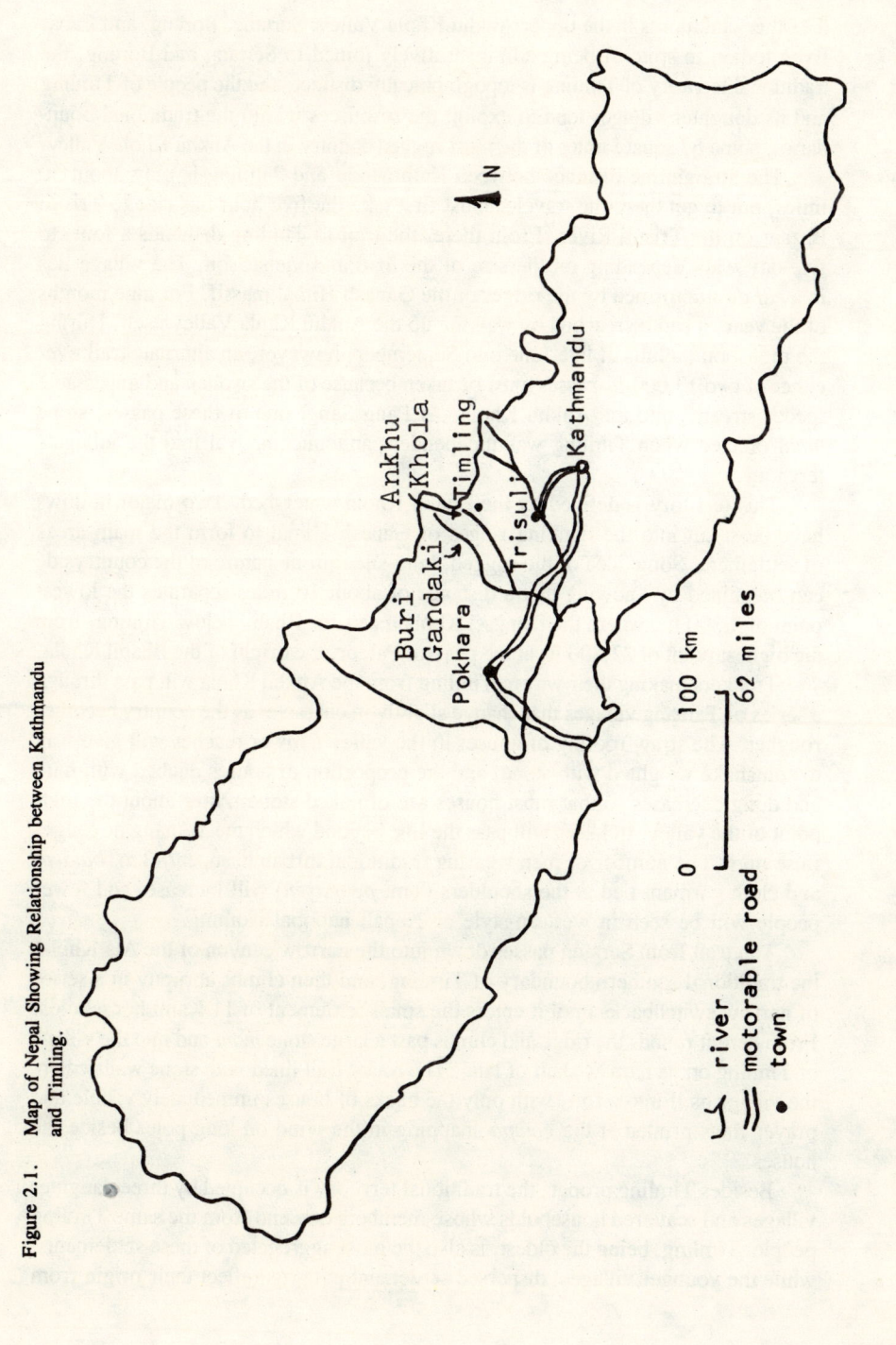

Figure 2.1. Map of Nepal Showing Relationship between Kathmandu and Timling.

the other chiefdoms in the upper Ankhu Khola Valley: Sertang, Borang, and Laba. Even today, in spite of being administratively joined to Sertang and Borang, the traditional territory of Timling is topographically distinct, and the people of Timling and its daughter villages tend to exploit the resources within the traditional boundaries, some 67 square miles of the most rugged country in the Ankhu Khola Valley.

The straightline distance between Kathmandu and Timling is only about 50 miles, but to get there the traveler must first take the five-hour bus ride to Trisuli Bazaar on the Trisuli River. From there, the trail to Timling demands a four- to five-day walk depending on the size of the load and the season. The village lies in a *cul de sac* formed by the ridges of the Ganesh Himal massif. For nine months of the year, it can be reached by walking up the Ankhu Khola Valley itself. During the monsoon months of late June into September, however, an alternate trail over either of two 13,000-ft. passes must be taken because of the swollen and impassable feeder streams into the Ankhu Khola. At Pang Sang, one of these passes, stone *mani* erected when Timling was independent announce arrival into the village's territory.

This territory is defined by the Bhabil Khola watershed. Two major hollows have been cut into the flanking ridges of Ganesh Himal to form the main areas of settlement. Some idea of the rugged, land-slide prone nature of the countryside can be gained by knowing that a distance of about 10 miles separates the lowest point of 5,300 ft., where the Dungsel Khola meets the Bhabil below Timling, from the highest point of 22,800 ft. at the peak of Paldor, the origin of the Bhabil Khola.

Trekkers making their way to Timling from the Ankhu Khola will pass through a series of Tamang villages that change slightly in character as the country becomes rougher. The straw roofing of houses in the valley's lower reaches will give way to splitshake weighted with stone, and the proportion of houses daubed with mud and dung decreases so that most houses are of naked stone. After about the midpoint of the valley, trekkers will pass the line beyond which the Tamang no longer raise pigs. The number of men wearing traditional turban headgear (Tm. *bajaro*) and cloth garment tied at the shoulders (Tm. *pengayen*) will increase, and fewer people will be seen in western-style or Nepali national clothing.

The trail from Sertang passes down into the narrow canyon of the Ata Khola, the traditional southern boundary of Timling, and then climbs abruptly in a series of narrow switchbacks until it enters the small settlement of 11 Kami households. From here it rounds the ridge and climbs past a large stone *mani* and into the village of Timling on its narrow shelf of land. The rocky trail lined with stone walls enters the village as if into a fort, with only the backs of houses immediately visible and prayer flags printed at the *gompo* snapping in the wind on long poles beside the houses.

Besides Timling proper, the traditional territory is occupied by three daughter villages and scattered households whose members descend from the same Timling people. Timling, being the oldest, is also the most aggregated of these settlements, while the younger villages' dispersed settlement patterns reflect their origin from

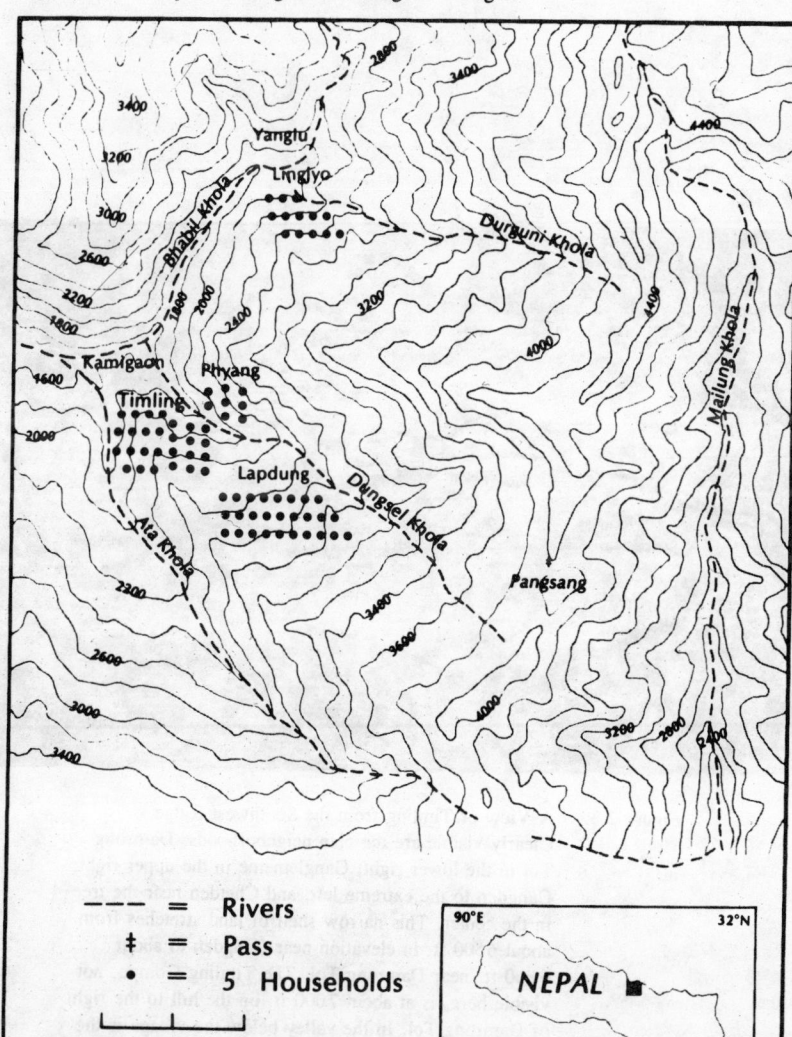

Figure 2.2. Map of Timling and Its Daughter Villages.

--- = Rivers
‡ = Pass
• = 5 Households

0 1 2 Km
Contour Interval = 200 Meters

former pasture and agricultural land. The people of all villages share one *gompo* in Timling, and all community land within the traditional borders is equally open to any person regardless of proximity to one settlement or another.

Lapdung, the largest of the daughter villages, lies directly up the slope toward Pang Sang and a 30-minute walk from Timling. Its 128 households sprawl between 7,000 and 8,000 ft. Phyang is a smaller settlement of 40 households on the slope

Figure 2.3. A View of Timling from the Southwest Ridge. Clearly visible are the clan neighborhoods: Damrong Tol in the lower right; Ganglememe in the upper right; Gangden to the extreme left; and Chetden near the tree in the center. This narrow shelf of land stretches from about 6 500 ft. in elevation near Gangden to about 6 800 ft. near Damrong Tol. The Timling Gompo, not visible here, is at about 7 000 ft. on the hill to the right of Damrong Tol. In the valley below the village is the Dungsel Khola.

directly across from Timling. Although residents of Timling and Phyang are close enough to shout conversations to one another, the walk to Phyang is about 45 minutes. Lingjyo lies around the corner from Phyang in the dark reaches of the upper Bhabil Khola. It is considered the least desirable place to live by the people of Timling, its 64 households stretching across a range of 6,500 to 8,000 ft. and exposed to the cold winds that come off the glaciers of Paldor all year around. An additional 24 households lie scattered throughout the area below Timling and between Phyang and Lingjyo, close to individual land-holdings.

The Village

Timling's 132 households are laid out in four distinct neighborhoods that roughly correspond to clan residences within the village. Within each neighborhood is a kind of plaza where people can gather to work, gossip, or take in the sun. Neighborhoods grow when sons leave their father's home and build new houses to the side, usually on clan lands of their inheritance. Each neighborhood has its own identity, at one time having its own headman (cf. Fürer-Haimendorf 1956). While the integrity of individual neighborhoods in Timling has been largely maintained, single households owned by other than clan members may be built on sold land.

The most ordered neighborhood (Np. *tol*), Ganglememe, takes up the southeast corner of the village at the edge of the shelf upon which Timling sits. Its dominant clan members, the Ghale, can trace their families back to a common ancestor and the large two-story houses here are arranged in three long lines of attached buildings. A fourth row of houses belonging to the Mepa clan joins theirs at a right angle.

On the hill to the southwest is Damrong Tol, named after the clan living there and dispersed across the ridge because the clan forebear instructed them to live there. These houses are less uniformly constructed than those of Ganglememe, being made from various materials and consisting of a mixture of single- and double-story dwellings. One reason for their relative dispersion is the frequent fires that have destroyed parts of the neighborhood in the recent past.

Gangden is the northernmost neighborhood inhabited by three clans: Mamba, Damrong, and Gomtsa. This *tol* is also the least orderly, with an array of winding paths between houses and the widest range of household quality. Some of the poorest members of the village live here in dwellings of woven matting or in houses plagued with leaking roofs and in need of repair.

In the center of Timling is Chetden, arranged around a large *mani* erected on top of a boulder and painted white. The households here, also belonging to Ghale clan members, tend to lie on either side of a single avenue, and again there is a mixture of single- and double-story buildings. A spur of houses away from the central *mani* is inhabited mainly by people of the Gomtsa clan.

A few houses have been built on the fringe of Timling outside of any neighborhood—mostly because the density of construction in the older parts of the village precludes any newer homes being built. Faced with the need to build a home and no available land near other clan members, a person will build on his land in another area. The village *gompo* also lies separated from the main village in a small grove of trees up the ridge. Here, the *gompo lama* and his family live in a single-story house next to the *gompo* itself. The *gompo* is a large, white building as high as a two-story house but open all the way to the roof and divided into two large rooms on the inside. In the first room, a kind of foyer, the former *gompo lama* and his wife have established residence since they have no house of their own and the present *lama* occupies the *gompo* house. Also in this grove of trees is the new school, built with communal labor some three years before.

The Tamang House in Timling

Within this area, most houses are constructed of stone and have roofs of splitshake, although the poorer Tamang families will make do with houses of cane matting or some combination of stone, wood, and bamboo. Tamang family life centers around the hearth—the best indication of economic independence for a son is that he has his own firepit, for which he must produce his own food. Although the Tamang ideal is that a son will move away from his father's house when he claims his inheritance and build his own home, some of the poorer families in Timling have not been able to afford the expense and have remained under a single roof. Yet, even here, a new firepit will be constructed at one end of the existing structure or on the second story, and the younger family will center its life around this second hearth. In some cases, an original single family house has been divided into four parts to accommodate all the brothers in a family.

Nevertheless, an ideal Tamang home exists in people's minds and, although only a few approach this ideal, it is worth describing. In Timling, people hope to build a home of stone quarried from a rock pit on the ridge directly above the village. The ideal dwelling should be about 40 by 50 ft. and have two stories. Although the roof will usually be built of splitshake, some people will bring slate back with them from the high pastures, and their roofs gradually become overlapping, leak-proof slate.

The upper story of a Tamang home is used for the storage of grains, while cooking, eating, and sleeping are done on the ground floor around the hearth set at one end of the building. The floors are constructed of loose rock overlaid by mud, and the area on both sides of the hearth usually has an additional layer of wood planking on which people sit and sleep. The smoke from the fire fills the room and escapes through the cracks in the roofing so that over the years all the inside surfaces become blackened.

During the day, the Tamang spend their time on the porch at the front of the house doing the work that can be finished at home. In most homes, the upper story, too, has a porch running the full length of the building, with a door opening onto it. During the wet months of the monsoon, some Tamang choose to sleep away from the damp ground floor and use this space. Windows are not considered an essential part of any house, but some people will include one or two shuttered openings in their walls to let in the light. Tamang doors are constructed of heavy wooden planking that can be secured from the inside with a heavy wooden cross-bar. Not all the people of Timling have locks, but some have hooks embedded in their door jams so they can lock the building when they leave.

Decoration is generally scarce although some people will carve designs into their doors and shutters, or pay somebody else to do the carving if they lack the skill. Homes of the Ghale clan are distinguished by enormous stone phalluses with varying degrees of realism. These stone *mle* (Tm. cock) that project from under the eaves terrify ghosts and other malevolent beings and dissuade them from performing mischief in Ghale households.

Although smoky, the Tamang home is designed to keep the wind and rain out and to be comfortably warm and dry in the cold months. Huge wooden chests for storing items that might be damaged by rodents line the walls, and wooden pegs for hanging clothing and tools out of the way are set wherever they may be needed. If a family has managed to save a little extra money and made it to a bazaar, a framed black and white photograph of some of its members, wearing borrowed western clothes and with their own or borrowed watches prominently displayed on wrists turned toward the camera, will hang over the door.

Apart from the house itself, the ideal arrangement will include a small courtyard where grain can be laid out to dry or various chores can be done when the weather is sunny. To the side of this, a small, open-sided shelter for the storage of fodder and a place to tether a cow or buffalo may be built. The final effect of this arrangement in the ideal is to distinguish an enclosed, family compound from those that surround it.

Clans and the History of Timling

Timling's people, like other Tamang, are organized into exogamous patrilineal clans. These are each identified by a common ancestral deity called *meme* (Tm. grandfather) and worshipped as the god of the hearth (Tm. *kulgi lha*) by household members. Marriage within the clan is forbidden, and the Tamang stress the need to know the patrilineage of all children, including those born illegitimately. Distinctions within the patriline are also recognized in Timling, as Höfer found in another Tamang village (1969:21-22):

> Within the clan, people sometimes distinguish between *santans*, a Nepali term meaning 'descendants' or, loosely, 'descent group', each having a common ancestor who lived in the sixth, seventh, eighth etc. generation. Another Nepali term, *dajyubhai* (brothers) expresses common descent from an ancestor in the third or fourth generation. *Dajyubhais* are bound to each other mutually, especially if one of them is indebted or dies before leaving behind orphans. Thus, *santan* seems to denote a major, and *dajyubhai* a minor clan segment.

Kinship terms are consistent with the stress on patrilateral and matrilateral cross-cousin marriage in Timling. Both sets of grandparents are referred to by the same

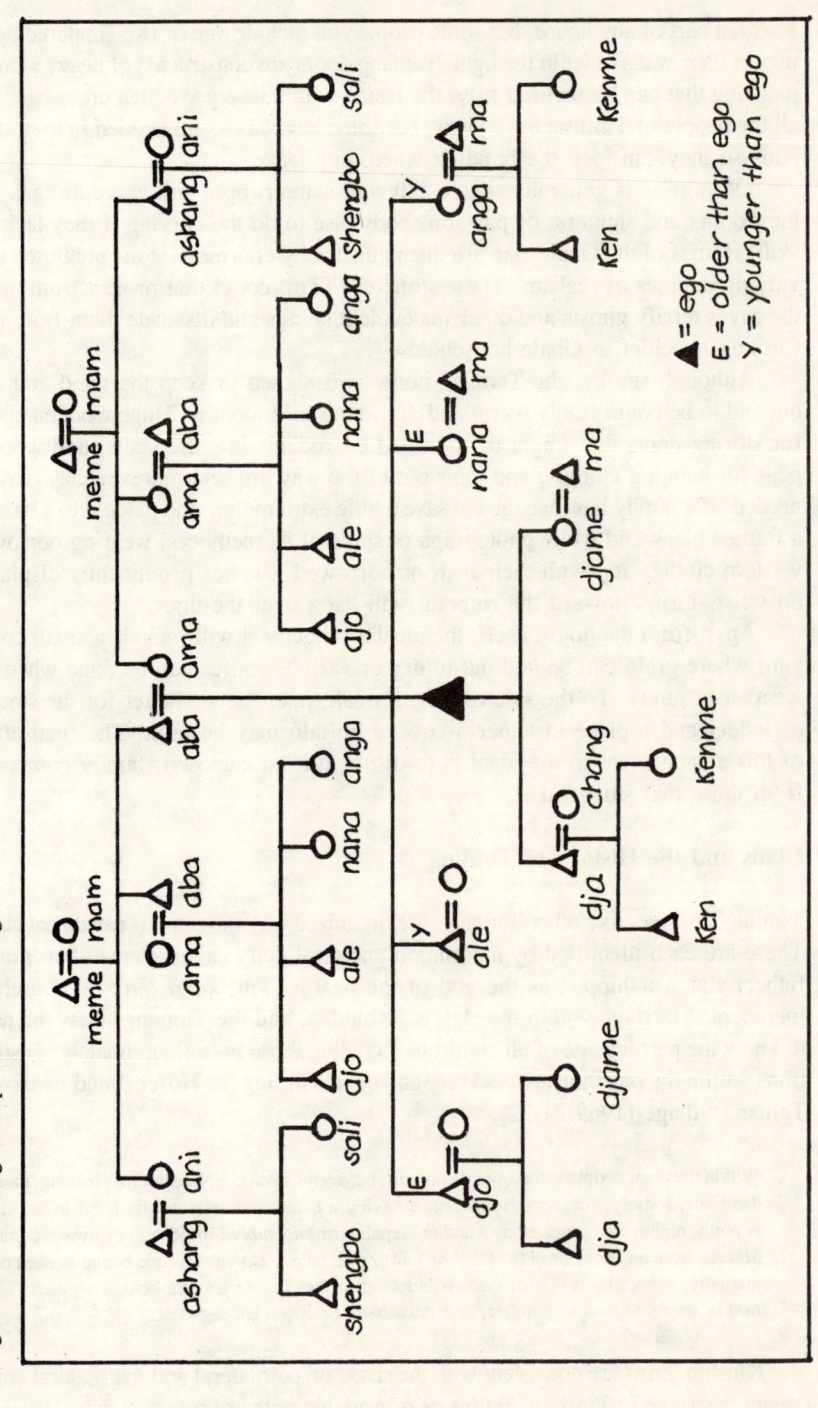

Figure 2.4. Tamang Kinship Chart for Timling.

names; ego's father's brothers are called by the same word as his or her father (Tm. *aba*); and mother's sisters are called mother (Tm. *ama*). Parents of marriageable children are distinguished, however. Thus ego's mother's brothers are all referred to as *ashang,* and ego's father's sisters are called *ani*. These terms are extended to father's sister's husbands or mother's brother's wives whether they hold that biological relationship or not (see figure 2.4).

Kinship terms apply to five generations and suffixes extend the basic terminology to account for age relationships. Thus mother's sister's husband is *aba gren* if he is married to an elder sister and *aba chengba* if the sister is younger. Similarly, older and younger sisters and brothers have different names while ego's own children are distinguished by birth order.

Clans do not own communal land in Timling, but the effect of inheritance rules is to create clusters of land belonging to patrilineal relatives. This land can be sold to non-clan members but it cannot be alienated at death even if a man dies without heirs. Inheritance rules will cause that land to pass into the hands of clan brothers in that event. The one exception to this is if a man without sons has brought a son-in-law; this man, who must be from another clan by the rules of exogamy, will inherit his land.

The 639 people of Timling are divided into four clans and one other group, the Ghale, who can be treated as another clan. Each of these clans has its own tradition about arrival in the village and worships its own deity (Tm. *kulgi lha*), represented by a stone near the hearth. The clans and their numbers in Timling are: Ghale (278), Damrong (elsewhere—Höfer 1969:21—spelled Dimduṅ but modified here to avoid unfamiliar diacriticals) (181), Mamba (77), Gomtsa (72), and Mepa (31). According to informants, the Gomtsa and Mepa are actually subgroups of the Lama clan and cannot intermarry; the traditional occupation of the Gomtsa is shaman (Tm. *bompo*), while that of the Mepa is *lama*. Each of the neighborhoods is to some extent defined by a dominant clan, and the various *tol* are often referred to by a clan name rather than by the more formal name of the area. Thus, Ganglememe might be called Ghale Tol in conversation.

The Ghale are a people set apart in the village even though it is convenient to call them Tamang for the purposes of this study (cf. Toffin 1976a:37; Dobremez and Jest 1976:144). They are considered separate from the Tamang even though they have intermarried for generations and speak the same language, except for a few differences in kin terms. For example, the Tamang term for older sister is *nana*, while the Ghale word is *namu*; for father, the Tamang say *aba*, the Ghale *yebe*. Apart from this, the effective difference between the two groups is dietary. Ghale, who still follow traditional dietary practice, will eat no meat except sheep, goats, or wild game, while the Tamang can eat any kind of meat including beef. A brief review of the village history will highlight some of the inter-clan relations.

Tradition has it that the first ancestors came across Pang Sang some 15 generations ago to settle in Timling, a name derived from *timnyu,* the Tamang word for monkey—so named because of the large number of monkeys that lived in the forests and rocks of the area. The first settlement was built on top of the ridge above the present village at a place called Tingang, and the original Tamang clan in the area, the Damrong, was joined later by the other clans. The Mepa ancestor is said to have flown in during the time when *lamas* had the knowledge of how to travel on the wind, a knowledge lost when the *lamas* of the *gompo* argued and burned the books with the empowering mantra.

One of the versions for the coming of the Ghale begins with the Tamang king, Bongzo Raja, who demanded so much from his subjects in Timling that they went in search of another king. One of the Tamang went off to the northwest where he found a group of children from all castes playing and, knowing that one of them would be the new king of Timling, he waited until they sat to rest. The child who sat so as not to get dirty was chosen as king, and the Tamang carried him back to Timling. His name was Khuruwa, the one who was carried. When he was brought to the village, Bongzo Raja was forced to leave, and his descendants still live in Chilime, a village on the other side of Pang Sang.

Whether or not this reflects the actual arrival of the Ghale in Timling, all people in the village insist that they are a separate group whose ancestors arrived from the northwest. The Ghale, also called Ghle or Khle, a Tamang word for king, are said to live in the ancestral lands as a people who dress and live like the Tibetans of the plateau. Ghale informants insist that they are distinct from the Gurung clan of the same name and that they intermarried with the Tamang out of necessity since only one exogamous Ghale clan is represented in Timling; these are the Geldang. The nearest Ghale clan with which they can marry is the Samre of Basunchet, some three days' walk away.

Even within the village of Timling, however, there is a distinction between those who live in Ganglememe and those who live in Chetden. The Ganglememe Ghale often speak disparagingly of the others as "those who do not honor the ancestors" because they violate ritual restrictions placed on them by their forebears. They are rumored to eat forbidden meats and are known to cook nettles inside their homes, a practice forbidden to the Ghale. On a more mundane level, the "jack Ghale" of Chetden live in poorer looking houses and have fewer possessions than the others.

Relative to other clans, the Ghale have a slightly higher status, which appears to have lost any real significance in day-to-day happenings. In the past, informants report, Ghale women commanded a slightly higher bride price than Tamang women, but this practice is no longer adhered to. The Tamang say that the Ghale were once much wealthier but that they are now more equal to the Tamang. Damrong tradition, in particular, tells of the shrewdness of a Ghale ancestor in alienating them from their richest lands in the lower valley. These are even today concentrated in Ghale hands.

Religious Life

Timling religious life shares the same mixture of Tibetan Buddhist (Nyingmapa, Tibetan: the old sect) and animistic elements found throughout the Tamang area.

Figure 2.5. Tamang Lama Administering Final Death Ritual.
This ritual is taking place on the ridge above Timling.

Religious specialists are equally divided between *lamas* and *bompo*, with 12 of each in the village. In addition, each clan has its own *lambu*, a specialist well versed in clan lore and knowledgeable of the minor rites for earth spirits. *Lambu* will sprinkle water over a goat so that it will be possessed before it is sacrificed, for example. Timling is dotted with *mani* throughout the village and the surrounding hills, although most of these are in disrepair. These stone monuments were erected over the remains of powerful *lamas* or secular men in the past. Newer *mani* are noticeably smaller, and this is explained as being the result of the great expense of having one built. A large *mani* will require the same expenditure of resources as a large house.

The Tamang ritual calendar meshes with the yearly agricultural and pastoral cycle, with the most important community events occurring at lulls in the work requirements. Significant rituals include the blessing of the fields by the *lamas*, who circumambulate the village terraces before the spring planting. *Barma*, a major cleansing of the village in July, requires three days and the cooperation of all village *lamas* and households. Major death rituals (Tm. *grel*) are performed at this time; *lamas* go on retreat in the village *gompo;* and a final day ritual in which the *lamas* dance through the main village paths and fling effigies of malevolent deities off a precipice outside of the village is enacted. The entire village follows the *lamas* out to the cliffs and, on the return, each person is brushed with pine boughs before entering Timling again.

Bompo are considered practitioners for the sick and specialize in propitiating local forest deities that can cause injury to Tamang villagers and their herds. Their ministrations are conducted in all-night rituals involving possession and the sacrifice of chickens or goats. Mothers and fathers of young children often seek the protection of *bompo* for their children while sickness will almost always involve their intervention.

Administration in Timling

Timling has been incorporated into the *panchayat* system that links all Nepali villages to the central government in Kathmandu. The *panchayats* have tended to join formerly autonomous villages into a single administrative unit, so that traditional lines of civil authority are altered when the *panchayat* leader comes from a different village. *Panchayats* are part of a civil hierarchy culminating in the king; the *panchayat* is itself the smallest unit in the national government to which funds are dispersed although it is further subdivided into wards along old neighborhood and village lines. The village of Timling is made up of three wards within the larger *panchayat*. Its elected leader (Np. *pradhan panch*) comes from the village of Borang about half a day's walk from Timling. Although the *panchayat* administration is officially responsible for the settlement of disputes within its borders, its effective responsibilities are to channel development funds to the local level and to assist in collecting taxes. Dispute resolution is still largely in the hands of traditional village

Figure 2.6. Grazing Cattle on Household Plots.
The cattle are grazing on plots above Timling after fall harvest.

Figure 2.7. Household Goats Grazing above Lapdung.

leaders, a council composed of clan elders and others whose status rests on their education or wealth. Often the deputy *panchayat* offices go to these men, and in Timling the highest *panchayat* official in the village is also the son of the former headman.

Administratively, Timling is today included in Sertang Gaon Panchayat along with the other formerly independent chiefdoms of Borang and Sertang. The people of Timling feel strongly that they are at a disadvantage in this setup and that Borang and Sertang benefit by being further downstream and more accessible to government officials. Most people feel that funds intended for the whole *panchayat* are unequally distributed between Borang, where the head of the *panchayat* lives, and Sertang, where other high officials and people related by marriage to the *panchayat* head live. People who live in the lower parts of the valley do, indeed, look askance at the people of Timling and consider them and their ways too rough to be acceptable.

One of the results of this is that Timling people will not visit the health post located in Sertang. Apart from the usual lack of medical supplies, the villagers report that they are charged for the medicine that is given to them when they know it is intended for free distribution. Although one of the health workers in Sertang, a Gurung, seemed sincerely interested in administering to the needs of the people in Timling, a more recent worker spoke to me in disgust of the Tamang there—of how they live in filth and are little better than bears of the forest.

The people are aware of their status in the *panchayat* and are actively seeking to form an administrative unit that would reflect the traditional borders of their territory. For the time being, they have forbidden the young men of Sertang from staying over night at Timling festivals, claiming that the people of Sertang impregnate their women and then refuse to admit paternity. The real reason for some of the antagonism may be the relative wealth of Timling in grass for cattle fodder and cane for matting, baskets, and temporary shelters. Sertang's position downstream means that it is effectively surrounded by other villages; its larger population must live on less land than that of Timling with the consequences that its people have used up more accessible stands of cane; in addition, the landscape around Sertang is less steep than Timling's, and most land is cultivated, while Timling possesses large areas of grassland on hillsides too steep for terracing. The people of Timling, in response to the feeling of being shortchanged by Sertang and to their own need for fodder, have forbidden people from outside the traditional territory to cut fodder or cane within the old boundaries; this prohibition has exacerbated the tension between the two villages. One result is that Timling men who go to *panchayat* meetings in Sertang go there prepared to defend themselves physically against some of the more enthusiastic members of the other village.

Within Timling itself, however, the operation of village politics proceeds a little more smoothly. Timling comprises three wards of the whole *panchayat,* and all of the wards have their own officials subordinate to the *panchayat* head. A kind

Figure 2.8. Members of Ghale Clan.
The clan is preparing to slaughter a ram for Dasain.

Figure 2.9. A Tamang Mother and Two Daughters.
The family is at a village fair in Lapdung.

of parallel administration exists with respected men from each clan, corresponding to the earlier clan headmen, meeting together to decide village affairs. They decide such matters as closing a large area of scrubland to cutting until the forest grows again, opening the grasslands to cutting fodder for village cattle, or imposing curfews within the village. These rules are enforced with the help of an informal police force of men chosen for their youth and strength.

For example, one person in the village was seen cutting grass on the communal wastelands before the season for cutting was announced by the clan elders. Four men in their 20s were called the next morning and told to confiscate the bales of cut grass and the tools of the man caught breaking the village law. The grass was then divided among those who had confiscated it and the man's tools stored until he paid a 10-rupee fine. Part of this fine was used to buy packets of cheap Indian cigarettes called *bidi* for these same young men and the rest kept by the highest ranking village official.

Most village grievances can be solved through this same informal channel, although antagonists in any argument have the option of pursuing justice through the official *panchayat* network if they are not satisfied. Unless the charge is very serious, though, there is little chance of that happening since most people distrust *panchayat* officials beyond the village boundaries. Indeed, a job as a *panchayat* official is seen as an avenue for enhancing one's personal fortunes, and occupants of these positions are not always trusted to make impartial decisions.

In summary, the people of Timling inhabit a niche far outside the Nepali mainstream. Even by Tamang standards, these people must be considered marginal, and the incorporation of the once independent chiefdom into the Nepali polity has had little effect on the lives of the people living there. A number of subjects remain to be touched on in the discussion of life in Timling—historical patterns in their changing economy, a changing orientation from Tibet to more southern and Nepali outlets for trade goods, and the events of birth, marriage, and death. All of these will be given fuller treatment in the more general discussion of productive and reproductive processes in Timling.

Age-Sex Distribution

In the next chapter I discuss the *lho* calendrical system and its use in assigning ages to Timling's people. While this method has probably not removed all error from the age estimates, it has substantially changed the kinds of error that do occur. More importantly, the *lho* system allows us to have confidence in these data to a degree not often found with illiterate populations. We are therefore more justified in attributing irregularities in the age-sex structure to real events than to problems in assigning ages.

Typical artifacts of age estimation in populations like Timling's are enumerated elsewhere (Weiss 1975:61-64, 1973; Howell 1974; Shryock and Siegel 1975:115). Among the problems we would expect *not* to find in the Tamang data are: strong evidence of age heaping or digit preference, a tendency to underestimate the ages

A Mountain Village in Nepal 49

of young women without children, and a tendency to place women with children in the middle age range. Table 2.1 presents the age distribution from the census, and figure 2.10 displays the age-sex pyramid for the same data.

We see from the age-sex pyramid that Timling's population lacks the extremely broad base relative to height associated with the most rapidly expanding populations. At the same time, it does not have the characteristic bell shape found in many industrialized nations. Like the Gurung of Thak (Macfarlane 1976:282), these Tamang are characterized by an intermediate age pyramid that we can associate with a population growing at a moderate rate. Macfarlane also writes that many

Table 2.1. Timling's Age and Sex Structure.

Age	Population in Interval N	%	Cumulative Percent
		Total	
0	18	2.8	2.8
1-4	69	10.8	13.6
5-9	66	10.3	23.9
10-14	73	11.4	35.3
15-19	54	8.5	43.8
20-24	71	11.1	54.9
25-29	45	7.0	61.9
30-34	31	4.9	66.8
35-39	43	6.7	73.5
40-44	43	6.7	80.2
45-49	26	4.1	84.3
50-54	26	4.1	88.4
55-59	14	2.2	90.6
60-64	23	3.6	94.2
65-69	18	2.8	97.0
70-74	14	2.2	99.2
75-79	3	0.5	99.7
80+	2	0.3	100.0
		Female	
0	11	3.4	3.4
1-4	36	11.1	14.5
5-9	31	9.5	24.0
10-14	35	10.8	34.8
15-19	32	9.8	44.6
20-24	35	10.8	55.4
25-29	22	6.8	62.2
30-34	16	4.9	67.1
35-39	21	6.5	73.5
40-44	21	6.5	80.0
45-49	14	4.3	84.3
50-54	12	3.7	88.0
55-59	7	2.2	90.2
60-64	13	4.0	94.2
65-69	10	3.1	97.3
70-74	6	1.8	99.1
75-79	2	0.6	99.7
80+	1	0.3	100.0

Table 2.1 (contd.)

Age	Population in Interval N	%	Cumulative Percent
		Male	
0	7	2.2	2.2
1-4	33	10.5	12.7
5-9	35	11.1	23.9
10-14	38	12.1	36.0
15-19	22	7.0	43.0
20-24	36	11.5	54.5
25-29	23	7.3	61.8
30-34	15	4.8	66.6
35-39	22	7.0	73.6
40-44	22	7.0	80.6
45-49	12	3.8	84.4
50-54	14	4.5	88.9
55-59	7	2.2	91.1
60-64	10	3.2	94.3
65-69	8	2.5	96.8
70-74	8	2.5	99.4
75-79	1	0.3	99.7
80+	1	0.3	100.0

Average Age
   Total   26.42
   Female   26.35
   Male   26.50

Population
   Total   639
   Female   325
   Male   314

Source: Timling Census.

developing countries have pyramids with 50% of their population under 20 years old. In Nepal, 52% of the population is 19 or younger (Banister and Thapa 1981:22), while the Tamang here have 43.8% below age 20. This compares with the Gurung of Thak with 39.6% below that age and the Dhingaba, a high altitude group from the northwest, with 45% (Ross 1981:37).

Figure 2.10 shows other interesting relationships. For example, the numbers in each age category do not smoothly decline with age as we would expect in the absence of random effects. On the other hand, nearly every age category shows a rough equality in the numbers of males and females, a pattern drastically violated only once. Moreover, the relationship of a particular age group with the one above or below it is generally the same for both sexes—deviations from the smooth age

Figure 2.10. Timling's Age-Sex Pyramid, 1981.

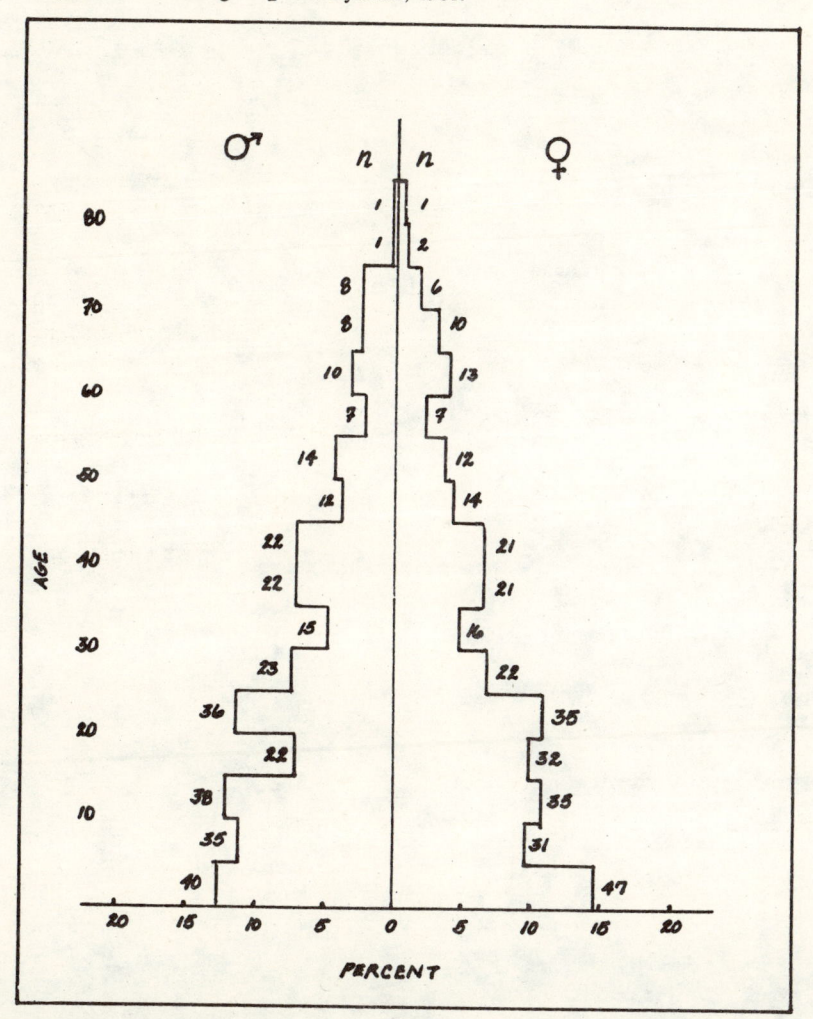

structure are in the same direction for both men and women. We might infer from this that these deviations are the result of random events, such as contagious illnesses, that equally affect both sexes.

These relationships will be discussed more fully in chapters 5 and 6. For now, it is enough to note the consistency of the Timling age data with what we would expect in a small population.

3

Data and Methods

This study's validity is heavily dependent on data quality, especially for event timing. I was unable to gather independent estimates of ages, for example, and the reliability of my estimates is contingent on the methods employed in the village. This study's focus on the processes of household formation, fertility, and economic adaptation requires information from both individual and household levels. I was able to take advantage of certain cultural features of Timling's population in gathering that information. Most significant for the problem of aging individuals in an almost entirely illiterate population was the still-current use of the Tibetan calendrical cycle (cf. Pignede 1966:315-17; Macfarlane 1976:281).

Briefly, the system involves a 12-year cycle with each year designated by an animal symbol (Tm. *lho*). Virtually all Tamang know the animal year of their birth and the number of cycles (Tm. *legar*) they have lived through. In addition, they often know the information for a wide circle of relatives and friends because age is a popular topic of conversation throughout the village and age distinctions are built into kinship terminology by adding suffixes to the generic kin designations.

Lho have a rough correspondence to full years in the western calendar since the new *lho* begins in the Nepali month of Magh, or about the second week of January in the western calendar. This varies slightly, but the overall pattern is close enough to make calculations in terms of western years. For this reason, I have converted *lho* to western years in this analysis. The chance of error in fixing events to a given year is very small, with only those occurrences in the first two weeks of January being affected, and there is no effect on figuring rates. The *lho* and their corresponding years for the last cycle are displayed in table 3.1. Thus if a person reported his *lho* to be *ta* (horse) and had gone through two *legar*, his year of birth would be assigned to 1954.

The use of this aging system contributed to a high degree of consistency in age reporting. Not only would individuals be able to report their birth years accurately, but their relatives and friends would independently give the same responses if asked the same person's *lho*.

The nature of this research involved a combination of standard anthropological techniques and more formal census and survey methods. Caldwell et al. (n.d.)

Table 3.1. Tamang 12-Year Calendrical Cycle with Tibetan and English Equivalents.

Year	Tamang Lho	Tibetan Lho	English
1970	khi	khyi	dog
1971	pha	phag	boar
1972	jiwa	byi-ba	mouse
1973	lang	glan	bull
1974	tah	stag	tiger
1975	yeh	yos	goat
1976	bruk	hbrug	dragon
1977	brul	sbrul	snake
1978	ta	rta	horse
1979	luk	lug	sheep
1980	pre	spre	monkey
1981	ja	bya	chicken

have called this kind of approach micro-demography to try to distinguish its hybrid nature from studies that rely almost entirely on either quantitative or qualitative data. My objective was to gather demographic information for all of Timling while the more intensive economic data were to be gathered for a representative sample of households.

Village selection was determined by my desire to work in a village at the earliest extreme of the demographic transition and relatively unintegrated into a monetized economy. This desire was balanced by a need to be within a reasonable distance of Kathmandu so that resupply trips would not take overly long. My walk up the Ankhu Khola convinced me that Timling represented a good balance of these factors, with the added advantage that its people welcomed me to live and work there. In order to identify the different households and assign identification numbers for compiling the questionnaires, I began my work by drawing a map of the village and numbering each household. These households were preliminarily defined by the presence of a separate cooking hearth even where walls did not separate living spaces.

Formal Survey Instruments and Procedures

Formal instruments for data collection included a village census form, a marriage and fertility history form to be administered to all women who had ever been pregnant or married, a household economic survey form, and a life history matrix that was originally intended for gathering information on life history events from all male household heads. The questions and categories of information for all of these instruments were developed before coming to the field, and modifications—such as those occasioned by my discovery of the *lho* system in Timling—were made in the village. Although Nepali is not the mother tongue of these people, my lack of proficiency in Tamang forced me to work in Nepali for most of my stay. To insure that my questions were completely understood, however, I employed an illiterate Tamang man to accompany me whenever I filled out forms. He was able to render the questions in Tamang while assuring the respondents of my good intentions.

Survey research is possible in marginal settings such as Timling, in spite of the frustration involved in locating people who are often away from the household. Questions can rarely be asked in a controlled setting with only respondents and interviewers present, but the collection of friends and relatives who sit beside the fire can be an advantage, lightening the occasion and correcting omissions. Interviews took place in the whole range of surroundings—around the hearth, sitting on the dirt in temporary cattle shelters, or along the trail. The work is hard on the survey forms, which invariably are rained on or covered with manure or burned with sparks from the fire, but the information can still be lifted from them. As work progressed, I was able to cross-check event histories for accuracy by comparing birth histories for family members. When discrepancies were noticed, I returned to the individuals and asked the questions again in light of reports from other people. For example, I could check the validity of birth years in the pregnancy histories by asking the children themselves when they were born. Once material was collected, I stored it in a rat-proof tin box in my house in Damrong Tol.

Timling Census

The Timling census was administered to all 132 households in the village. It was designed to obtain basic demographic information on the sex and age structure of the village as well as to identify individuals for the administration of the other survey instruments. Accompanied by my assistant, I introduced myself to any adult member of the household and asked them to allow me to record the census information. As it happened, the year of my visit coincided with the Nepali National Census, and most villagers were familiar with the type of questions I asked. Responses on my census were generally from the household head or his wife. In cases where people were not home at the first visit, I would try to get the information from a neighboring household, often a brother's. Close kinship suggested highly reliable responses. A brother's children, for example, are categorical children in the Tamang kinship system. Nevertheless, I would return to the household to check information with actual household members when they were home. The census is *de jure;* information was obtained for household members living in the village as well as for those away for extended periods even if their return was not expected.

Marriage and Fertility Histories

From the census I was able to determine those village women who had been exposed to the risk of pregnancy through marriage and cohabitation. In one case, a woman was pregnant and unmarried. The marriage and pregnancy histories follow the format used by the Hulls in their Java study (T. Hull 1975; V. Hull 1975) and were designed to gather information on marriage patterns and village fertility. Their reliability for Timling rests on incorporation of the *lho* system to determine ages and the timing of events, along with the eagerness of women to talk about their birth histories and marriages. Sexuality is a topic of easy conversation in Timling, and no woman found it embarrassing to discuss these events with a male researcher and his male assistant. The social setting is such that sexual joking along the lines found among the Lepcha (Gorer 1967) is a frequent and enjoyed event. Even obvious premarital pregnancies were admitted to with wry smiles. Marriage and fertility histories were gathered from 150 women in Timling. One woman did not participate because of senility. Another woman had never married and was probably sterile while another sterile woman had left the village for Lingjyo when her sister married her husband.

For each woman, I collected general information on her age, marital status, and number of pregnancies. Separate sheets were then filled out for each pregnancy and marriage she reported. Additional information was asked on the desire for children and family planning, but these sections of the questionnaire were often bewildering to the women of Timling. No woman reported the use of family planning methods, traditional or otherwise, although they were all aware of them. The most frequent response to a question on desire for additional children was a deep laugh and a joke. I pressed the issue, however, and was able to come up with responses in most cases although my overall impression is that women don't think about the number of children they'd like to have.

Additional information included that for mortality. The ages at death for all children who died were recorded along with the causes of death. Similar information was gathered for husbands if the respondent had been widowed. This mortality information for children ever born is the basis for the mortality discussion in chapter 6.

The reliability of these data is very high. Living adult children of interviewed women were asked for their birth years in the census, and this was corroborated with the reports of their mothers. It is possible that errors of recall skew the results, but the analysis in chapter 5 suggests that there is no pattern here that can be attributed to the age of women. The advantages of the public interview are clearest here where forgotten miscarriages or births of children who subsequently died were inserted by neighbors and relatives present during the survey. My assistant's knowledge of recent history in the village (he was 27 years old at the time of fieldwork) was also useful here.

Timling Economic Survey

By far the most sensitive information I gathered from the point of view of the villagers was the household economic information. The people of Timling have a natural distrust of outsiders, and questions that impinge so directly on their livelihoods are considered threatening. For this reason I saved these questions until I had established myself as a regular part of village life. My intention was to gather information that would allow a comparison of the economic standing of village households along with a description of the village economy that could be generalized. The reticence of household heads in supplying that information and the frequent revisits required to get all the data made it necessary to select a random sample of 30 households. These were chosen with a table of random numbers and the household numbers assigned during the census. Most information about household possessions was easily obtained, but the questions relating to herd size and land holdings were occasions for the most outrageous lies. My assistant was able to help a great deal here, and herd sizes were easily checked by walking out to the pastures close to the village since this survey was conducted at the close of the high pasture season and village herds were grazing in the terraces around Timling.

The problem of obtaining land estimates was more frustrating, however, and I was nearly ready to give up when one of the wealthier men reported that he owned

58   Data and Methods

barely enough land to feed the poorest household in the village. My breakthrough came when one of the Ghale elders discovered me trying to elicit the land information from his brother. When he heard the man's reply, he laughed and chided him for not telling me the truth when my work would help the village. He said that I had come to write a book about their lives and that I needed to have the truth. How would the people of my country know how hard their lives really were if they made them sound so onerous as to be unbelievable? Then he added that I would only discover the truth anyway by going to the district headquarters and checking the land records there. So why be unreasonable? After saying this, he sat down and told me to take out one of my forms and ask him the questions. Before I could even begin, he told me what land he had inherited, what land he had bought, and the size of his herds.

Most people were more forthcoming after that encounter. I was, however, able to check their answers. I added questions on the questionnaire to discover the amount of seed planted for each crop the previous year. I had long before discovered roughly how much seed was required for a given area of land by crop and could convert seed into units of land. Moreover, I asked these same people in an independent questionnaire, the life history matrix, to tell me how much land they owned in *hal* (described in chapter 4). The land area in *hal* agreed with my calculations based on seed area, suggesting that both sets of responses were accurate. A further check was made by using information from members of more than one generation of a single patriline. My random survey provided me with three intergenerational sets as well as with sets of brothers, and I was able to compare the reports on inherited land. Since inheritance is equal among sons, I expected them to report the same quantity in their *angsa* (Np. inheritance). These reports were consistent. Even more, I was able to sum the inheritances of brothers to come up with land totals that agreed with the reports of their fathers' holdings. I argue, therefore, that my information on land holdings has a high degree of reliability.

Life History Matrix

The advantages of the life history matrix (LHM) approach to collecting information on event timing for individuals have been described by Smith and Chapon (1978) and Lauro (1979). My own experience with this method strongly supports their conclusions and expands the potential for its use from the relatively accessible populations they studied to more marginal survey environments such as Timling's. Essentially, the life history matrix consists of a grid with ages or years down one side of the page and event categories across the top. An interview consists of a loosely directed conversation in which events are marked at the intersection of age and category on the sheet. Only change in status needs to be marked on the grid so that relationships among events are readily apparent to the eye. The relationships among events will elicit memories of other occurrences in much the same way that an event calendar can be used to get at age in the census. I modified the age column by using *lho* instead of age and began by filling in the easily remembered years of birth. The timing of other events such as marriage, inheritance, and movements outside of the village was then related to these benchmarks.

Some of the powerful advantages of the LHM in the Timling setting included the conversational style of the interview, the short time needed for an interview, and the ability to cross-check event timing with other occurrences in the lifetime of the person being interviewed. Lauro (1979:50) reported high accuracy in responses from a Thai village.

My original intention was to administer the LHM to all adult men and women in Timling, but time constraints and the impossibility of finding a literate research assistant in the village as I had intended forced me to modify this goal. Additionally, the LHM was administered after the fall ploughing, and the extreme mobility of men at this time forced me to abandon the random sample of households and take life history data from any household head I could. These data cannot be considered statistically representative for this reason. They are useful, however, in allowing me to illustrate processes in the life cycle of Tamang men by referring to selected cases. I use the life history matrix extensively in chapter 8 in the discussion of household developmental cycles in Timling.

The LHM was administered to 50 male household heads. Only 17 of these were from the randomly selected sample households. Its use for illustration of the larger trends is, however, encouraging evidence of its potential for microdemographic study.

Informal Methods

Other categories of information were gathered outside of the survey format. Following more traditional anthropological methods, I relied on people with whom I had a special relationship for most of these. My principal informants included my 27-year-old male research assistant from a middle wealth Damrong family, a 57-year-old Ghale male who had spent some time in the British army in the Second World War, an 82-year-old Ghale male from the wealthiest village patriline, the 37-year-old Gompo Lama of Timling, and two women—one, the 25-year-old Ghale wife of my assistant, and another, a 22-year-old Ghale woman. A large number of other people were especially helpful at various times, including a 30-year-old Mepa *lama* and two Gomtsa shamans.

Information gathered from these people includes lineage histories, village stories, and information on agricultural and planting techniques. My data on the time investment in various activities come from a comparison of three detailed reports from my field assistant, the Gompo Lama, and the 57-year-old Ghale. Information for past conditions in the village and the trade with Kyerong comes from older village members. A great deal of data was also gathered through simple observation and participation in village ritual life and work. Questions about village organization and rules arose naturally out of this process; answers were sought from whoever was present.

4
The Subsistence Economy

We are people of the ridgetops. Our life is hard, but that is the way of this country.
—Norgay Damrong, age 27

Resources

Timling's agro-pastoral economy is organized to fulfill the subsistence needs of its people rather than to produce a marketable surplus. In the past, the people of the village were largely successful in providing for themselves although they have never been entirely self-sufficient. A robust salt trade with the Tibetans of Kyerong, for example, continued until at least 1959, when the Chinese closed the border. The present trade orientation is to the south at Trisuli Bazaar, a four- to five-day walk from Timling. Here the periodic need to buy grain can be satisfied and certain commodities from India can be obtained. While the closing of the border probably hastened the reorientation of Timling's trade links, it is possible that this would have occurred a few years later in any case, when a motorable road connected Trisuli and Kathmandu and opened the door for market expansion to the south. The important change in the Tamang economy, however, has been a steady movement toward a cash economy, along with a correlative need to buy basic foodstuffs in bad harvest years.

A full understanding of Timling's economy can be gotten only by keeping in mind that the present adaptation is the culmination of at least 15 generations of history in the area. Changing historical processes in a mountain village like this can be masked by the apparent regularity of the agro-pastoral cycle. To the observer, a world where the autumn ploughing season is opened with the blowing of thighbone trumpets and ritual by the *lamas* of a particular clan, or where spring planting is preceded by the circumambulation of village fields, is one of precise timing and balance. Nevertheless, the dangers of assuming a steady-state adaptation have been shown by Salisbury (1975), and part of the goal of this analysis will be to examine changes in the Tamang adaptation.

Brush (1977:69) reminds us that at least two levels of integration and analysis are relevant to the study of peasant economies. At the level of the village, large-scale patterns in a people's adaptation become clear. Here, the general set of constraints and resources available to all of Timling and a common set of responses to the environment can be examined. This focus on a kind of average condition that no household may actually approach ignores the variability of reality but helps to establish the context for other units of analysis and allows gross comparisons with other populations.

In peasant societies the household represents a critical unit of analysis because it is at this level where production, consumption, and reproduction processes overlap (Macfarlane 1978a) and where variability in a wide range of characteristics is expressed. For example, slightly variant strategies for satisfying household needs might be expected on the basis of differential land holdings. A complete explanation must incorporate this variability into the discussion of more general patterns.

The strategy for this analysis will be to begin with some of the most general environmental factors constraining and offering opportunities to the whole population. This is partially justified for Timling by the still dominant importance of local resources to Tamang subsistence. Given the level of Tamang technology and the relatively marginal environment, it is reasonable to expect the major features of the ecosystem to channel adaptive behaviors more closely than in an oil-based technology, for example. The second part of this chapter will deal with the actual patterns of behavior that characterize Timling's population.

Vertical Zones in Timling

Mountain environments throughout the world take much of their character from the striking changes in altitude over short distances. The immediate effect of this contour is to collapse a whole range of ecological zones into a relatively small area; these zones generally separate vertically along mountain slopes (Peattie 1936:79; Brush 1976a; Price 1981). Not only are natural ecosystems strongly affected by this vertical zonation, but human systems, too, take much of their shape from the variety of resource possibilities within a restricted area. The idea of verticality has been successfully applied to the Andean region (Murra 1972; Brush 1977:6–11) and has logical relevance to the Himalayan context as well. (This is the general condition for mountain environments, but see Goldstein and Messerschmidt [1980] for some exceptions.)

Vertical zones in the Upper Ankhu Khola Valley can be constructed on the basis of climate (Thouret 1977), vegetation (Yon 1976), or a combination of natural and cultural use areas (Alirol 1976, 1977; Toffin 1976a:39). In fact, years of human activity in the region have obscured the differences between classifications based on human use and those that pretend to be natural. The lower parts of most of the region have been extensively altered by cultivation and terracing while the upper margins show the effects of cattle and sheep grazing. Nevertheless, it is useful to explore the significance of undomesticated plants as a means of defining the environments.

Thouret (1977:60) divides the area into sets of thermal zones based on the movement of air during the months of May through August, just before and during the monsoon. Alirol's (1977:534) scheme, on the other hand, is based on a combination of ecological and human use factors:

Vertical zones based on climate
1) tropical	1805-2950 ft.	(550-900 m.)
2) sub-tropical	2950-6560 ft.	(900-2000 m.)
3) temperate	6560-8860 ft.	(2000-2700 m.)
4) mountain	8860-12,140 ft.	(2700-3700 m.)
5) Himalayan	12,140-14,270 ft.	(3700-4350 m.)

Vertical zones based on use
1) cultivated	5250-8500 ft.	(1600-2600 m.)
2) forest	8500-12,500 ft.	(2600-3800 m.)
3) pasture	12,500-15,420 ft.	(3800-4700 m.)
4) high mtn.	15,420+ ft.	(4700+ m.)

None of Timling's territory is as low as the tropical zones although the lower reaches fall well into the sub-tropical elevations and receive no snowfall even in the coldest months of winter.

The identity between the two classifications illustrates the extent to which different factors are related. For example, the upper limit of the temperate zone closely corresponds to that of the cultivated zone, while the mountain and forest zones are nearly the same. Finally, the pasture zone begins at about the same elevation as Thouret's Himalayan zone. These parallels reinforce the application of verticality as an organizing concept.

During the coldest months of December and January, snow falls as low as 5900 ft. (1800 m.), although the length of time it remains on the ground is dependent on the exposure of the slope. Yon (1976:34) measured the snowline in May at about 11,500 ft. (3500 m.) in the upper forest zone and moving rapidly higher during the summer months. By June, the snowline is at about 14,750 ft. (4500 m.), and it reaches its highest point of 15,750 ft. (4800 m.) in July and August before turning downward again. Paldor, whose peak is at 22,800 ft. (6950 m.), is glaciated on two sides. One of these glaciers extends as low as 15,100 ft. (4600 m.) and into the high pasture area.

During the monsoon season temperatures in the pasture zone generally range from 35.6° F (2° C) at night to 53.6° F (12° C) during the day (Yon 1976:28). Nevertheless, shepherds report occasional frost and snowfalls during these months. Alirol (1977:566) writes that the cultivated and forest zones are nearly always warmer than freezing and that the pastures are covered with snow from November until May of every year. In fact, frosts occur frequently in Timling from November until the spring and the ground around the village is frozen through the winter months. Additional factors such as narrow valleys that funnel cold air down from the higher elevations increase the sense of extreme cold that the Tamang report.

Natural vegetation in the upper zones is characteristic of the Central Himalaya (Mani 1978:13–17). From about 8000 to 9500 ft. the forest zone is populated by stands of oak (*Quercus semacarpifolia*) and maple (*Acer sterculiaceum, A. cardatum*) and conifers such as hemlock (*Tsuga dumosa*). Dominant species in the 9500 to 11,600 ft. range include fir (*Abies spectabilis*) and a variety of rhododendrons, giving way to stands of white birch (*Betula utilis*) up to about 12,300 ft. Above this elevation, a number of subalpine species dominate, including stunted growths of rhododendron and juniper (*Juniperus indica*). A complete inventory of high pasture vegetation has been compiled by Yon (1977). Three important species with medicinal uses—*Nardostachys jatamansi, Pichroriza scrophulariifolia,* and *Swertia multicaulis*—are important sources of cash when sold to merchants at Trisuli (cf. Dobremez and Jest 1976:182–84).

Although human use has largely obliterated the natural forest in the lower elevations, species such as barberry (*Berberis asiatica*) are reestablishing themselves on abandoned terrace areas. The type of vegetation characteristic of the upper areas suggests that the natural vegetation at all altitudes was typical of the middle sector in the Nepal Himalaya in which species from the more humid eastern and drier western sectors tended to mix (Mani 1978). A reconstruction of the native vegetation up to about 6500 ft. would include a number of flowering shrubs and trees such as chestnut (*Castinopsis indica, C. tribuloides*) and "chilaune" (*Schima wallichii*). The landscape from this level up to the present forest zone would have been essentially an extension of the rhododendron-oak-maple forest that exists now.

The area of Timling includes three broad use zones that will be examined in more detail in the next section. Some idea of the extremely rugged terrain of this area can be had by looking at the relative sizes of the various zones. Timling's approximately 67 square miles consist broadly of a zone of habitation and cultivation extending up to about 8500 ft. (2600 m.), a forest zone from here to about 12,000 ft. (3700 m.), depending on exposure, and a high pasture and high mountain zone extending above. A rough computation of the amount of land in each zone yields the following: the lowest zone includes about 14.5 square miles or 22% of the total area; the forested zone is the largest, at about 38 square miles or 57% of the total; the highest zone is roughly the same size as the lowest, with about 14 square miles or 21% of the total area. While these relative figures offer a good idea of the critical constraints on the shape of Timling's economy, further refinement is necessary to determine the actual resources available.

Field, Forest, and Pasture

Locally available resources are essential to subsistence in Timling and its daughter villages. Although it is necessary to caution against rigid adherence to these categories, natural resources can be usefully divided into forest, grazing, and arable land. These categories break down, for example, when considering the use of forest resources as fodder or the graze available to landholders on the spaces between terrace plots (cf. Macfarlane 1976:35).

A gross measure of resource availability can be obtained by first looking at population density. For Timling and the surrounding area, such a measure is unsatisfactory for a number of reasons. A major drawback is that large areas are too steep for intensive use. Nevertheless, such a rough measure is useful for comparison with other populations even though the relative densities may have more to do with terrain than with actual resources. For Timling, we know that 639 people live in 132 households, for an average household size of 4.84. If we take this as characteristic of all 388 Tamang households in the area and add 68 for the 11 Kami households, then the total population supported on this 67 square miles is 1,946. The ratio of 29 people per square mile is low for even the mountain region in general (Banister and Thapa 1981). Further refinement of these figures will demonstrate, however, that the number of people supported by the productive land in Timling is similar to other areas in Nepal.

Altitudinally based zones give the general boundaries within which major resources are distributed but fail to give a full picture of the actual complexity. Forest cover, for example, is not uniformly distributed within a single altitude range, nor is the quality of pasture consistent throughout the highest zone. A more complete description of resource availability is possible using the one inch to a mile maps of the Indian survey in conjunction with a walking survey of Timling's territory. With the help of these guides, it is possible to make some inferences about natural resources.

Communal grazing land is available in all vertical zones, but the high pastures above 12,000 ft. contain the largest contiguous portions. Of this total acreage of about 8960, roughly half is used as pasture. The remainder is located above 15,000 ft., or it is too rocky or exposed for herding. The seven square miles of high pasture are grazed by about 20 herds of sheep and goats from May until mid-September, during the time when about 90% of the vegetation flowers in the higher altitudes (Alirol 1977). Timling and its daughter villages contribute eight of these herds, with the others belonging to the people of villages as far as Kimtang, three to four days' walk away. In addition, the people of Gotlang bring their herds of yak-hybrids to graze in the area. During the season of peak use about 4,000 sheep and goats, a third of the herds in the entire Ganesh Himal (Alirol 1976:53), graze within Timling's traditional boundaries. The village of Timling alone accounts for three of these herds, consisting of 750 sheep and goats. The earlier practice of raising yak-hybrids was discontinued in the early 1960s when trade with Kyerong was cut off.

Additional grazing land in the forest and cultivated zones augments the high pastures at other times of the year. In the forest zone, for example, open meadowland is used for graze when the sheep and goat herds are in transit from other areas. With the cultivated zone, patches of grassland are opened to grazing at other times

The Subsistence Economy

when the herds are being massed for movement to the low pastures around Kimtang, where Timling shepherds are given grazing rights in exchange for summer pasture rights in their own territory. In the cultivated zone, an additional 700 to 900 acres of communal grazing land is available near Timling itself while an unknown amount exists near the other settlements as well. This is in addition to the privately held household plots. The timing of village access to these lands is, however, rigidly controlled by the ruling body of elder clan members.

Forest resources are essential to the livelihood of the Tamang. Fuel for cooking fires and warmth, lumber for roofing, floor planks and household timbers, and the raw material for the whole array of household and farm tools come from the extensive forest areas within Timling's borders. The extent of the forests in this area is massive compared to the deforested areas further south in the middle hills, yet it would be misleading to assume that all 24,448 acres of the forest zone provide this wood to the Tamang. In fact, within the broad band of forested land, four major concentrations of dense forest provide resources to the settlements here.

Timling and Lapdung gain the major portion of their wood from the large stand of forest that lies toward Pangsang Pass. A smaller forested area lies to the other side of this ridge and is now largely unused. Together, these two stands of timber take up some 7000 acres of land, nearly 11 square miles. Even within this restricted range there is no uniformity in forest cover though. Permanent cowsheds are spaced throughout the forest, and cleared meadowlands have grown around these as the cowherds have cut trees for their own needs.

Two other concentrations of forest lie further to the north near Lingjyo. Taken together, they cover over 6000 acres, or more than 9.5 square miles of land. Much of this huge tract is unused, with the smaller concentration near the settlement covering nearly 2750 acres, about four square miles. As in the zone above Timling and Lapdung, this area is spotted with permanent cattlesheds for the summer pasturing of animals.

This total area of 20.65 square miles represents over 54% of the land within the forest zone and still only refers to areas with the densest cover. Stands of timber in other areas are deliberately ignored in the following calculations as a partial corrective for the cattleshed clearings. The total area of forest considered here, 13,216 acres, may actually be an underestimation of the real reserves in Timling.

Without question, Timling's forests can supply more than enough wood to keep the 388 Tamang and 11 Kami households supplied with wood in perpetuity. A closer look at production and consumption will demonstrate this more clearly. Using the same figures for growth rates of wood that Macfarlane (1976:44) uses for the temperate forest of Thak, we can assume that the growth rate for wood is approximately 20 cubic meters per hectare, or 10.61 cubic yards per acre a year. On this basis, the forests of Timling produce 140,221 cubic yards of wood each year.

Estimates of wood consumption are necessarily rough since some occasional needs are difficult to account for and the number of observations of actual consumption were limited to three households over a short time. The following figures are based on actual observation for one week in July, reports of amount stored for the monsoon, and reported consumption by household heads. The unit of consumption is the amount an adult male can carry, a load of about the size reported in Macfarlane (1976:42–43): 3 ft. long by 1 1/2 ft. around.

Fuel consumption varies by season in Timling. During the cold months of November through February, households burn nearly one load a day, while a load will last close to five days in the other months. Yearly consumption of wood for fuel, then, is about 149 loads in a year. This compares well with the estimate of 120 loads per year for the Gurung village of Thak located at a warmer elevation (Macfarlane 1976:43). An additional two loads are consumed in the Gurung village for building materials and tools. Similarly, the people of Timling consume four loads for roofing and building. Assuming that the need for wood is the same as in Thak plus the addition of roofing (Gurung households at the elevation of Thak are roofed in thatch), the Tamang use an additional five loads of wood a year. The total household consumption is 154 loads.

Within the Timling area, then, 399 households use about 30,723 cubic yards of wood a year. This amounts to only 22% of the yearly growth. In fact, the situation is not so healthy as this would imply since western styles of forest management are not practiced. In the harvest of timber, Tamang men are free to cut anywhere in the communal forests above the zone of cultivation. The rollback of the forest edge is manifest in the expansion of daughter settlements onto land once occupied by forest and isolated cattlesheds. Older villagers report that 60 to 70 years ago the village of Lapdung was a dense stand of forest, and they point to timbers in their own houses that came from the ridge above Timling. This same ridge is covered by scrub brush and scattered trees today. Three years ago, village leaders closed this deforested stretch to cutting in the hope that timber would grow back—indicating that some village attitudes are swinging to more planned use.

Arable land, the final resource to consider, is the critical limiting factor in the present adaptation. As with other mountain peoples (Brush 1976a; Messerschmidt 1976a), Timling's economy has changed through the years until agriculture has become dominant. Thus we must consider this resource in some detail. The zone of cultivation and habitation is similar to the others in that the total area overstates the actual resource potential within its bounds. Even more than the others, slight variation in altitude contributes to major changes in production.

Timling's people recognize three broad subdivisions of cultivable land corresponding to altitude. The best from their point of view is the lowest, from 5300 to about 6000 ft. This relatively high quality basin land below the snowline is the most intensively farmed, suitable for the intercropping of finger millet and maize. A middle division that centers roughly on the Timling *gompo* runs from about 6000 to 7000 ft. and is planted in maize, potatoes, millet, and barley in an alternating cycle. Above this lies the poorest land, called *lekhko khet,* running from 7000 to 8500 ft. Potatoes and wheat are planted here in a three-year cycle that includes a year's fallow. Estimates from a contour map of the area show that the lowest zone contains only 1.13 square miles, or 7.78% of the cultivated zone; the middle area contains a slightly larger 3.36 square miles, or 23.16% of the entire zone; and the highest and poorest land includes 10.02 square miles, or 69.06% of the zone.

Although this breakdown gives a far better indication of the relative amounts of land quality the Tamang have to work with, other factors further reduce the amount of potentially cultivable land. Some of the land within this zone, for example, is too steep for cultivation; other parts have been taken away in landslides; and trails and houses take away another significant part. An extremely rough calculation of actual production and habitation zones suggests that only 4.14 square miles are actually in use throughout the entire territory. This area must be further reduced to account for the area devoted to households, threshing floors, the *gompo* and its surrounding land, the dense network of trails, and areas taken up by the *mani* as well as scattered uncultivable spaces within otherwise arable land.

From a random sample of households in Timling itself, it is possible to estimate the amounts of land per household. While the Tamang of this area have no way of measuring actual land area (cf. Caplan 1970:205-6), they do have ways of talking about relative amounts of land in terms of the time it takes to plough them. One *hal* of land refers to the amount of land it takes a team of oxen (Np. *hal*) one day to finish ploughing. Although this area can be expected to vary with soil quality and other factors such as slope, most people in the area who have traveled to other parts of Nepal agree that a *hal* is roughly equivalent to three *ropani*. Informants were asked to estimate the amount of grain needed to plant one *hal* in a given crop. The areas were then computed on the amount of grain sown. In spite of the obviously crude measure that results, it is worth discussing the figures for Timling and comparing them for other areas.

Sample households in Timling owned an average of 24.34 *ropani* apiece. If this area is expanded for all of the 132 households, then a total of 3212.88 *ropani* (417.67 acres) are actively cultivated in the village. This figure does not include fallow land or small garden plots within the village, yet it amounts to .654 acres per person. In terms of land area alone, the people of Timling are essentially the same as the 100 sample households in Thak with their .64 acres per person (Macfarlane 1976:47). This is better than the situation for Nepal as a whole; converting the figures provided by Banister and Thapa (1981:20) into acres per person shows that in 1971 arable land per capita for all of Nepal was .427 acres. For the mountain region, there was .211 acres, .247 for the hill region, and .735 for the Terai.

The accuracy of these estimates for Timling is supported by the comparison with the Gurung and by internal evidence. Separate information was gathered on the number of *hal* per household. Based on these figures each household owned an average of 25.85 *ropani* of land. Thus, although these estimates are rough, we can safely take them as indications of actual landholding.

A further breakdown in terms of the five major crops shows that the average household puts 26% of its land into maize, 16% into millet, 15% into wheat, 28.9% into barley, and 15% into potatoes. In area, this works out to:

maize   .823 acres
millet   .506 acres
wheat   .475 acres
barley   .914 acres
potatoes .475 acres

Data from other sources suggest that households can produce enough for their subsistence requirements on these average holdings (Macfarlane 1976:46–47; Clark and Haswell 1970:119). In Uchucmarca, Peru, for example, average household lands are of similar extent. Total holdings amount to 3.90 acres, while the number of acres devoted to potatoes, corn, wheat, and barley is 3.48, compared to 3.16 in Timling (Brush 1977:88). Average household size in Uchucmarca, however, is also a little smaller than in Timling, with 4.09 compared to 4.84. Nevertheless, although detailed medical surveys were not carried out, signs of severe malnutrition were not observed in the village. The reported production totals in sample households also suggest that the average household produces a slight surplus. In 1980, sample households produced an average of 400 *pathi* of grain each, roughly 1300 kilograms.

The final point to be made here is that in spite of the vast amount of land not yet opened in the zone of cultivation, the people have effectively reached the limits of arable land. Land in the lowest zone that is not already cultivated is unsuitable for production. Informants report that no large tracts of new land have been opened in the past 50 years. More evidence for increasing pressure on the already open section of land in the territory is found in the recent attempts by Lingjyo's people to have the *gompo's guthi* lands opened to claims by their households.

Household Capital Other Than Natural Resources

In addition to the natural resources of the area, each household must have at its disposal livestock, agricultural tools, and a variety of household articles to enable its members to gain their livelihood. The calculations in this section are based on information gathered in the economic survey. Although comparison with Macfarlane's Gurung data suggests that the estimates for Timling's households are reasonable, some caution must be exercised in accepting these figures too readily. First, respondents were less forthcoming about actual possessions than they were when they spoke about amounts of grain sown. Most of the reports for larger household items could be readily verified by a quick glance around the room, but small articles such as jewelry are generally concealed; thus estimates for these items are probably understated. Nevertheless, there is reason to believe that the Tamang possess less jewelry than the Gurung of Thak since they have had less opportunity to engage in outside employment and are generally poorer than the Gurung. Additionally, many women have begun selling their jewelry to an entrepreneur from the south in the last few years.

A final reason for a generally smaller amount of capital per Timling household concerns the nature of the two economies. Thak is considerably closer to a major market center, about six hours' walk from Pokhara. This and the greater involvement of the Gurung in the national cash economy mean that a number of household items can more easily be assigned a cash value. In Timling, on the other hand, many items are simply made by household members using materials near at hand. Some equivalent market value could be arrived at for some items but this was impossible for a great many. In Macfarlane's case, for example, a firetongs is valued at three rupees, while in Timling every household includes a homemade set of tongs from split cane. Since it takes about 30 seconds to make from readily available materials, the Tamang will not put a price on it. Other articles not sold locally, however, can be given a price since people from other villages are willing to pay for them. Grain baskets, for instance, are made from the locally abundant cane and sold in villages further south. Appendix 1 includes a basic inventory of household items and their prices if available. The articles to be discussed here can be expected to vary more generally in their abundance among households.

Apart from agriculture, the most important part of Tamang adaptation is the pastoral economy. A significant part of household capital is bound up in livestock. Unlike land, the value of livestock owned by a household is subject to considerable fluctuation from year to year, and even between seasons. The few buffalo kept by the Tamang provide milk but are otherwise productive only when they are slaughtered. Cows and oxen are used for traction, on the other hand, and cannot be legally slaughtered in Nepal although they often fall from the steep slopes of the forest zone where they are pastured. The Tamang butcher and eat the meat of these already dead animals. Goats, sheep, and chickens are not only subject to loss from accident but are also slaughtered as offerings during illnesses and on religious occasions. Chickens, in particular, are the frequent victims of influenza and other sickness in the human population. After a time of unusual ill health, their numbers are noticeably reduced. Other factors influencing the numbers of livestock include predation by natural enemies such as jackals, bears, foxes, and tigers.

Figures for livestock were gathered in October, after the Dasain holiday, which was celebrated in September. It is possible that the inventory given here therefore represents a low in the annual cycle; not only were animals butchered during the holiday, but some households were selling part of their stock just prior to it to gather money for rice purchases outside the village.

Table 4.1 presents the actual numbers of livestock reported for each household, the average number per household, and the average number considered adult under Macfarlane's assumptions (1976:89) about the proportion of adults to juvenile animals. For sheep, goats, and cattle it can be assumed that 3/4 of the animals are adult; for chickens, 1/4; the proportion of adult buffalo was actually observed. The total head of sheep and goats per household, 5.9, agrees with Alirol's findings that each household owns from 5 to 6 head (1976:53). It is less clear, however, how the total number of cattle per household compares. Alirol (1976:54) states that these animals are gathered into family herds of about a dozen while the data here show that each household has an average of 4.4 head. The discrepancy may be accounted for by assuming that Alirol was referring to the practice of related households joining their herds together in pasture. Finally, very few people in Timling raise buffalo. The Tamang report that the animal does very poorly in Timling, and they agree that this has something to do with the elevation, pointing out that the higher settlement of Lingjyo has no buffalo at all.

Comparison with figures from two Gurung villages in table 4.2 shows Timling's population to be more pastoral, with more capital invested in livestock. It is also interesting to note how the proportion of cows to oxen is reversed in the Tamang case, although the significance of this cannot be explained here. Finally, if the presence of buffalo can be taken as an indication of orientation to more southern, "Hinduized" values, then the Tamang are clearly less a part of the mainstream than the Gurung of these two villages.

The final task is to assign to the livestock a cash value so that relative capital investments in the different parts of the economy can be estimated. Table 4.3 presents prices for adult and juvenile animals in Timling and gives the total and average household investment in the various species. These are idealized figures since prices vary with respect to age, the quality of the animal, and the desire to sell or buy at a given time.

These cash values demonstrate that the major part of the Tamang commitment to livestock is related to their agricultural cycle. Since the major value of cattle is for traction, the capital investment in traction animals is fully 59% of the total livestock capital; the investment in sheep and goats, raised for their own sake as sources of food and wool, is only 35%. Yet the economy is clearly more pastoral than that of Thak, with its 10% investment in sheep and goats (Macfarlane 1976:89).

In addition to livestock, the household inventory includes a number of items that insure survival and aid in gaining a livelihood. Standard items of clothing are owned by all households; the numbers of these articles depend largely on the number of people over the age of 12 in the family. In general, clothing is manufactured within the household although dyed thread for women's skirts is now bought in Trisuli. In the entire village, only one woman owns a *sari*, and this was bought by her husband when he recently returned from 20 years of service in the Indian army. Appendix 1 presents the essential wardrobe for men and women in Timling along with the value of the articles of clothing.

The total value of clothing for a fully dressed male is about 350 rupees, depending on the exact mix of purchased or locally produced thread. For an adult female, the total is about 300 rupees, again depending on the exact clothing worn. The Tamang also consider it prudent to have two sets of clothes for each adult. The second set is older and can be considered to be worth half the value of the new. For the Tamang male, this amounts to an additional 50 rupees worth of clothing

The Subsistence Economy

Table 4.1. Total Livestock Owned in Sample Households.

Animal	N	X̄	"Adults"
Sheep	82	2.73	2.05
Goat	108	3.60	2.70
Cow	67	2.23	1.67
Ox	66	2.20	1.65
Buffalo	9	.30	.23
Chicken	111	3.70	.93

Source: Timling Economic Survey.

Table 4.2. Household Livestock in Three Villages.

Animal	Timling 1981	Thak*1969	Mohoriya*1958
Sheep	2.73	---	---
Goat	3.60	3.02	1.47
Cow	2.23	1.66	2.27
Ox	2.20	.73	.68
Buffalo	.30	2.23	1.05

Source: Timling Economic Survey and *Macfarlane (1976:90).

Table 4.3. Rupee Value for Livestock, Timling 1981.

Animal	N	Adult Value	Juvenile Value	Total	%	X̄
Sheep	82	450	150	30,750	18	1025
Goat	108	300	100	27,000	16	900
Cow	67	900	600	55,275	32	1843
Ox	66	800	400	56,200	27	1540
Buffalo	9	1200	500	9,400	6	313
Chicken	111	25	15	1,943	1	65
Total				170,568	100	5686

Source: Timling Economic Survey.

since it is unusual to have a second jacket, while the female Tamang would have another full set of clothing worth about 150 rupees. An extremely rough estimate of the value of clothing for the average household, then, would be about 1300 rupees.

The quality of houses in Timling varies considerably, both in the raw material used for construction and in the amount of space available to each household. Although buildings are all about the same size in Timling, available space varies

Table 4.4. Household Capital in Timling and Thak.

	Timling 1981			Thak* 1969		
Type	Rupees	$US	%	Rupees	$US	%
Land	24,340	2896	61.9	28,150	3350	68.5
Livestock	5,685	677	14.5	1,423	169	3.5
Housing	4,950	589	12.6	5,060	602	12.3
Household goods, tools	3,049	363	7.8	5,617	668	13.7
Clothing	1,300	155	3.3	856	102	2.1
Total	39,324	4680	100.0	41,106	4891	100.0

Source: Timling Economic Survey and *Macfarlane (1976:109).

because of the practice of poorer families subdividing a larger structure among brothers. It is not unusual to find buildings that originally held a single household now divided to hold four. The range of prices for a new house will depend on the materials used in construction, the number of stories, and other features such as location and ornament. A two-story house with a splitshake roof costs the builder approximately 10,000 rupees to build in Timling, although a house built during my stay in the village cost 8000 rupees because its owner secured much of the labor by calling in debts and his father donated the land. For the evaluation of households in the sample, all these factors have been considered together to assign a value. The investment in houses, then, is about 5482 rupees.

Finally, table 4.4 presents the total capital for the average household in Timling. Excluded are communal lands and labor resources for each household. Comparisons with Thak are illuminating in that they show a rough correspondence in capital value. This similarity should, however, be accepted with caution since inflation and regional variation in prices mean that items such as clothing, livestock, and household goods tend to be more expensive in Timling.

The final picture that we get from this review of resources shows that the Tamang, while not as richly endowed as the Gurung of Thak, are not yet in a desperate situation on the average. In terms of the natural resources of timber and grazing land, they appear to be quite well off. Yet this picture obscures some of the variation in the fortune of individual households and still needs to be placed in the larger context of adaptive processes and social change. The next section will examine the kinds of work that the Tamang actually do while another chapter will discuss variation within Timling in greater detail.

Ways of Working in Timling

Work in Timling is a matter of survival. Each household can be thought of as an independent economic unit defined by the need to produce food for the hearth.

The Tamang perceive themselves as having to work harder than people in the lower valleys, but it would be misleading to picture them living lives of unremitting toil. Even necessary work is not especially onerous when done with friends and relatives. People often choose to emphasize their work in one section of the economy for no other reason than a fondness for the task. Thus, men speak of the pleasures of tending cattle in the forest zone where large parts of the day are devoted to smoking tobacco and gossiping, punctuated by occasional breaks to check on the cattle or chop wood for the fire.

Work within the village territory can be divided into agricultural, pastoral, and maintenance. All households are, without exception, involved in these categories. Some households include members who engage in the additional work of ritual specialist—*bombo* or *lama*—and are active throughout the year placating gods, ghosts, and witches while working their own fields and caring for their own livestock. Their work tends to be divided among them all although some individuals are sought out for their exemplary performances. The *gompo lama* is often pressed into service for death rituals, for example, because of his ability to read the Tibetan texts.

Work outside the village is becoming an increasingly important component of the village repertoire as some families send members afield to seek wage labor in portering or road work as far away as Bhutan. This part of the economy promises to expand in spite of its mostly supplemental status for present households.

The Subsistence Calendar

The timing of subsistence activities in Timling is rigorously determined by meshing the different requirements of cultigens and livestock with the openings provided by the environment and local climate. The Tamang hold this exploitation of multiple environments in common with other mountain peoples. Table 4.5 presents the general calendar of activities. Although much of it is obvious, some features need to be highlighted.

One very important function of this schedule is to join the agricultural and pastoral segments of the economy at mutually beneficial intervals. Thus, sheep, goats, and cattle are permitted into the village and cultivated zones only at times when they are least threatening to maturing plants and when they provide the benefits of manure for fertilizer. In the case of oxen they also provide traction for ploughing. In practice, this might be more accurately thought of as keeping the animals out of the cultivated zone during the four summer months when arable land is in crop and there is no space for freely roaming herds. The strategy is one of taking the livestock to their fodder rather than the more intensive one of bringing fodder to the livestock. Those months when livestock are kept in the village area are the same months when they can be fed inedible parts of the harvest or when household members are free from other agricultural tasks and can more easily collect fodder.

Table 4.5. Timling's Agro-Pastoral Calendar.

	Jan	Feb	Mar	Apr	May	Jun	Jul	Aug	Sep	Oct	Nov	Dec
Corn			PS	W	W	W		HC	HC	C	PC	PC
Millet₁	C	C	C	PC	S	W	T	W	H		C	C
Millet₂	C	C	C	PC	S	W	W			H	HC	C
Barley			W	HC	HC	C			P	P	S	W
Wheat				W	H	HC	C		P	P	S	W
Potatoes			PS	W	W	W	HC	HC	HC	P	P	P
Soybeans				S	W	W			H	C	C	

T = Transplanting
H = Harvest
C = Primarily Consumed

P = Plough
S = Sowing
W = Weeding

	Jan	Feb	Mar	Apr	May	Jun	Jul	Aug	Sep	Oct	Nov	Dec
Sheep & Goats	S	V	V	V	VF	F	P	P	PV	V	V	VS
Cattle	V	V	V	V	VF	F	FV	FV	FV	V	V	V

V = Village Zone
F = Forest Zone

P = High Pastures
S = Southern Pastures

76   The Subsistence Economy

Table 4.6.   Ritual Holidays in Timling.

Month	Holiday	Days
January	Magh Purni	2
July	Barma	3
	Saon Sakranti	1
August	Baddo Purni	2
October	Dasain	3
	Tiwari	3
December	Jatra	3
Total Days		17

It is apparent from the calendar that grain harvests occur throughout the year. The seasonality of harvests for particular grains is reflected in the seasonality of diet for the Tamang. Predictably, the months of Phagun and Chait (mid-February through mid-April) are considered the hardest months, when some households experience shortages; the period from Baddo through Mangsir (mid-August through mid-December) is the time of greatest abundance, when the diet is supplemented by other garden produce in addition to the variety of grains. The intersection of times of scarcity with the period of low labor requirements in the village makes the time from Pus through Phagun (mid-December through mid-March) an ideal time for the Tamang to leave the village in search of wage labor. Coincidentally, this is also part of the peak trekking season in Nepal and a time when porters are most likely to be employed. The result is a reduction of mouths to feed in the village during scarce times and a potential addition of supplemental funds to the household when the need is greatest.

Even those times of year when production activities are most essential to subsistence in Timling are not without interruption. The Tamang follow an intricate ritual calendar in addition to that patterned by agro-pastoral activities, and the year is filled with non-work days. The full and new moon days of each month, for example, are considered rest days by the people of Timling. A number of major holidays mark the year. These days are in addition to the 22 already taken off, for a total of 37. Other days are viewed as non-work days for the village but occur irregularly. For example, nobody in the village will work in the fields when a death has occurred in the area, and other days are taken off for reasons such as illness or travel to Trisuli Bazaar for supplies. The result is that of the approximately 300 days when agricultural work in the village is done at least 29 are regarded as nonwork days for ritual reasons and an additional number are taken off for deaths, illnesses, and other reasons.

Household Work

A large part of work in Timling has to do with the maintenance of buildings and tools, manufacturing items for use, and the domestic tasks of cooking and caring for children and the sick. Except for cooking and childcare, most of these chores can be managed at the convenience of household members although there might be a mild seasonality of tasks when the subsistence calendar permits. Of the standard inventory of household items listed in appendix 1, it is important to remember that the need for them is somewhat flexible; they will be made if the household can spare the labor or obtained in other ways if it cannot.

Necessary domestic tasks for every household include making clothing, cutting firewood, fetching water, and some household maintenance. Some necessary items that may not be made in the household where they are used include the different kinds of bamboo matting that have uses from temporary shelters to walls to sleeping mats. These are mainly produced by older men in the household. Younger men will also make them if they have the time or are recovering from an illness and can do light work.

Taking into account those tasks that must be performed in all households, it is possible to establish the approximate person-days per year required by each task. We have already seen that the average household requires some 154 bundles of wood a year. Although a variety of methods is practiced for gathering the wood during the year (cf. Macfarlane 1976:134–35), it generally takes about half a working day to cut and haul one bundle of wood back to the village. This is true even though at certain times of the year groups of men cut wood together to lay in a large supply before the monsoon and winter months. The principal benefit of working together in this way is in camaraderie since little effort is saved and the rate of hauling and cutting is unchanged. One popular method of laying in wood is to spend five or six days in the forest cutting and tossing the logs into the Dhungsel Khola, which flows below the village. There a team of men removes the lumber for splitting. This method is popular more for obviating the need to haul for long distances on the back than for any great savings in time. The approximate number of person-days of labor for an average household's lumber supply is thus some 77 days.

All households in Timling need to cook for themselves. While it is difficult to arrive at an average figure for the time spent in cooking and related chores each day, my impressions agree with Macfarlane's estimate of about half a person-day per household. This includes the work of keeping the fire going, fetching the water, and actually cooking the food. Tamang cooking is far from elaborate. The basic meal consists of flour and water boiled and stirred together to form a thick porridge called *dhiro*. Salt may or may not be a part of the meal and, depending on the season, the side dish might consist of a sauce prepared from stinging nettles. Likewise, pots and utensils are seldom cleaned, and the dried porridge on the inside of the pot is simply picked off and eaten by whoever wants it during the day. Two major meals are eaten in the morning and evening with a smaller snack eaten toward mid-day. On this basis a very rough estimate of the time spent by a household in cooking and related tasks is about 182.5 person-days per year.

Women manufacture clothing for each household's members during the year. While not all of these articles need yearly replacement, the average household needs about four new garments in that time. Each garment requires about five days for the weaving alone. In addition, turbans and cummerbunds must be replaced about every two years, and the tight weaving for these requires about ten days of work. Assuming that the average household requires four of these articles every two years suggests that an additional 20 person-days per year are required for the manufacture of clothing. Thus the total labor input for all clothing is 40 person-days a year.

If this were all that were required for each household, then the total person-days for household work would amount to 299.5 in a year. But other work must also be done even if every household does not participate in it. We might add labor time sufficient to replace two cane mats and two new baskets each year. This would add 10 days to the average household's labor requirements.

Agricultural Work

The most important subsistence work is agricultural. While the pastoral and wage labor portions of the economy are able to provide supplementary foods, the day-to-day food requirements of these villagers are almost entirely dependent on what they grow in their fields. Consequently, even though pastoral work has higher prestige for Tamang men, they are quick to admit the importance of agriculture. As one man put it: *Alu chaina bhane, sas pani chaina* (Without potatoes, there would also be no life). The same could be said for any of the major crops grown. Table 4.7 shows the major domesticated plants of the village. Other than the grains and potatoes, not all of these plants are grown by all households. Another edible plant, the stinging nettle (Tm. *polo*), grows wild throughout the area.

Swidden agriculture is no longer practiced extensively, and the Tamang consider most of the worthwhile arable land to be already open. Asked about the possibilities of growing potatoes in the open areas around the permanent cattlesheds, they replied that the heavy monsoon rains at that elevation caused the tubers to rot in the ground. Consequently, most of the agricultural work for Timling is directed to ploughing and raising crops on already open land. Each of the different subdivisions within the zone of cultivation is appropriate for a different set of plants, and even different areas at the same elevation differ in the crops rotated on them.

Crop rotation also means that the proportion of land in a particular crop will change from year to year. Although almost all households will plant the same array

Table 4.7. Domesticated Plants in the Upper Ankhu Khola.

English	Tamang	Nepali
Finger millet	sanga	kodo
white	tar sanga	seto kodo
red	ola sanga	chamre kodo
black	chup sanga	kalo kodo
Millet	andewola	kodo
Maize	makai	makai
white	tar makai	seto makai
yellow	ur makai	pahelo makai
Barley	cahku	jau
Wheat	wah	gaun
Potato	teme	alu
Soybeans	thowa	bhadmas
Beans	pruntung	simi
Squash	parsi	pharsi
Taro	pindalu	pindalu
Pepper	kurcanyi	khursani
Amaranth	mendo	latthi

of grains and potatoes each year, the amount of seed sown for any single crop can vary considerably. Nevertheless, broad patterns do define the different crop zones.

The lowest cropland below the village is the most desirable by Timling standards; it is also the least abundant. Less than half the sample households own any land there at all, but two of the holdings amount to more than two *ropani* (.26 acres). In this area of most intensive farming, millet and maize are intercropped from year to year without fallow. The procedure is first to plant the maize sometime in March. The millet (*andewola*) is planted in small nursery plots in late April and early May and transplanted between the maize stalks in July. After the harvest and during the coldest months of the year, village cattle are pastured on these plots, and the heavy pasturing allows their dung to, in part, replenish the soil.

The middle division of agricultural land centering on the *gompo* is devoted to the rotation of maize and potatoes, barley, and red finger millet (*olasanga*). Black finger millet (*chupsanga*) is grown in the cooler, less sunny areas toward Lapdung; while finger millet (*tarsanga*) is grown on the slopes around Phyang, where the sun exposure is best in spite of medium quality land. All of these varieties of finger millet are processed in the same way and are not transplanted as the millet in the basin land is.

In 1981, maize and potatoes were planted in the middle division during March. The plots had been ploughed twice, in November and December, and once again just before the planting. After the harvest in September and October, the ground was again ploughed and planted in barley, which would be ready for harvest in May of 1982. After yet another ploughing, the red finger millet would be planted and ready for harvest in November for the completion of the two-year cycle.

In fact, different parcels of land within this zone are at different phases in the cycle, and while the timing above refers to village territory in the *gompo* area and toward Lapdung, the land in the other direction toward Kamigaon was planted in finger millet instead of maize. Each household owns several parcels of land throughout all of the zones (apart from the lowest) and grows a variety of plants every year. The Tamang consciously reason that they are spreading their risks by doing so since there is a high probability that some of the crop will be reduced by hail, excessive rain, blight, or foraging animals.

The upper fields are also planted in a two-year cycle, but one that includes a lengthy fallow period between the wheat harvest and the planting of potatoes. For example, a field planted with wheat in October of 1981 will be harvested in June of 1982 and allowed to lie fallow until April of 1983, when it will be planted in potatoes. These potatoes will be harvested in September and October of that same year, and the cycle will continue again with the wheat planting. As with other lands, all phases of the cycle are occurring at any given time.

It is difficult to come up with estimates of person-days devoted to agricultural activities in Timling. The method used here is identical to that used by Macfarlane (1976:127) in that I asked two people how long it would take to perform various tasks on a given area of land. Person-days were then calculated by dividing the estimates by 10. (The length of a person-day is considered to be 10 hours here, except in the case of ploughing when it is taken to be six hours.) The number of person-days per *ropani* for the various crops and tasks is given in table 4.8. Because these figures represent the labor intensity per *ropani*, they need to be multiplied by the actual number of *ropani* devoted to each crop to give the total agricultural labor requirement for the average household. The last two columns give these figures and the percentage of labor devoted to each crop. Total person-days devoted to agricultural production amount to some 203, if we consider only production-oriented tasks. The actual total would be higher since the hours devoted to simply watching the field to protect it from theft or the predations of monkeys and bears have not been figured in. This total is, nevertheless, a useful one for comparison since it incorporates the labor time for the production of each crop.

Pastoral Work

Although we have seen that pastoral work is secondary in importance to agricultural work in Timling, a substantial portion of household capital is invested in livestock,

Table 4.8. Labor Inputs (Person-Days) per Land Unit and Percent of Labor by Crop.

Crop	Manure	Plough	Plant	Weed	Harvest	Other	Total per rop.	Total per crop	%
Corn	3	0.60	0.15	2.60	1.30	1.00	8.65	48.04	24.7
Millet$_1$	4	0.33	0.50	4.80	4.00	1.45	14.63	7.14	3.5
Millet$_2$	1	0.33	0.50	1.90	1.60	0.05	4.93	16.13	7.9
Barley	2	0.67	0.50	1.50	1.60	0.65	9.97	72.08	35.5
Wheat	2	0.67	0.50	1.50	1.60	0.65	9.97	36.99	18.2
Potatoes	4	1.17	0.10	0.60	0.70	----	5.57	22.66	11.2

Total person-days for an average household = 203

Source: Timling Economic Survey and field notes.

and each household must devote labor to the care of these animals. The average household is not in a position to devote a constant amount of labor to the maintenance of its livestock, especially when the demands of the agricultural cycle are at their peak. In addition, the different animals themselves require different strategies of pasture, as when sheep and goats are separated from the cattle herds in the summer and winter months. The strategy of joining the livestock of more than one household and dividing herding responsibilities greatly reduces required labor inputs during those times of year when it is least available.

It is easy to show how livestock can potentially increase household labor requirements in the absence of cooperative herding. Of the 365 days in a year, sheep, goats, and cattle can only be herded together for about 185 days. Assuming that each household would need to devote one person-day of labor to these herds for each day, a year would require 185 person-days plus two times the remaining 180 days when one person is needed for each separate herd. These 545 person-days would be more than twice the labor investment required by agriculture.

Two strategies permit a solution to this dilemma. The first is the practice of delaying the splitting of herds when a son claims his inheritance. Most sons will demand only their share of the land when they establish their own households; they continue to retain joint interest in livestock although they will be able to identify particular animals as their own. In practice, this means that an average herd is an amalgam of three households. A second strategy pursued by those households with full control over their own herds but lacking labor resources for herding has the same affect. These households will link with others of their choice to form a communal herd and share their labor.

Further reductions in labor requirements are possible during the time of year when sheep and goats are herded separately. Since large numbers of sheep and goats are easily herded by a few shepherds and a few good dogs, these animals are massed into three large herds for the village. Each herd of about 250 animals consists of the sheep and goats from about 42 households but requires the labor of only two people for those 180 days they are together. Thus the labor requirements for cattle can be divided by three while those for sheep and goats can be divided by even more since they add no person-days of labor when they are divided into their individual households and herded with the cattle. The pastoral economy, then, requires an average investment of roughly 130 person-days per household in a year.

In fact, the actual investment of labor is probably slightly more for each household, since the average composition of household members in the permanent cattle sheds is one fully productive adult along with a young boy of about age 12.

A partial accounting of the average labor requirements per household, then, amounts to 632.78 person-days. If we assume that the average household has 2.59 production units who are available for work about 300 days out of the year, then 777 person-days of labor are available for each household. Of these, 144.22 are left for tasks other than those we have considered.

Working for Wages

A final category needs to be considered here although both the number of households involved in it and the amount of time devoted to it are highly variable. More and more of Timling's households send members from the village to participate in the wage labor economy of Nepal for short periods. As a rule, this occurs during the months of Pus through the beginning of Phagun (late December through February), when the labor requirements in the village are reduced and when porter work is most available. In addition to porter work, the Tamang often make the difficult trip to Bhutan where they obtain jobs on Indian government road construction crews.

Working outside is a high risk undertaking since wages are low and the availability of jobs cannot be guaranteed. In addition, this is the only part of the Tamang adaptation that places people in competition with thousands of people from other hill villages seeking the same kinds of work at about the same time. Timling's relative remoteness and the high rate of illiteracy place its people at a disadvantage for some jobs. Jobs such as *sirdar* for trekking parties, for example, might require the ability to read and write and even to speak rudimentary English. In practice, this means that the Tamang often work at the most menial jobs for about 10 rupees a day if they are lucky enough to obtain work to begin with.

Other avenues for wage labor include employment as Gurkha soldiers in the British and Indian armies. While this is a high prestige occupation, very few households from Timling have had members take advantage of it, and only one person in the village managed to stay in the army long enough to earn a pension. The reasons for this have to do with the British army policy of favoring Magar and Gurung tribesmen over the Tamang in the past. Added to this is the recent requirement for minimum schooling to join the Indian army. The consequence has been that, but for one member of the Damrong clan, only a few Ghale from Timling have served as Gurkhas. As Ghale, they would be able to pass for Gurung, who also have a clan of that name, and be more highly rated than other Tamang recruits. The importance of Gurkha service to the people of the Ankhu Khola area is discussed more fully in Toffin (1976b) and Höfer (1978). The role of this type of work for Timling will be taken up again in the discussion of a particular household history.

5

Demographic Processes I: Fertility

Issues in Fertility Analysis in Small Populations

The analysis of fertility is critical to any discussion of a community's adaptation to its environment. Fertility and mortality schedules together determine the major characteristics of a population closed to migration—such as age distribution and growth rate—that have a direct bearing on household economy and the balance between community size and resources. In addition, community level fertility data are lacking in Nepal and, although the situation is improving, it is still necessary to accumulate as many studies as possible (cf. Macfarlane 1978b). Timling's population practices no effective method of conscious birth control. As Leridon (1977:104) notes, the conditions that frustrate the gathering of reliable demographic data are often the same as those that encourage a natural fertility regime. Analysis of Timling's fertility therefore has more general value as a contribution to the study of natural fertility.

Although the value of fertility data is not in doubt, the small size of the populations that anthropologists typically study raises questions about how far analysis can go. One major concern is unique to small populations: that of random fluctuation in vital rates or other population characteristics through time. While minor disruptions in more general trends can be masked by the sheer weight of numbers in large groups, chance events will have a more visible impact in smaller groups. If the special explanations for anomalous rates or distributions aren't known, the analysis of data can be seriously affected. Other problems can be more easily dealt with. For example, defining the population and finding methods appropriate to the data are concerns peculiar to small populations (Carroll 1975:3; Feeney 1975:21). Otherwise, demographic analysis presents much the same set of difficulties for any size unit. As Feeney (1975:44–45) cautions: "In practice, all data are in error. The issue is never whether or not error is present, but what the magnitude and the direction of the error are and the significance of this magnitude and direction for any particular analysis."

Thus there is no *a priori* reason to believe that the demographic analysis of anthropological populations is without value. A growing body of technical literature (Howell 1974, 1976b; Weiss 1973, 1975) suggests just the opposite, and substantive studies have been carried out in populations of varying sizes: a Thai village of 1,718 people (Lauro 1979), a Malaysian group of 733 people (Fix 1977), a !Kung population of 569 (Howell 1979), and a highland New Guinea people of about 1,500 (Wood et al. 1985).

The Experience of Women of Completed Fertility

If rates are not changing drastically in Timling, then the experience of women who have completed their fertility is the best indicator of the present and future fertility performance for all women in the village. The 56 women in the Tamang sample who have completed their fertility represent an age span of 31 years, from age 45 to age 76 at the time of fieldwork. At one extreme, this means that one five-year cohort is still technically in the fecund period since a few births do occur between 45 and 50, while at the other extreme is a group of women who have been past the fecund period for at least 25 years. Within this kind of range it can be reasonably assumed that the reported experience of older cohorts will suffer from the effects of memory bias.

Table 5.1 presents the parity distributions for these five-year cohorts. Although this breakdown creates extremely small groups, it provides a manageable way to examine the completed fertility record for trends in the total number of births per woman.

The first thing to notice in this table is that there is no evidence of a trend in any direction in total number of births. In fact, the largest average number of births has been reported by the oldest cohort—evidence to contravene any suggestion of memory bias. The cohort experiencing the low average of 3.57 births per woman is somewhat anomalous in relation to the other cohorts; but, although its small size makes a firm conclusion difficult, it is worth noting how the number of women who completed their reproductive careers at two births distorts the spread and that the number of women of low parity is approached by only one other cohort, whose greater size lessens the impact on the overall average.

From this table, then, it can be seen that the total number of births to women of completed fertility has remained fairly constant over the 30+ years of experience represented here. The cumulative experience of all women 45 years and older shows a roughly regular distribution around the mode of five births per woman.

Table 5.2 presents the age-specific fertility rates for these 56 women as if they represented a single cohort's experience. The rationale for this apparent deviation from good demographic sense is that the rates can be significant only if they represent the experience of some maximal number of women or woman-years in a small population. Since we can conclude that no obvious trends are visible from the data in table 5.1, this table merely expands the scope of that conclusion to vital rates.

Table 5.1.   Parity Distributions for Five-Year Cohorts of Women 45 Years Old and Older.

Number of Births

Age	(N)	0	1	2	3	4	5	6	7	8	9	10	11	$\bar{x}$
45-49	(13)	0	1	2	1	1	2	2	2	1	1	0	0	5.00
50-54	(11)	0	0	0	1	2	3	2	2	0	1	0	0	5.55
55-59	(7)	0	1	3	0	1	0	1	0	1	0	0	0	3.57
60-64	(9)	0	0	1	1	2	1	0	2	0	1	0	1	5.78
65-69	(8)	0	0	1	0	0	4	2	0	1	0	0	0	5.25
70+	(8)	0	0	0	1	2	0	1	2	1	0	1	0	6.13
Total	(56)	0	2	7	4	8	10	8	8	4	3	1	1	5.25

Source: Timling Marriage and Fertility History.

Table 5.2. Age-Specific Fertility Rates for Women 45 Years Old and Older.

Parity

Age	1	2	3	4	5	6	7	8	9	10	11	Total	At Risk	ASF
15-19	7	2	0	0	0	0	0	0	0	0	0	9	280	.032
20-24	34	15	4	0	0	0	0	0	0	0	0	53	280	.189
25-29	13	27	19	8	1	1	0	0	0	0	0	69	280	.246
30-34	2	8	15	17	10	2	1	0	0	0	0	55	280	.196
35-39	0	1	8	13	16	13	5	2	1	0	0	59	280	.211
40-44	0	1	1	5	8	8	8	5	3	1	0	40	280	.143
45-49	0	0	0	0	0	1	3	2	1	1	1	9	274	.033
Total	56	54	47	43	35	25	17	9	5	2	1			

Total women 56
Total births 294
Mean parity 5.25

Source: Timling Marriage and Fertility History.

It thus follows the practice of Howell (1979) and others (cf. Macfarlane 1976; Fix 1977) who have worked with "anthropological" populations. The table gives information for age of mother at birth parity x in addition to age-specific rates, which are figured by dividing the number of births to women in an age period by the number of woman-years in that period. The slightly reduced number of years in the 45–49 year group accounts for the small number of woman-years left to have all 56 women move out of the theoretical fecund period.

This table presents a remarkably regular picture of Timling women's fertility, considering the small size of the sample. The low rates at the beginning of the fecund period, followed by swift ascent and slow decline in age-specific fertility, are consistent with the record for natural fertility populations in general. Where the anomaly exists in the table, the higher ASFR for the 35–39 age group than the 30–34 age group, the small number of births involved and the random fluctuation that can affect the results for small numbers of people can easily explain the pattern.

Figure 5.1 graphs the age-specific fertility rates and compares them to the various regional rates within Nepal (Banister and Thapa 1981). Once again, a noticeable feature of the Timling rates is their remarkable consistency. Of particular interest is the close correspondence between Timling's rates and those of the mountain region in comparison with those of other regions of Nepal. The full explanation for the fertility experience of Timling women will be discussed later, but it is worth noting here that Timling's cultural and economic history aligns it more closely with the peoples of the mountain region of Nepal than with those of the hill region, which includes a wide range of more Hinduized and less pastorally inclined groups.

Another way to look at this same information is to compare the average fertility experience of Timling women at a given age with the experience of other women in Nepal. Table 5.3 presents this information for Timling and the separate regions of Nepal. It shows how many children a woman can be expected to bear on the average by the end of the age period. The similarity between Timling and the mountain region is again borne out in these figures. The final column presents a hypothetical cumulative experience for the average woman in Timling if the age-specific rates for the earliest five years in the fecund period were to match those of the mountain region. The even closer correspondence that results suggests that Timling's fertility is dampened relative to that of the mountain region in the first five years when age-specific rates are more susceptible to the effect of marriage rates. More will be said about this in a later section.

Finally, table 5.4 presents average ages for first and last births and average reproductive spans for the women of Timling who have completed their fertility experience. Once again, there is no obvious trend that may be inferred for the six cohorts although age at first birth is slightly later in the youngest age group in comparison to the oldest.

Figure 5.1. Age-Specific Fertility for Timling and Three Regions of Nepal Compared.

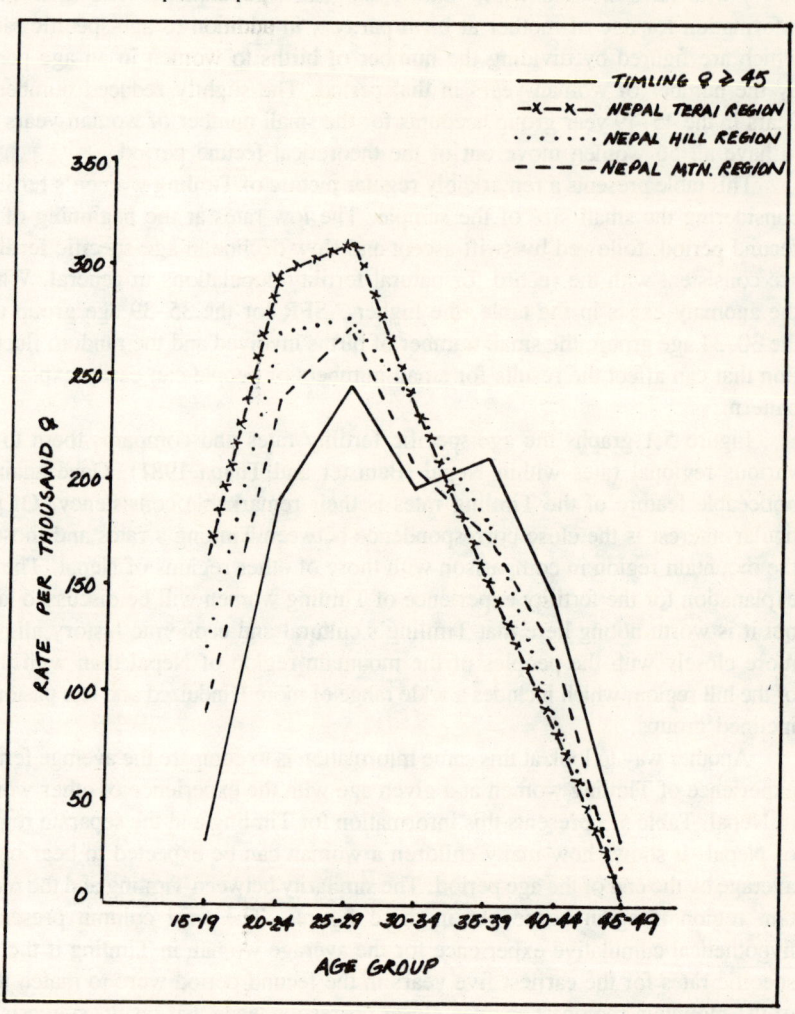

——— TIMLING ♀ ≥ 45
—x—x— NEPAL TERAI REGION
·········· NEPAL HILL REGION
— — — NEPAL MTN. REGION

Reproductive span is here defined as the number of years between ages at first and last birth, since the best indicator of entry into a fecund state is the first pregnancy and the best indicator of secondary sterility is the failure to produce more children. The reproductive span is, thus, not be be confused with the fecund period, a biological concept less subject to the effects of social structure. Reproductive span is at best a very rough indicator of the fecund period, with the age at entry influenced almost entirely by the age of marriage and cohabitation while the age at last birth is equally susceptible to such factors as absence or death of spouse.

Table 5.3. Cumulative Fertility for Timling and Selected Nepali Populations.

Age	Timling[a]	Terai[b]	Hills[b]	Mtns.[b]	Timling*
15-19	.160	.815	.600	.450	.450
20-24	1.105	2.290	1.985	1.640	1.395
25-29	2.335	3.840	3.380	3.005	2.625
30-34	3.315	5.000	4.605	4.020	3.605
35-39	4.370	5.765	5.475	4.870	4.660
40-44	5.085	6.180	5.885	5.475	5.390
45-49	5.245	6.220	5.975	5.625	5.550

*Assuming the same ASFR in the 15-19 group as in the mountain region.

Sources: [a] *Timling Marriage and Fertility History* and [b] *Banister and Thapa 1981*.

Table 5.4. Average Age at First and Last Birth and Length of Reproductive Span for Women 45+.

Age	1st Birth $\bar{X}$	SD	Last Birth $\bar{X}$	SD	Reproductive Span $\bar{X}$	SD
45-49	22.85	2.97	38.69	7.16	15.85	7.97
50-54	22.91	3.83	40.00	4.29	17.09	2.51
55-59	24.86	1.78	36.71	6.08	11.86	10.24
60-64	21.78	2.33	38.78	7.23	17.00	7.60
65-69	23.25	2.82	40.38	5.29	17.13	6.56
70+	21.63	3.38	40.88	4.16	19.25	4.03
Total	22.82	2.92	39.27	5.79	16.45	6.82

Source: Timling Marriage and Fertility History.

A comparison of tables 5.1 and 5.4 suggests a relationship between reproductive span and parity. Those cohorts with an average of over five reported births per woman are the same cohorts with at least 17-year reproductive spans. The shortest reproductive span of 11.86 years is that of the cohort with the least number of average births per woman; a closer look at table 5.4 shows that this reproductive span was truncated at both ends, with the latest average age at first birth and the earliest average age at last birth.

The main point from these 56 reproductive histories is that there seems to be no trend toward either higher or lower fertility over the 30+ years encompassed by these women's careers. The average number of births per woman is 5.25, a low total for a natural fertility population but one that invites comparison with the 5.63 births attributed to the average woman in the mountain region in the Nepal Fertility Survey during the 1971-75 period. Age-specific fertility rates for these women also follow the expected pattern although they tend to be lower in the earlier ages than those of other populations. Most of the measures of fertility for women of completed fertility show a strong internal consistency that argues well for the quality of the Timling data.

Fertility Performance over Time: Measures of Period Fertility

An alternative way of picturing Tamang fertility in Timling is to use the reproductive histories to look at fertility during specific periods. This allows us to analyze fertility during the particular years or groups of years while also forcing us to confront the reliability of the data in other ways.

By checking the TFR for the five-year periods for which women occupy every age group, we can gain a longer perspective on the data. The TFR for the 1957–61 period, an average of 6.35, effectively challenges the notion of a long trend toward increasing fertility. For the next five-year period, an average TFR of 5.05 suggests, if anything, that the dominant pattern is one of a fertility peak at the end of decades with slightly lower fertility at the beginning.

Goldman et al. (1979) have suggested that the accuracy of data in the Nepal Fertility Survey can be checked through the assumption of unchanging cumulative fertility in the different cohorts. By establishing rates for the most recent period and comparing those of other periods with them, we can determine the extent of omission in particular years. One major and not unreasonable assumption here is that events in the most recent period are more accurately reported because they are still fresh and not as easily forgotten. This applies to errors caused by omission, which lower the TFR for a period, as well as those due to displacement, which can shift age-specific rates to higher and lower numbers in different age categories or inflate the TFR for one year and deflate it in another.

Fertility measures for Timling have already been shown to fluctuate through time. A closer look at the age-specific rates by period should allow us to say more about how these changes work. Table 5.5 presents age-specific and total fertility

Table 5.5. Timling's Age-Specific Fertility Rates for All Women by Period.

Period

Age	42-46	47-51	52-56	57-61	62-66	67-71	72-76	77-81
15-19	.000	.027	.014	.051	.022	.025	.022	.037
20-24	.303	.071	.164	.282	.172	.220	.138	.207
25-29	.212	.182	.286	.274	.155	.313	.330	.263
30-34	.211	.212	.182	.214	.178	.197	.232	.275
35-39	.412	.184	.173	.242	.258	.205	.197	.273
40-44	.176	.132	.154	.030	.143	.137	.141
45-49	.059	.053	.038	.030	.000	.027
TFR	5.05	6.35	4.27	5.67	5.28	6.12

Source: Timling Marriage and Fertility History.

rates for five-year periods in the past by age group. Columns in this table present period rates while diagonal cells will give the experience of a cohort of women. If adjacent cells are compared horizontally, the experience of different cohorts can be compared for a particular age-set. Thus, the same group of women who have an ASFR of .273 in 1977-81, when they were between 35 and 39, experience an ASFR of .232 in 1972-76, when they were between 30 and 34.

Depending on our opening assumptions, these data permit a number of interpretations. While Goldman et al.'s assumption that the most current period will most accurately reflect actual fertility is reasonable, especially for the Nepal Fertility Survey data, it would force a strained interpretation of the Timling data. Following this assumption, one would expect rates to decline in the earlier years through the effects of omission. Since there appears to be no such general decline in the rates for Timling, we would have to conclude, for example, that the TFR for the 1957-61 period was even higher than that of the most recent period. Further, the more recent periods would not be adjusted upward as much as the earlier ones, increasing the range of fluctuation in TFRs. The result would be an even more jagged picture than the data presently suggest. Both the lack of clear trends in Timling's rates and the long-term residence in the village that went with data collection argue against recourse to the constant effects of memory bias to explain or adjust rates.

Figure 5.2 gives a graphic idea of the trends in total fertility rates throughout the five-year periods for which data exist in all age groups. It clearly demonstrates the lack of patterned change in rates over five-year periods while also showing the general consistency in the timing of births over these same periods. Once again, the 1962-66 period appears to be the most depressed in relation to the others. Although the shape of the graph for this period would be consistent with event displacement to the 35-39 year age group for reported births, the lack of any evidence for such displacement in other years, coupled with a method of aging and placing events that should be largely free of age heaping, point to some more specific cause for the pattern.

The 1962-66 column, like all others with a complete set of age groups represented, gives the experience of seven five-year cohorts of women. By comparing these rates with those to either side, we are able to compare the experience of different cohorts as they pass through the same ages. Such a comparison reinforces the attempt to lay the cause of dampened fertility on factors specific to this period. Four of the seven cohorts experienced markedly reduced fertility for their age class during this period. If the age-specific fertility rates for women of completed fertility are taken as a yardstick, the rate for the 20-24-year-old group during 1962-66 is .017 below the average; for the 25-29-year-old group .091 lower, for the 30-34-year-old group .018 lower; and for the 40-44-year-old group .113 lower than the average. This would mean a total fertility of 1.20 children fewer than the average. That the reduced fertility during this period was not a function of lower levels of fecundity in these cohorts is suggested by a return to near-average rates for their age groups during the next period.

96 Demographic Processes I

Figure 5.2. Cumulative Fertility for Five-Year Periods—
Synthetic Cohorts.

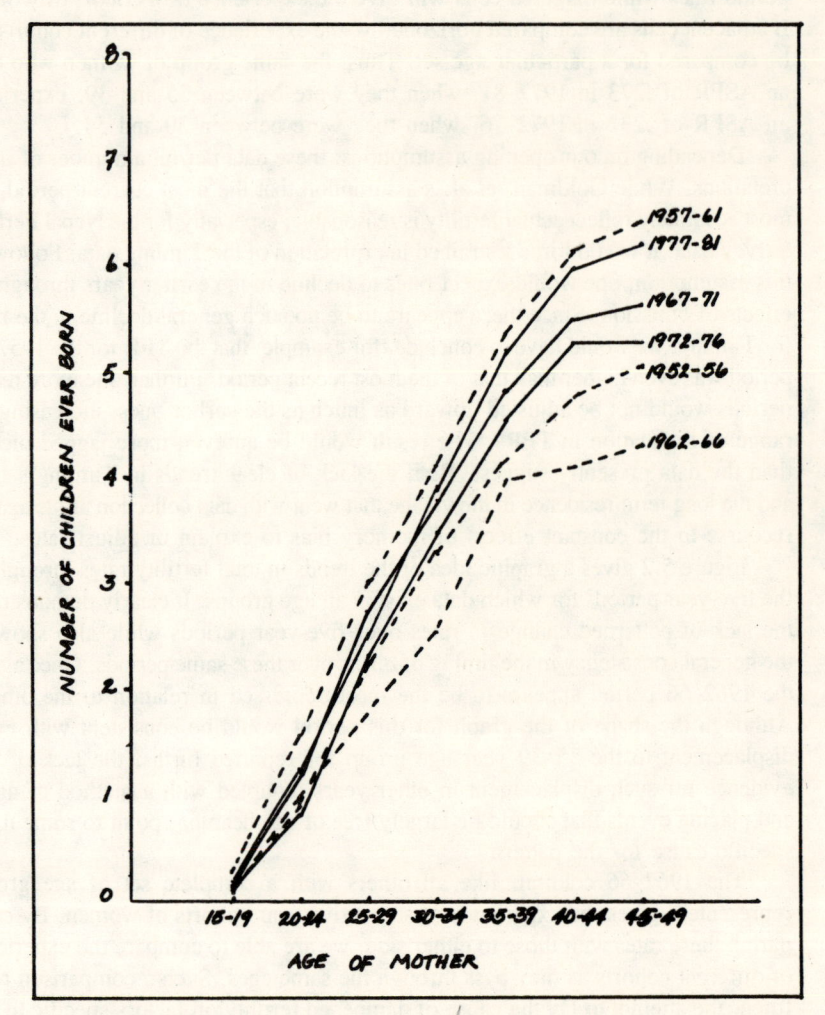

Table 5.5 reveals no further trends. Each cohort experiences roughly similar rates at a particular age range, with some unpatterned fluctuation. The irregular patterns for period ASFR in more recent years are related to the smaller number of woman-years in the past. Where a total of 560 woman-years is represented in the 1977–81 column, giving an average of 80 for each age group, the 1942–46 period includes 182 woman-years, for an average of only 36.4 in each of the five age groups. Not surprisingly, the earliest years on the record are the most open to the effects of random variation.

Figure 5.3 presents the mean age of childbearing in 1977–81, the most recent five-year period, along with the mean ages of childbearing for five-year cohorts of women between 25 and 49 years old at the time of the survey. The averages for age groups with incomplete fertility careers are based on the completed rates up to the time of the survey and thereafter on synthetic rates from the last five-year period. For this reason, the youngest two cohorts are omitted since their schedules are most heavily influenced by the period rates, resulting in a mean age at childbearing equal to that of the 1977–81 period. If the timing of events were displaced toward the date of the survey, the mean age at childbearing for the older cohorts should be higher than the average for the last period. Since this is not the case and the variation in mean age is not large, the data once again suggest a high degree of consistency and little change through time.

The crucial issue of changing rates seems to be answered with little evidence for any trend. Without this evidence, the small fluctuations that do occur can be explained as random fluctuations of the kind that we would expect to be most apparent in small populations such as Timling's. Thus the best indicator of the underlying fertility pattern in the village is the pooled experience of all women. Table 5.6 presents this information for 152 Tamang women who have ever been exposed to the risk of childbirth. Figure 5.4 displays the ASFRs that would result from the pooled experience of these women and compares them to those for women who have completed their childbearing careers and those who haven't.

Finally, we arrive at a picture of fertility that will allow us to make generalizations about the effects of childbearing on other features of Timling's human ecology and to make comparisons with other populations. Timling's demographic history is characterized in this most recent period by a high degree of consistency across time despite the fluctuations that would be expected to result from random processes in a small population. The average Tamang woman gives birth to just over five children in her reproductive career, and the pattern of childbearing follows the general experience of natural fertility populations. By the time the average woman has reached the age of 25, she has borne at least one child and continues to have them at a high rate for the next 20 years. The 35-year reproductive period between 15 and 49 results in an average of 5.43 births per woman, but the years of highest fertility are between 20 and 39, when 4.36 of these children are born.

The causes for this particular pattern remain to be determined. An especially important feature is the low number of births that occur in the absence of contraception. The next section will deal with this problem in terms of Davis and Blake's framework (1956) and more recent statements about human fertility and its determinants (Leridon 1977; Bongaarts 1975, 1978).

Proximate Determinants of Fertility in Timling

Faced with a total fertility rate of slightly over five children for Tamang women in Timling, a figure on the lower end of the observed range in natural fertility

98 Demographic Processes I

Figure 5.3. Mean Age at Childbearing for Most Recent Five-Year
Period and for Five-Year Cohorts.
Most recent cohorts based on synthetic rates (see text).

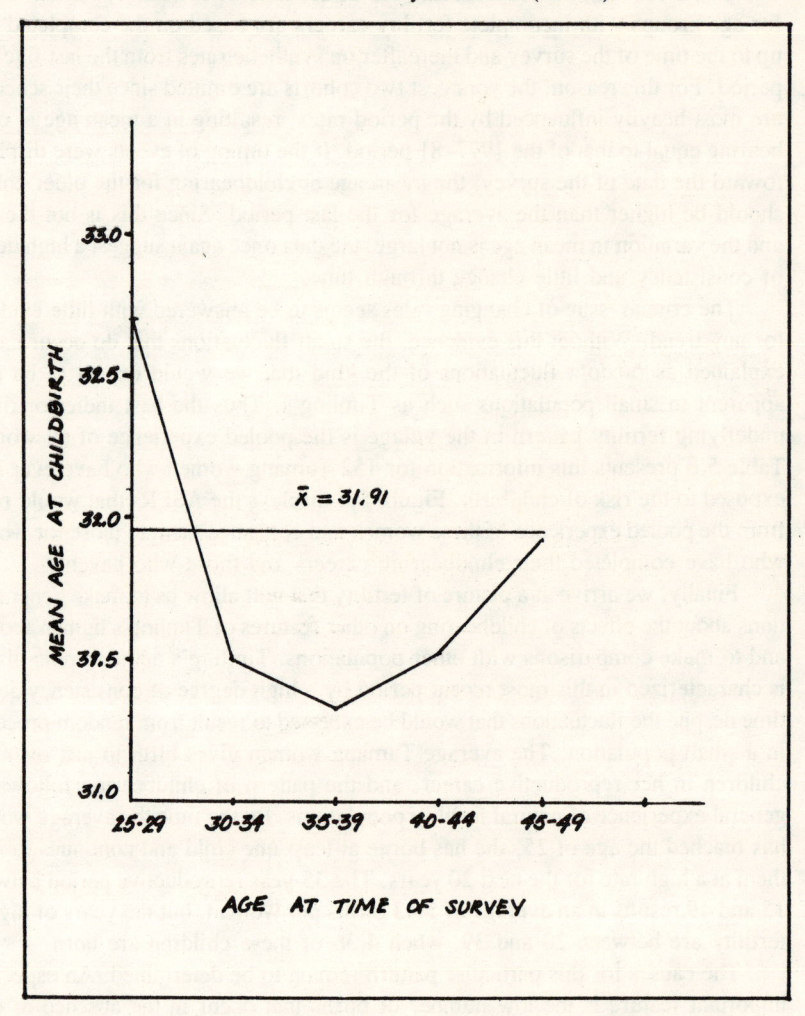

populations (cf. Leridon 1977:106–10), we must next explain why fertility is expressed at this level. The crude birth rate for 1981 in Timling was 41 births per thousand people, while for the 1976–81 period it was about 37 (assuming a base population of 600 for every year of the period and that those births on the reproductive histories were the only ones to occur). These figures again suggest that Timling's fertility falls at the lowest end of the range for highest fertility levels. Bongaarts (1975:290–91) places the range of highest observed crude birth rates

Figure 5.4. Age-Specific Fertility for 152 Tamang Women and for Women Younger than 45 and Older than or Equal to 45 Separately.

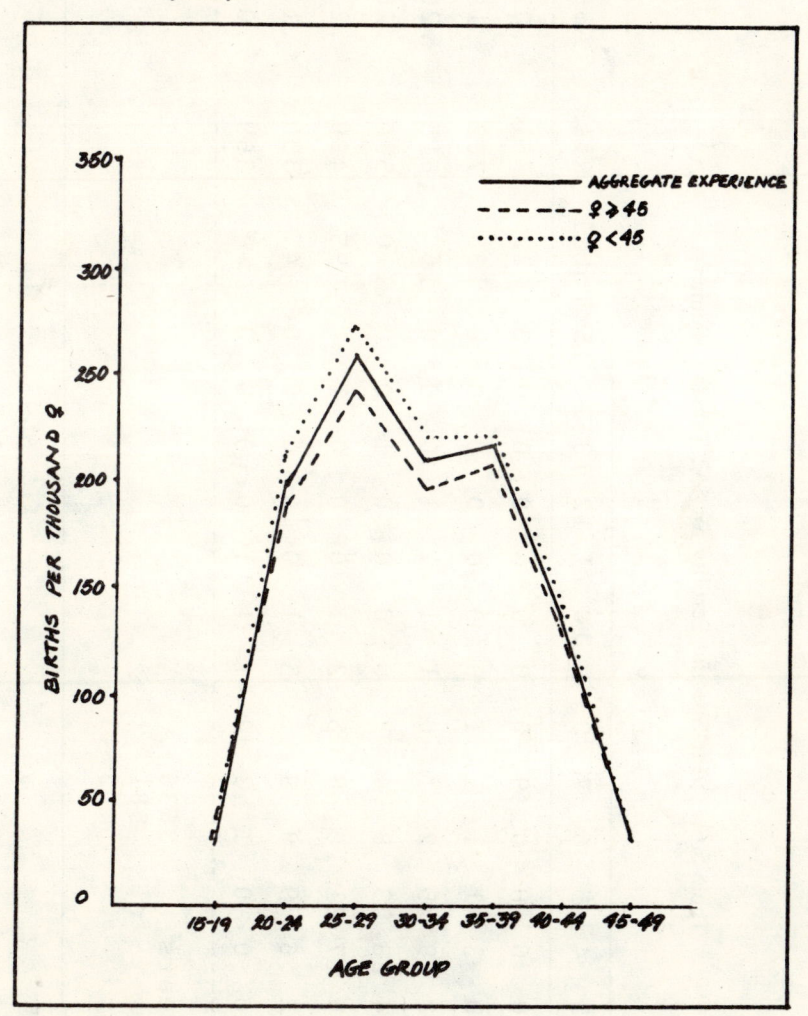

at from 40 to 50 births per thousand and writes that populations at the upper end of this range have an almost complete absence of contraception and induced abortion while crude birth rates closer to 40 usually imply some use of birth control. Yet the people of Timling reported no use of birth control. The question we must ask ourselves is: Why is the result of natural fertility so low among the Tamang?

The biological limits of the reproductive span are usually taken to be the years from 15 through 49. But as Leridon notes:

Table 5.6. Age-Specific Fertility for 152 Tamang Women.

Parity

Age	1	2	3	4	5	6	7	8	9	10	11	12	13	14	15	Total	At Risk	ASFR
15-19	18	4	0	0	0	0	0	0	0	0	0	0	0	0	0	22	751	.029
20-24	78	43	10	3	1	1	1	1	0	0	0	0	0	0	0	138	702	.197
25-29	33	54	42	19	5	2	1	0	1	1	1	1	0	0	0	160	615	.260
30-34	5	15	24	28	23	8	4	2	0	0	0	0	1	0	0	110	530	.208
35-39	2	3	15	17	21	19	8	5	2	1	0	0	0	1	1	95	439	.216
40-44	0	1	2	6	9	9	9	5	5	1	0	0	0	0	0	47	330	.142
45-49	0	0	0	0	0	1	3	2	1	1	1	0	0	0	0	9	269	.033

Total woman-years 3636
Total births 581
TFR 5.43

Source: Timing Marriage and Fertility History.

the total length of the reproductive life could be longer than 35 years, if we consider the complete interval between puberty and menopause; actually, however, . . . the fecund period is on the average only 27–28 years, and in addition both the beginning and the end of fertility seem to be progressive processes. (1977:10–11)

The highest level of natural fertility within that period is reported for Hutterite women married between 1921–30. These women bore an average of 9.5 children each (Leridon 1977:107). Even in Timling we have examples of women who have given birth from 10 to 15 times. As Bongaarts (1975:289) writes, if we were to take the minimum interval between births as nine months, a woman could theoretically bear as many as 40 children in her 30 reproductive years.

Clearly, the expression of fertility must be influenced by factors outside of the simple nine-month gestation requirement. Given an average reproductive span of 30 years and a total of 5.35 births to the average Tamang woman, only 48.2 months, or 13.4% of the reproductive period, are spent in a pregnant state (cf. Bongaarts 1975:294–95), which states that women in typical natural fertility populations are pregnant for about 16.7% of their reproductive years).

The factors that reduce the hypothetical limit to a woman's fertility are both physiological and behavioral. First, certain biological requirements and probabilities act to limit the number of children a woman can actually bear. Interacting with these are a number of behavioral components that can act to maximize or further reduce fertility.

For a complete discussion of the measures used to describe these variables, the reader should refer to the original article by Bongaarts (see also Bongaarts 1975, 1976). The following discussion is confined to an application of the indices and measures to the Tamang, and I will be able to make use of a much simpler version of the model. For example, Bongaarts has created measures to get at the effects of marriage, contraception, abortion, and lactational infecundability; since the Tamang report no use of contraception or abortion in Timling, we can simply ignore these variables. This model is additive in that we will be starting with the expressed TFR and inflating it to show the effect of each variable.

The most important variable affecting fertility in non-contracepting population is exposure to the risk of pregnancy. In practice, this is most easily determined by looking at the number of women married at each age of the reproductive period. Thus exposure is a function of (a) age at marriage, (b) age at cohabitation, and (c) separation due to divorce or death of husband. Bongaarts' measures subsume all of these effects into one index, which he calls the index of proportion married (C_m). This is calculated as the weighted average of the age-specific proportions married, with the weights given by the age-specific marital fertility rates (Bongaarts 1978:109).

We have seen that fecundability changes with a woman's age. It follows that non-exposure to the risk of pregnancy will have a different impact on a woman's final fertility experience depending on the ages at which she is not exposed. The index of proportion married simply takes account of this differential and gives us the proportional reduction in fertility due to exposure factors by themselves.

Some features of the Tamang society and culture require us to modify the meaning of this index. At one end, the index assumes that marriage marks the beginning of sexual intercourse while a related assumption is that a woman does not engage in sexual relations in the absence of her spouse. These assumptions break down somewhat when applied to the Tamang. First, premarital sex, while not actively encouraged by Tamang parents, is not severely disapproved of and is even expected. Boys and girls have frequent opportunities to get together during all-night shaman rituals or during dances near the *gompo*. Here, a boy and girl will silently drop out of the circle of dancers to slip into the trees that surround the *gompo* and stone *mani*. Their friends will continue to dance and sing and make amused comments about their whereabouts for the half hour or so they are gone.

Likewise, spouses are frequently separated at other times during their married lives, and I am aware of at least two cases in which children were conceived when the women's husbands were at least a two- or three-week trek from Timling. In one of these cases, the husband returned to find that he had a new son, an event that he quietly and happily accepted. The other case involved a more complicated settlement, but the problems did not revolve around the woman's infidelity.

Nevertheless, while premarital intercourse is condoned, pregnancy nearly always leads to a swift marriage with the child's father or some other agreeable male. The Tamang place great stress on knowing a person's clan membership, and this can be determined only through the father. Very strong pressure is brought on an unmarried pregnant girl to name the father of a child, and subsequent pressure on the father almost guarantees marriage, or support if he is already married and not able to take a new wife.

I have used the experience of all Tamang women to calculate the Bongaarts measures since it includes the greatest range of data and should be the best reflection of the typical village pattern. Table 5.7 provides a summary of the relevant fertility measures by age for all woman-years in the reproductive period and for exposed woman-years only. Other information for calculating the index of proportion married is also given. We can see from the figures for age-specific fertility and age-specific marital fertility how greatly exposure can affect a woman's childbearing. These figures also indicate that marriage behavior in Timling has the effect of moving the peak reproduction rates from the biologically most fecund 20–24 year period to the next, slightly less fecund period. Looking again at figure 5.1, we can see that the much lower ASFR for the 20–24 year age group in Timling, compared to the Terai and Middle Hills regions, would disappear were it not for the exposure effects of marriage practices.

Figure 5.4 gives a more graphic presentation of the same information for all women 45 years old and older and for woman-years exposed to the risk of pregnancy. We can clearly see here that most dramatic exposure effects occur in the first 10 years of the reproductive period. Were all women exposed to the risk of pregnancy throughout these years, some 1,095 additional children would be born per thousand women in those years. Far smaller exposure effects are felt in the last 25 years, when only 515 additional births per thousand women would occur. A breakdown of Bongaarts' index will make this even more obvious.

The index of proportion married is easily computed from the information in table 5.7. We simply multiply the proportion of exposed to total woman-years in each age class by the corresponding ASMFR and divide these by the sum of the ASMFR alone. The resulting proportion, .771, tells us that average fertility is reduced 22.9% because Tamang women are not exposed during parts of their fecund period. For these women of completed fertility, this translates into the difference between having an average of 5.43 births and an average of 7.04 births per woman. Because I have used the age at cohabitation rather than the age at marriage, the interpretation is slightly different from straightforward "marriage" effects, but it is more accurate given the possibility of delaying actual cohabitation after arranged marriages.

We can break this down even further if we wish to distinguish between the effects of age at cohabitation and of separation from spouse due to his death. We could do the same for separation due to divorce, too, but only three divorces occurred in this group of women. In one case, the woman remarried in the same year, and I have no way to break down woman-years into smaller units. In the other two cases, the women divorced their husbands before cohabiting with them, and those effects are included as a part of age at first cohabitation. Table 5.8 presents the woman-years of exposure that would result using three assumptions.

In assumption one I take the given age pattern of cohabitation and ignore the deaths of husbands. The second assumption does the reverse and takes it that all women are married at the beginning of the reproductive period, with unexposed years resulting from the given pattern of widowhood and remarriage. I have included a third assumption to discover the kind of pattern that would result were the Tamang to marry at the beginning of the reproductive years and not practice widow remarriage. A glance at the proportions of years exposed to the risk of pregnancy under the different assumptions suggests that the pattern of cohabitation has the greatest impact on fertility; this is borne out when we calculate Bongaarts' index of proportion married following the same procedure as above. When we assume that exposure is affected only by the age at cohabitation, we get an index of .829. The first mortality assumption produces an index of .969. Even when we assume the current pattern of mortality without widow remarriage, this is only slightly reduced with an index of .922. Thus, the exposure effects of Tamang marriage and cohabitation patterns are to reduce potential fertility almost 20%, while the effects of widowhood and remarriage reduce it an additional 3%.

Figure 5.6 shows the childbearing experience of the average Tamang woman given the different assumptions. The top line shows how many children would be

Table 5.7. Age-Specific Fertility, Age-Specific Marital Fertility, and Woman-Years of Exposure for All Tamang Women.

| | \multicolumn{7}{c}{Age Group} |
	15-19	20-24	25-29	30-34	35-39	40-44	45-49
ASFR	.029	.197	.260	.208	.216	.142	.033
ASMFR	.144	.301	.295	.222	.236	.163	.046
Woman-years							
Total	751	702	615	530	439	330	269
Exposed	153	458	542	496	402	288	196
Exposed/Total	.204	.652	.881	.936	.916	.873	.729

Source: Timling Marriage and Fertility History.

Figure 5.5. Age-Specific Fertility and Age-Specific Marital Fertility for 152 Tamang Women.

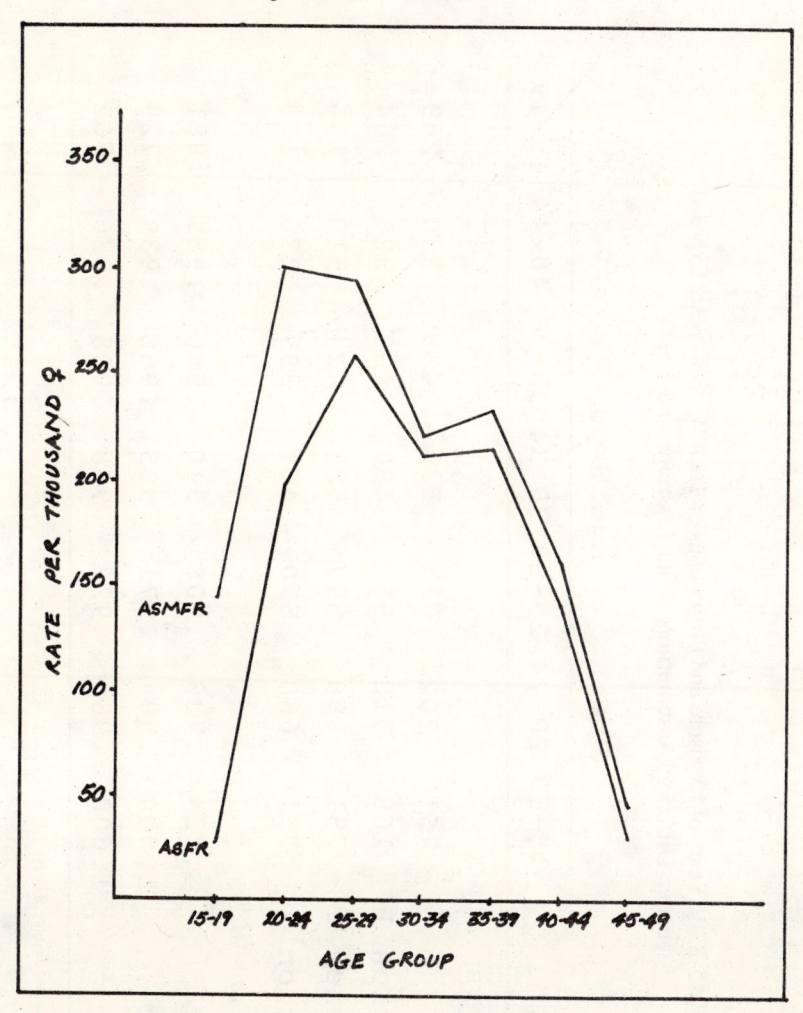

born per woman were she exposed throughout the reproductive years; the bottom line traces the actual course of fertility in Timling. The total number of births per woman demonstrates the large fertility dampening effects of exposure variables:

```
Total marital fertility ................................................. 7.0 births
Widowhood with remarriage ............................................. 6.8 births
Widowhood, no remarriage .............................................. 6.5 births
Cohabitation effects alone ............................................. 5.8 births
Actual fertility ...................................................... 5.4 births
```

Table 5.8. Years of Exposure and Proportions of Total Woman-Years Exposed under Differing Assumptions about Marriage and Death.

Age Group

	15-19	20-24	25-29	30-34	35-39	40-44	45-49
Woman-years							
Total	751	702	615	530	439	330	269
Assumption 1	168	512	557	498	433	325	264
Assumption 2	751	698	597	522	424	310	196
Assumption 3	751	680	570	481	399	276	178
Ratios							
1/Total	.224	.729	.906	.940	.986	.985	.981
2/Total	1.000	.994	.971	.985	.966	.939	.729
3/Total	1.000	.969	.927	.908	.908	.836	.662

Source: Timling Marriage and Fertility History.

Figure 5.6. Cumulative Fertility for 152 Tamang Women under Different Exposure Assumptions.

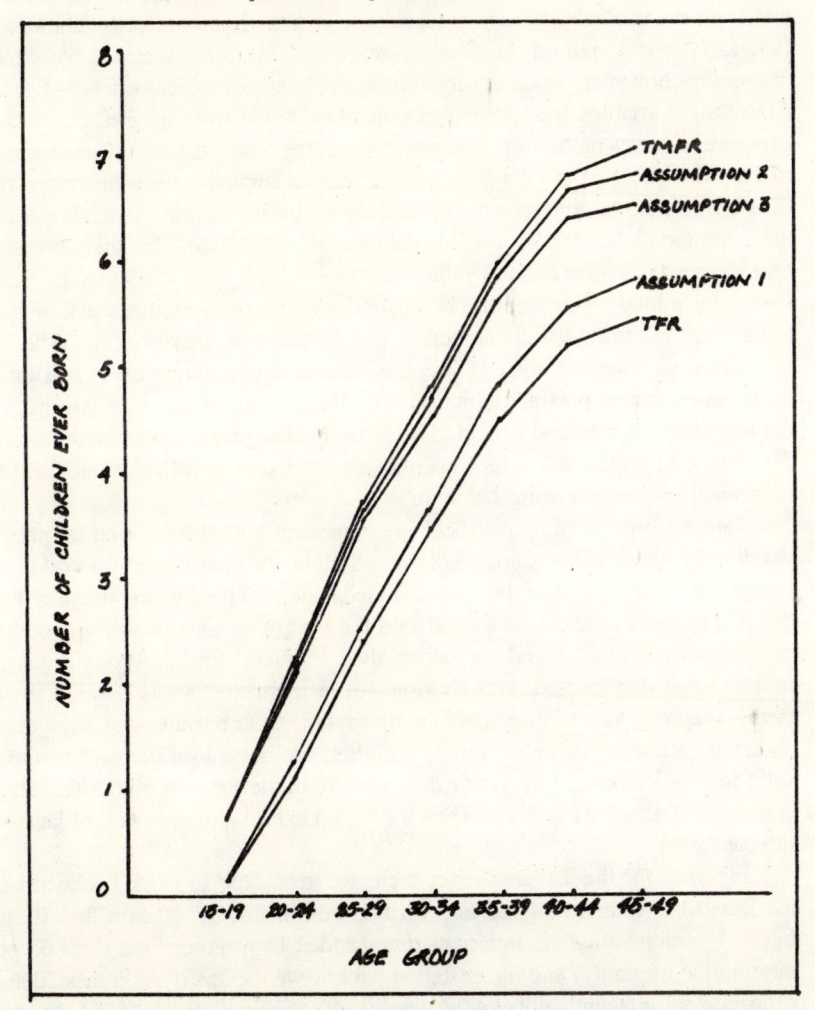

While these exposure factors reveal some of the reasons why Tamang fertility is so low, the total is still vastly smaller than the potential for natural fertility populations. Yet no woman in Timling reported contraceptive use or recourse to abortion. Even if some women concealed abortions in their past, we can be confident that the fertility dampening effects would be trivial since the only reason to abort would be to escape the consequences of a premarital pregnancy. Tamang attitudes toward premarital sex and pregnancy are not especially oppressive. For this reason there is no need to consider the Bongaarts index of non-contraception or his discussion of abortion effects.

The next major index that Bongaarts has developed is the index of lactational infecundability (1978:116). Because detailed data on breastfeeding were not gathered, my use of this index must rely more heavily on the assumptions of the Bongaarts model than on the discussion above. This is not a strong blow to this discussion, however, since the model incorporates the typical effects of fertility dampening variables from known populations. Aside from the impact of known exposure variables on fertility, discussed above, the remaining intermediate variables include the effect of (1) the infecundable period immediately following a birth, (2) waiting time to conception, (3) time added by intrauterine mortality, and (4) the nine-month gestation period (Bongaarts 1978:115). In the absence of breastfeeding, the time added by these factors is 1.5, 7.5, 2, and 9 months, respectively, for a total of 20 months. Bongaarts' model simply assumes that any additional time in the infecundable period is a function of breastfeeding. The index of lactational infecundability (C_i) is the ratio of this minimal 20-month interval to the same period plus additional time in the infecund state. We assume, then, the length of the infecund period to be the only changeable factor on the average. The index of lactational infecundability then tells us to what extent fertility is dampened by breastfeeding behavior.

Tamang breastfeeding practices are consistent with those found in other less developed countries (Bongaarts 1978:116). That is, the breastfeeding period is much longer than that of most of the industrialized nations. The Tamang themselves feel that it is proper to breastfeed a child until the next pregnancy, and I have observed children as old as five and six taking their mothers' breast. Women generally reported that they nursed their children for at least three years or until the next birth. They explained longer periods by saying, "Oh but that was my youngest child; of course it got more milk." Children are nursed on demand, even after solid food is introduced into their diet, usually in the form of premasticated rice, at the age of about six months. Thus we would expect a long period of lactational infecundability.

Figuring for the Tamang case, then, we need only to work backward from the Bongaarts estimate of the interval between births, 3.38 years for all closed intervals. Subtracting the invariant times added by waiting time to conception, intrauterine mortality, and the gestation period, we then arrive at a mean duration of lactational infecundability of 22 months (40.55−7.5−2−9 = 22.05). In spite of the problems of small sample size and the crude estimate of months in the birth interval that we get by converting years into months, the mean duration is amazingly close to that observed in Bangladesh (18.9 months), where very similar breastfeeding practices prevail (Bongaarts 1978:116). The index of lactational infecundability for the Tamang works out to .493, indicating that breastfeeding reduces fertility to about half of what it would be in the absence of breastfeeding. Thus the total fecundity rate, defined as maximum fertility of the Tamang in the absence of these dampening factors, is equal to the total natural marital fertility rate divided by this index (7.0/.49), or 14.3 births per woman.

We thus can conclude that the lower natural fertility estimates reported by this survey can be explained by age and rate of cohabitation, lessened exposure due to separation, and periods of infecundability due to lengthy breastfeeding practices. Timling's population has not been faced with the conscious need to limit births up to the present time since there has been no compelling limitation in the amount of new land left to open. The fertility level is the unreflected consequence of behavior not specifically directed toward fertility control. Indeed, Tamang women report a desire for as many children as possible, yet they reduce their potential childbearing by more than one birth through marriage and cohabitation effects alone. Caldwell's point about pre-transition societies being "seamless" (1976:343) has some indirect support here. One indication of a breakdown in the supports for high fertility would be consciously relating intermediate variables to the number of children born and then directing behavior to control that number.

6

Demographic Processes II: Mortality and the Tamang Life Table

I have devoted much discussion to Tamang fertility, in part because the marriage and fertility histories through which the data were gathered make this set of information among the most reliable for the people of Timling. In addition, a woman's fertility experience is an important element in her own fortune as well as that of her husband and of the rest of the household. The household developmental cycle to be discussed in the next chapter is largely dependent on the fertility of Timling's women, and the replication of Tamang social structure through the generations depends on the bearing of children. Nevertheless, other essential elements of Timling's population structure need to be discussed. Fertility itself is only half the equation that determines the shape of Timling's population. Mortality is the other half. (I am assuming here that the effects of migration are minimal.)

Lotka (1907) showed that an unchanging age distribution and rate of growth characterize a population closed to migration and subject to unchanging age-specific fertility and mortality. This will occur regardless of the initial age distribution. Thus, the parameters of a population are mathematically dependent on each other and, if the assumption of unchanging rates can be met, certain features of a people's demography can be inferred from the presence of others.

We can never hope exactly to satisfy these assumptions with real populations subject to random fluctuation of vital rates. Anthropologists, especially, working with small populations of a hundred to a few thousand, may doubt the application of stable population theory to their needs. Yet these problems apply to any population, and the unusual nature of anthropological data is only one of degree (cf. Feeney 1975:44–45, cited above). Nancy Howell puts it well:

> Stable population models are like the "friction free" models in physics: Their usefulness is not restricted by the observations that no real human populations continue to operate under unchanging mortality and fertility schedules for long periods of time and few human populations are closely bounded (or "closed"). Stable population models show us what would happen, precisely, under given conditions, and tell us what to expect on the average in real populations that can be closely modeled. (1979:20–21)

Even though we cannot hope to find an empirical case that will duplicate the model, we can hope to find models that fit better than others, and we can surmise the underlying demographic processes that help shape a population.

Fortunately, demographers have already used Lotka's insights to construct tools for this kind of analysis. Through observation of the regularities found in large numbers of studied populations, a range of model life tables has been constructed (United Nations 1955; Coale and Demeny 1966; Weiss 1973). All of these sets of tables embody different data bases and represent variant assumptions about mortality. While the United Nations and Coale-Demeny life tables have been constructed from national populations (Shryock and Siegel 1975:485–86), the Weiss tables are uniquely constructed from various anthropological data sets and are designed for use with the fragmentary data with which anthropologists are usually confronted (Weiss 1975:4). Howell's (1979:75–80) review of the merits of the various model tables is recommended to the reader who wishes a more detailed discussion. I will recapitulate a few of her points here.

First, all of these models are organized according to the level of mortality and the age pattern of mortality. The expectation of life at birth serves as a handy index for mortality levels while age-specific mortality can vary within levels. In spite of this, striking parallels in the pattern of age-specific mortality are evident across all levels and even among different sets of tables. This pattern typically shows a high probability of death in the first year, declining rapidly until the tenth or fifteenth year, after which it begins to rise again to the high probabilities of death after age 45. Second, Howell suggests that the points of similarity in mortality patterns indicate a biological regularity; people are susceptible to biological stresses to varying degrees throughout their life course. Differences in the patterns of mortality can be the result of different kinds of exposure to these stresses, and there can be both ecological and sociocultural reasons for this.

Like Howell, I prefer to use the Coale-Demeny "West" series of model tables for the analysis here. These tables represent the broadest range of known mortality experience while other tables are confined to populations that diverge somewhat from this "normal" range. In addition, the little mortality data that can be teased from the pregnancy histories are more consistent with the age patterns of mortality represented in the "West" series. This is not to suggest that Weiss' model tables are without practical advantage. To the contrary, very successful application has been made with these tables (Neel and Weiss 1975; Fix 1977). Their advantage seems, however, to be best realized where limited data will make for very rough estimation and where the data "do not warrant the complex methods of national demography, designed to extract another decimal point from the data" (Weiss 1975:4). The Tamang data, however crude, are of sufficient detail and range to allow application of those other models.

My procedure will be to take the data that do exist for Tamang women and to derive as many measures as possible from them. These measures will then be compared with a range of tables from the Coale-Demeny series and examined for *overall* consistency (Fix 1977:77). We have already seen that real populations cannot be expected to conform exactly to any one model's predictions; this will be even truer for a population of Timling's size. It will be gratifying, then, to find a table that allows generalizations about those demographic processes for which we do not have data.

Mortality

I have mentioned that, other than fertility, mortality is the next important determinant of a population's age structure. Very little data exist for Nepal on the causes and pattern of dying other than a few health surveys (cf. Worth and Shah 1969) and analyses derived from other data sources such as the Nepal Fertility Survey (cf. Thapa and Retherford 1982). Similarly, the analysis for Timling must be derived from the marriage and fertility history data, particularly since I did not stay in the village long enough to make it possible to generalize from the deaths that occurred.

The high ritual significance of death in Tamang culture is a good indication of the impact it has on family life. Illness and the possibility of accidents abound in Timling, and the *gompo* are continually involved in placating the supernatural causes of sickness with night-long ceremonies and impromptu blowing of *mantra*. The Tamang have very little access to western-style medicines. Part of the reason is that the government health post in neighboring Sertang is often out of stock and, even were it in stock most of the time, Timling's people would not use it often because of their feeling that they are abused and unfairly charged by the health workers there. If medicine must be bought, they would rather buy it from the small settlement of Newar merchants in Sertang or even make the trek to the hospital in Kathmandu. Very little use is made of medicinal plants gathered in the high pastures, although those who know of their uses will store some away for stomach cramps and similar problems. In practice, then, Timling's people do not intervene in the course of illnesses except for the social and psychological ministrations of the shamans and *lamas*.

By western standards, Timling is a dangerous and dirty place. Children and sometimes adults defecate freely wherever they choose, even though some of the neighborhoods have designated sheltered areas away from their water supply as public latrines. During the monsoon, one of the central paths of the village is turned into a running stream that spills into the springs from which the lower households gather their water, and the danger of contamination is heightened. In addition, cattle quench their own thirst in the same springs that are the village water supply, increasing the risk of parasites for villagers.

The risk of accident is also high within the village and the surrounding area. Trails are in serious disrepair in many areas, and sharp, slippery rocks combine with the monsoon rains to make them especially dangerous. During my stay, I treated cuts and gashes from these rocks so often that I had to reserve an hour in the morning for everyone but those needing immediate attention. Risk of infection multiplies the danger of cuts and sores from the leeches that afflict everyone during the monsoon. With few exceptions, the people of Timling are not fond of bathing, especially in the colder months when the water is uncomfortably icy. One of my hardest fought battles was to get people whose wounds I had treated to keep them clean.

In spite of these problems and the often inadequate clothing that people have to protect themselves from rain and cold, Timling's environment can be considered relatively healthy in other ways. Too high for mosquitoes, the village has never been exposed to malaria, while leeches, lice, and fleas are seasonal problems dispelled by the dry season or the winter cold. The people are themselves aware of this and speak disparagingly of the unhealthy lowlands and the poor quality of water below their ridges. Periodic epidemics do come through Timling. One of the Ghale men, 55 years old, reported three times in his life when major illnesses took more than one life in the village; the last episode was in the early 1960s. But the major continuous threats to health seem to be the result of infection and poor sanitation.

The Tamang of Timling have only vague notions about the "causes" of death and illnesses. They are as likely to attribute them to ghosts (Np. *bhut*) as to anything else. For example, the death of one man in the Dungsel Khola below the village when the monsoon rains had gorged it is attributed to the need of the god of the place to feed on human flesh. I attempted to gather information on the causes of death, but the classifications in table 6.1 make clear that I had little success.

Causes of death were classified by their symptoms as reported by the mothers of children who died. The table shows that a high percentage of reported deaths are attributed to supernatural causes—in these cases, informants were unwilling or unable to specify symptoms. The second major category, however, refers to symptoms related to stomach problems and diarrheal diseases such as dysentery. Respiratory ailments include tuberculosis and pneumonia. In spite of the extremely crude nature of these categories, we see that a high percentage of deaths are related to sanitary conditions and exposure, a pattern similar to those reported elsewhere (Worth and Shah 1969; Macfarlane 1976:266).

These other areas where similar conditions prevail are all characterized by high mortality, although the actual level varies in Nepal with regional and other factors. Molnar reports for a Kham Magar population to the west that 47% of the children born to a sample of women in the village died before reaching adulthood (1978:28; although Molnar does not define the age at which adulthood begins, I assume she means around age 20). Ross reports only slightly smaller percentages of deaths to children of women of completed fertility, with about 40% to 45% of Dhingaba children not surviving (1981:39). A yet smaller percentage of deaths among children of women 40 years or older is reported for the Gurung, where 33% died (Macfarlane 1976:272). We would not be unjustified, then, in expecting similarly high percentages of deaths in Timling.

Table 6.1. Reported Causes of Death for Children of Surveyed Tamang Women.

Cause	N	%
Flu	46	29.9%
Ghost	49	31.8
Respiratory illness	14	9.1
Sores, wounds	10	6.5
Accident	10	6.5
Other	25	16.2

Source: Timling Marriage and Fertility History.

While these mortality statistics indicate high death rates for their respective village populations, they are not strictly comparable since they are subject to the effects of local age distribution. More finely calculated mortality statistics are necessary if we are to relate the demographic parameters of various populations to each other. In the case of Timling, we are able to examine age-specific mortality using the data gathered in the marriage and pregnancy histories and following standard demographic practice, as Howell did with similar data for the !Kung (1979:80–82). Table 6.2 displays the mortality experience of children ever born to interviewed Tamang women.

In order to calculate these mortality figures, I have made an assumption similar to that made in the calculation of fertility rates: the underlying pattern of mortality has remained consistent throughout the lives of these women and their children. This assumption allows us to aggregate the experience of different cohorts to increase the number of cases with which to calculate rates. Reviewing the table, we find that 580 children entered the first year of life, but that 20 of these were born in 1981 and were still subject to the risk of death within the first interval. These are excluded from the calculation. Of those remaining 560 children who were born a year or more before 1981, we find that 114 have died. Simple division gives the probability of dying in the first year of life: .204. The remaining two columns show the number beginning the interval (l_x) and how many will die in that interval (d_x) under the given probability of death. If we divide l_x by 10, we get the survivorship probabilities up to age x. Thus the probability of survival from birth to age 1 is .796; from birth to age 15 it is .682. A final feature of this table that needs to be kept in mind is that the numbers will become decreasingly reliable as we move down the column because of the rapidly declining number of cases we have to work with.

Table 6.2. Mortality Measures on Ever-Born Children of Surveyed Tamang Women.

Age Death	Began Interval	In Int'l	Compltd Int'l	Died	q_x	l_x	d_x
0	580	20	560	114	.204	10000	2040
1	446	65	381	32	.084	7960	669
5	349	58	291	14	.048	7291	350
10	277	58	219	4	.018	6941	125
15	215	41	174	6	.035	6816	239
20	168	47	121	2	.017	6577	112
25	119	30	89	4	.045	6465	291
30	85	21	64	2	.032	6174	198
35	62	27	35	2	.057	5976	341
40+	33	33				5635	

Source: Timling Marriage and Fertility History.

Tamang mortality is very consistent with mortality patterns in other known populations. The first year of life is characterized by a relatively high risk of dying that rapidly declines and begins creeping upward again during the middle years of life. It we take age 20 to be "adulthood," we find that about 34% of these children have died before reaching that age, a much smaller percentage than Molnar reports in a Kham Magar village. Looking at survivorship to age 40, the age at which all deaths to ever-born children have already occurred, we see that about 44% of these children have died, indicating a level of mortality similar to the population studied by Ross if we assume equivalent age structure and age-specific fertility.

Infant mortality is an especially interesting indicator of a population's mortality level since much of the increase in the expectation of life at birth is related to a reduction in mortality during the first year of life. In Nepal as a whole the infant mortality rate has been declining since at least 1960, although it still remains high (Banister and Thapa 1981:41); analysis of the Nepal Fertility Survey shows a great deal of interregional variation (Thapa and Retherford 1982). Table 6.3 compares infant mortality in Timling to that in other areas.

Timling's is the highest of all these areas, although we note that it is once again most consistent with the mountain region. Infant mortality for the Gurung of Thak is unusually low relative to the other areas, a fact that Macfarlane also notes (1976:275) but does not try to explain. If we accept the validity of this figure, we might attribute it to the enviable economic and ecological position that Thak enjoys relative to most places in Nepal. The high infant mortality in Timling is not surprising if we consider that the areas surveyed for the NFS were chosen, in part, for their accessibility (NFS 1976). We might reasonably expect this accessibility to be correlated with greater exposure to government health posts and village sanitation projects. Looking at the figures for the mountain region (Thapa and Retherford 1982:74), we see that infant mortality has declined from 238 deaths per 1000 births in the 1960–64 period, an indication of some sort of intervention. Timling, on the other hand, has experienced no similar benefit during this period for reasons already mentioned.

The limited number of cases we have to work with makes it difficult to analyze mortality differences among many different groups in Timling. Nevertheless, the possibility of differential mortality by sex needs to be examined before we leave the subject. Not only will different behaviors on the part of the child itself subject males and females to different risks of mortality, but the different values that parents may place on children because of their sex can affect the investment they put into that child. When this investment includes health care, we will expect different probabilities of survival for each sex. Recent explorations of this issue (Scrimshaw 1976; Simmons, et al. 1982) have demonstrated that the value of children to their parents is reflected in mortality experience. The range of known mortality differentials includes the extreme case of northwestern India (Miller 1981), in which intricate cultural and economic supports for a strong male preference are reflected in strikingly unbalanced sex ratios. Historical data from German villages, on the

Table 6.3. Infant Mortality Rates for Timling and Nepal.

Region/Village	Infant deaths per 1000 live births	Period
Nepal[a]	156	1970-74
Terai[a]	165	1970-74
Hill[a]	143	1970-74
Mountain[a]	188	1970-74
Thak[b]	86	***
Timling[c]	204	***

Sources: [a] *Thapa and Retherford 1983*, [b] *Macfarlane 1976:276*, and [c] *Timling Marriage and Fertility History.*

other hand, do not conclusively demonstrate that peasant populations there favored one sex over the other (Knodel and De Vos 1980).

As in other hill populations of Nepal (Molnar 1978, 1982; Jones and Jones 1976), women enjoy a great deal of equality with men in Tamang society. People express a slightly greater desire for male children in Timling. This is consistent with a social organization in which people obtain their clan identity through their fathers and where men inherit most of the property and care for their aging parents. In spite of this mild cultural tilt toward sons, however, I have never witnessed a case where male children were obviously favored over female. On the contrary, the affection given to infants of both sexes has struck me as being the same, and the grief of parents at the death of a child of either sex has appeared equally deep.

Figuring the mortality measures by sex exactly as I did for all children in table 6.2 yields inconclusive evidence. We can see in table 6.4 that there are very slight differences in the age-specific mortality of males and females, but the number of cases is so small that it is difficult to make firm statements based on this. Knodel and De Vos (1980) have suggested that even equivalent age-specific probabilities of death between the sexes would not rule out male bias since females are biologically stronger and more resistant to stresses than males. With that in mind and the slightly higher probabilities of death for females, we may infer that some small behavioral differences are reflected here. But we have no evidence of the drastic differentials in the treatment of males and females that are found in some areas of India.

We are probably safer in noticing the general pattern of mortality experienced by each sex, although here again the small numbers confound any firm conclusions. Still, it is interesting to note the sudden upturn in mortality of females after their 25th year, when the dangers of childbirth increase the risk of death. Male age-specific mortality, on the other hand, shows an upturn after age 15 that would be consistent with greater exposure to accidents and the risk of infection as they begin their working life outside the immediate village. It is at about that age that they are considered ready to work in the high pastures or even to make the trek to Bhutan in search of road work.

Tamang mortality in Timling, then, appears to be higher than in other areas for which we have comparable information. This is at least the case for the first year of life, when mortality is highest for all populations. We can infer that the conditions that cause this initially high mortality continue to keep mortality rates at older ages higher than the average for other areas. Except for the differences discussed above, male and female mortality is roughly the same in the village. The pattern of mortality is such that, for both sexes, somewhat fewer than two out of three children survive to age 30; some of the consequences of this will be discussed in a later chapter. Our next task here is to use the mortality information to help fit a model life table to Timling's population.

Table 6.4. Mortality Measures on Ever-Born Children by Sex.

Age at Death	Started Interval	Still in Int 1	Completed Interval	Deaths	q_x	l_x	d_x
			Females				
0	273	12	261	54	.207	10000	2070
1	207	32	175	16	.091	7930	722
5	159	25	134	6	.045	7208	324
10	128	24	104	2	.019	6884	131
15	102	25	77	2	.026	6753	176
20	75	22	53	1	.019	6577	125
25	52	15	37	3	.081	6452	523
30	34	10	24			5929	
35	24	23	11				
40+	11	11					

			Males			
0	306	8	298	59	.198	10000 1980
1	239	33	206	16	.078	8020 626
5	190	33	157	8	.051	7394 377
10	149	34	115	2	.017	7017 119
15	113	16	97	4	.041	6898 283
20	93	25	68	1	.015	6615 126
25	67	15	52	1	.019	6489 123
30	51	11	40	2	.050	6366 318
35	38	14	24	2	.083	6048 502
40+	22	22				

Source: Timing Marriage and Fertility History.

Figure 6.1. Survivorship of Male and Female Children Born to 150 Tamang Women.

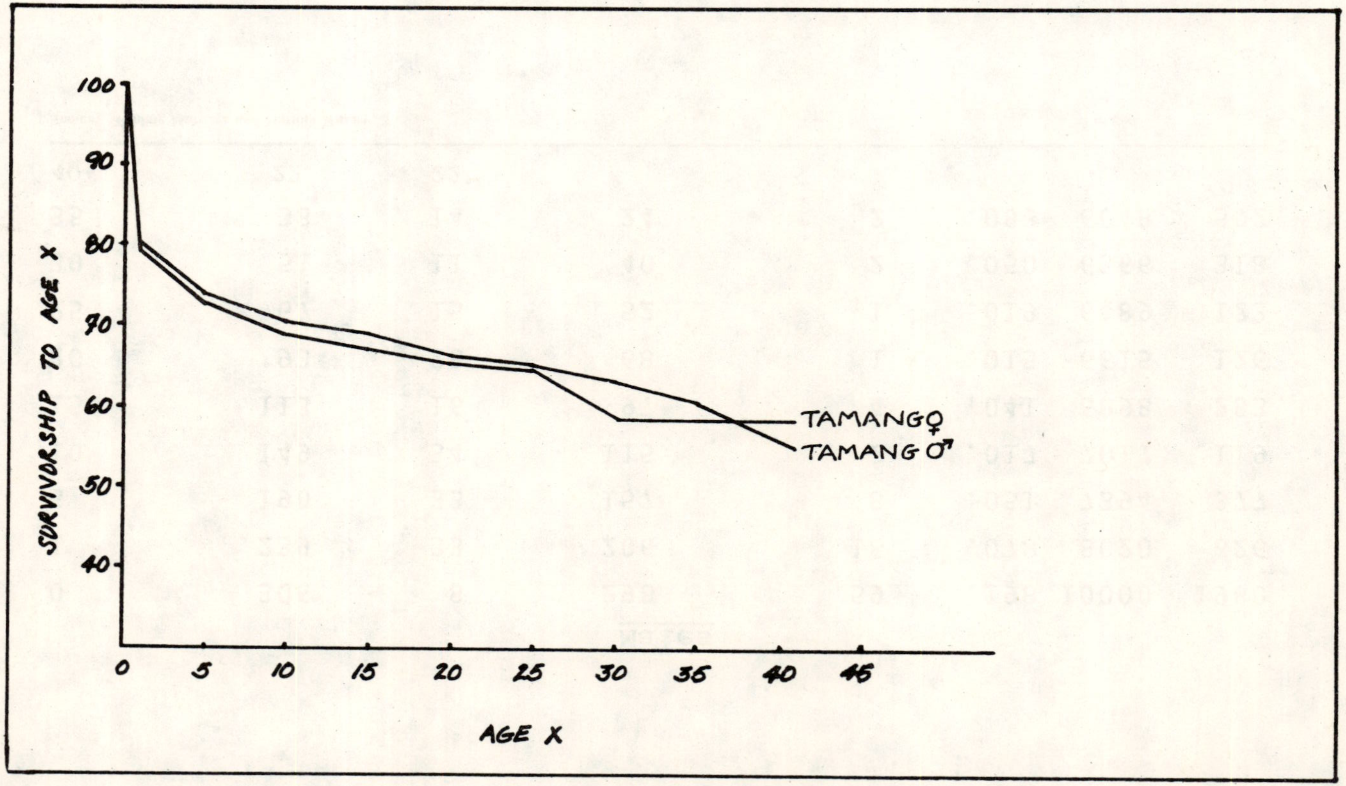

A Tamang Life Table

In order to account for the possibility that males and females are subject to slightly different mortality experiences in Timling, I will fit the life tables for the two sexes separately. Weiss (1973:65-69) has shown that it is possible to fit tables using extremely fragmentary data but that our confidence in choosing a particular model over another will always increase with the amount of empirical data we have. In the case of the Tamang, we are confronted with a relatively rich supply of demographic information, yet in the absence of mortality information for every age category it is not possible to construct a life table based on the data alone. Hence, our desire to describe population processes more completely leads us to rely on model tables where they help to fill in the gaps.

My first step is to compare the survivorship curve for Tamang females with a range of curves in the Coale-Demeny "West" series. Figure 6.2 graphs the outcome of this comparison and suggests a number of points. First, we can see that the general pattern of Tamang female survivorship is quite consistent with the model relationships in spite of the small numbers we have to work with. Second, the graph shows us that the pattern of survivorship up to age 40 is consistent with expectations of life at birth of between 37.5 and 42.5 years (levels 8 through 10 mortality in the model series). If we suspected that Timling's population were stationary, we could simply stop here and compare the proportion of the actual population in each age group with the model values, choosing the closest table as representative of Timling's underlying demographic regime. But there is strong reason to believe that Timling's population is growing, as the existence of daughter villages throughout the traditional territory testifies. Since the proportion of the population in each age group will vary with the rate of growth (Weiss 1973:71), it is necessary to approximate the intrinsic rate of natural increase for Timling's population so that we can choose a range of model life tables for comparison.

My procedure has been to use a range of mortality assumptions coupled with the fertility rates given in the last chapter to calculate the set of demographic statistics we can use to describe the population. Using these assumptions I have calculated different estimates of the following values:

a) GRR (gross reproduction rate)
b) NRR (net reproduction rate)
c) m (average length of a generation)
d) r (intrinsic rate of natural increase)
e) b (crude birth rate)
f) average age of population

All of these values can be compared with model values for each level of mortality and rate of increase in tables calculated by Coale and Demeny (1966). The explanation for the various calculations is given in Lingner's handbook (1974:86-91).

Figure 6.2. Survivorship of Female Children with Three Survivorship Curves from Coale-Demeny Female West Models.

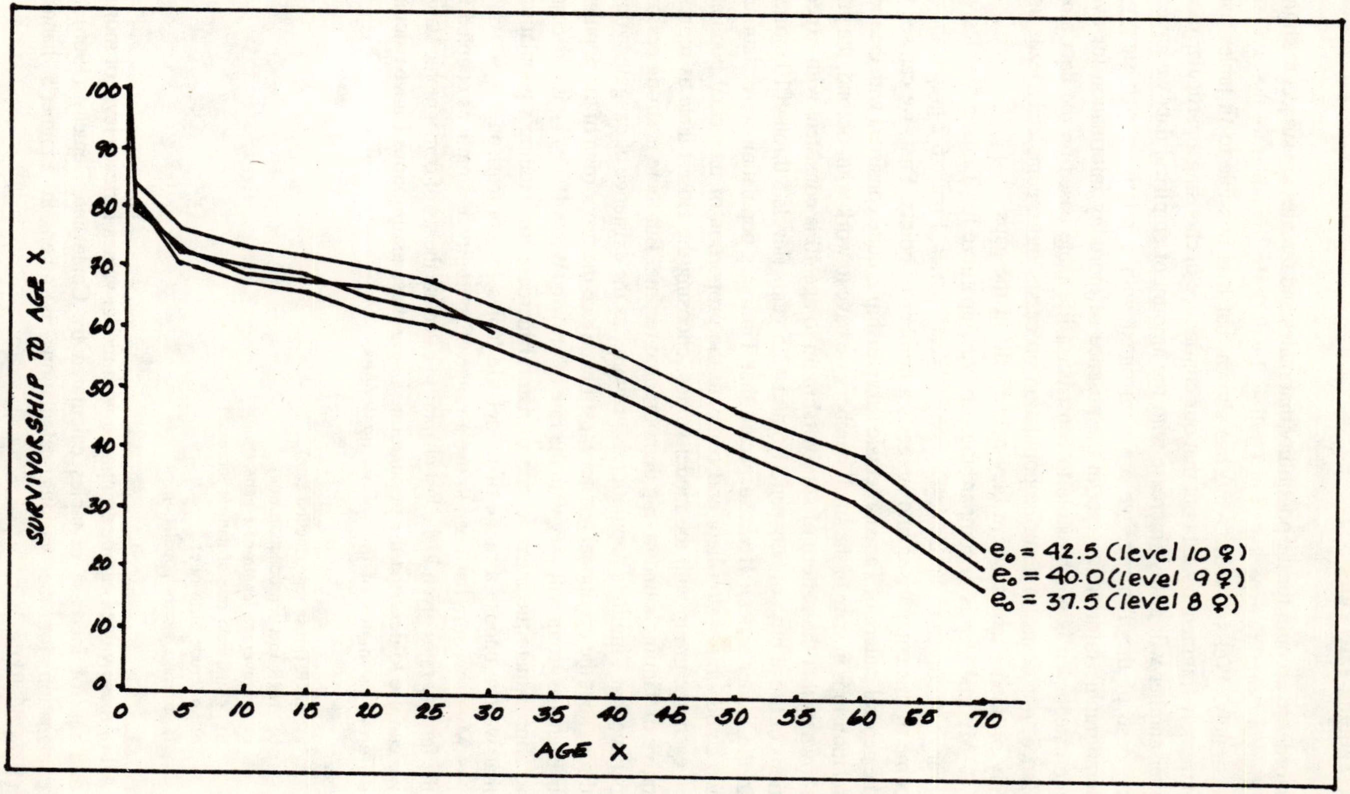

Table 6.5. Estimates of Demographic Measures under Different Female Mortality Assumptions.

Measure	Level 8 A	Level 8 B	Level 9 A	Level 9 B	Level 10 A	Level 10 B
GRR	2.51	2.51	2.51	2.51	2.51	2.51
NRR	1.39	1.47	1.47	1.50	1.55	1.55
$\bar{m}$	29.90	29.66	31.14	30.97	31.20	31.21
r (%)	1.1	1.3	1.2	1.3	1.4	1.4

A = Assuming model mortality throughout female lifecourse.
B = Assuming mixture of model and empirical mortality.

Sources: Timing Marriage and Fertility Schedule and Coale-Demeny Model Life Tables.

Table 6.6. Comparison of Empirical Case with Different Stable Population Model Parameters at Given Rates of Population Growth and Mortality Level.

Age	Timling	Level 8 (r=1.1)	Level 9 (r=1.2)	Level 10 (r=1.4)
		Proportions up to Age (x)		
1	.034	.032	.031	.038
5	.145	.136	.135	.138
10	.240	.251	.250	.255
15	.348	.357	.356	.362
20	.446	.453	.452	.459
25	.554	.541	.539	.546
30	.622	.619	.617	.624
35	.671	.689	.687	.693
40	.735	.751	.749	.754
45	.800	.806	.803	.807
50	.843	.854	.851	.854
55	.880	.895	.892	.894
60	.902	.929	.926	.927
65	.942	.956	.954	.954
Birth Rate		36.59	35.47	35.44
Death Rate		25.59	23.47	21.44
e_0^0		37.5	40.0	42.5
GRR ($\bar{m}$=31)	2.51	2.51	2.44	2.46
Average Age	26.35	26.50	26.65	26.37

Sources: Timling Census, Timling Marriage and Fertility History, and Coale-Demeny Model Life Tables.

I have used three sets of mortality assumptions based on mortality levels 8 through 10 of the Coale-Demeny "West" life tables. In each case, I have taken advantage of the mortality information that we do have for females and figured two sets of measures. The first of these is based entirely on the model survivorship probabilities while the second incorporates the empirical survivorship probabilities for those age groups for which information is available. Table 6.5 presents a range of measures based on different mixes of empirical and model assumptions.

Figure 6.3. Survivorship of Male Children with Three Survivorship Curves from Coale-Demeny Male West Models.

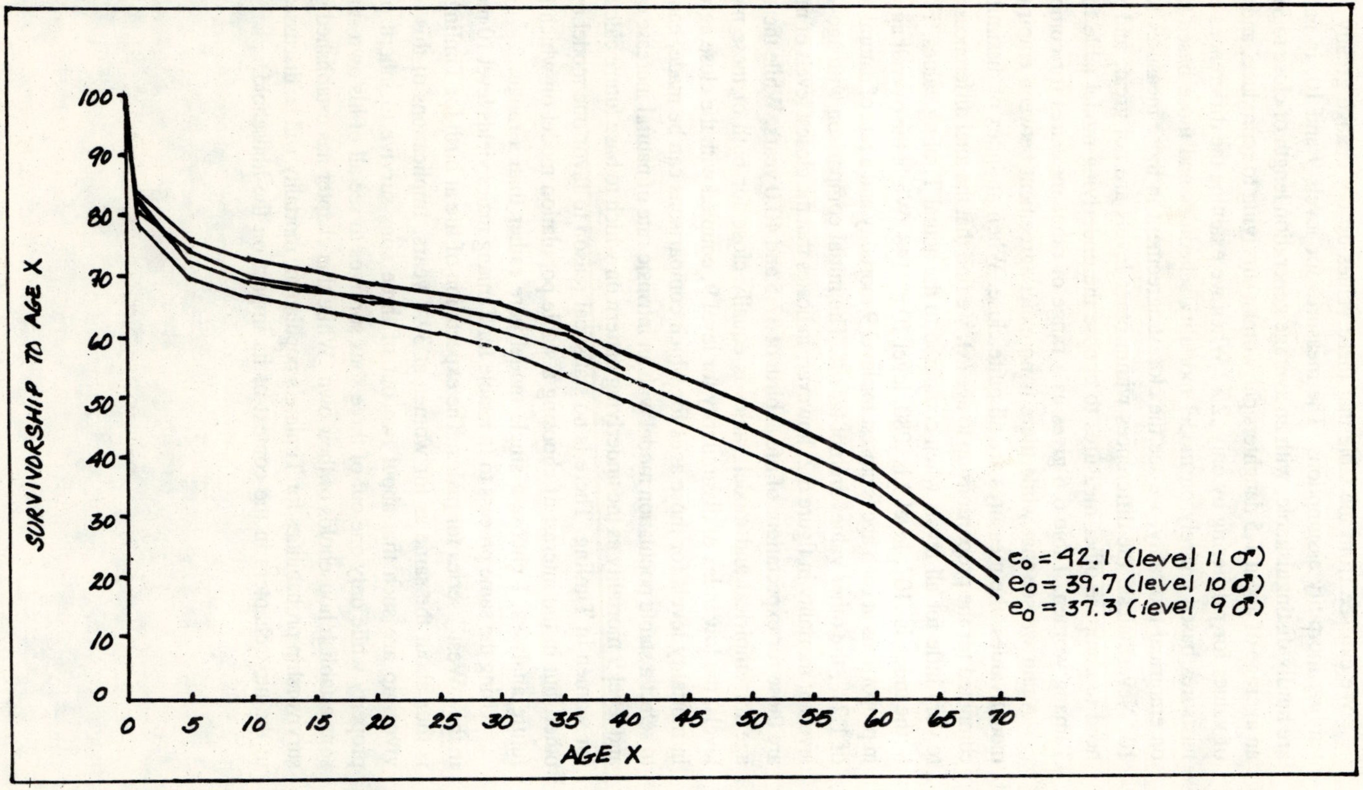

$e_0 = 42.1$ (level 11 ♂)
$e_0 = 39.7$ (level 10 ♂)
$e_0 = 37.3$ (level 9 ♂)

We can see from the table that these values do not change greatly with the varying mortality assumptions. The measures for levels 9 and 10, in particular, are hardly distinguishable, with an average generation length of close to 31 years, an average of about 1.5 daughters per woman surviving to reproduce, and a range of values for r differing by only .2%. When we examine the differences between measures based entirely on model mortality schedules and those based partially on empirical mortality, we see the closest agreement in those measures for level 10. Nevertheless, the differences within other levels are not great, and we will need to compare other measures to choose the underlying model table for these Tamang women. Table 6.6 gives us a range of other measures for comparison.

Again we see that while there is no exact agreement between empirical and model values, the measures are all quite close. When an index of dissimilarity is computed for the proportions up to age (x), we find that the total differences amount to very little for all levels when compared to the actual Timling values. For level 8, the index is .107; level 9 is .080; level 10 is .143. While the overall agreement in proportions at each age is closest for level 9 mortality and a rate of natural increase of 1.2%, the other values are not far off. The initial comparison with age-specific levels of mortality in figure 6.2, however, indicates that the closest levels of mortality are those for expectations of life at birth of 37.5 and 40.0 years. While the average age for empirical and model values is equally close for both of these mortality levels, the low index of dissimilarity for level 9, coupled with the close agreement in mortality levels for those ages for which comparisons can be made, causes me to select a stable population model with an intrinsic rate of natural increase of 1.2% and level 9 mortality as the underlying pattern on which to base future calculations for women in Timling. There is no statistical reason to favor one model over the other, but in the interest of choosing a stable population model on which to base future analyses, I choose a single model here rather than a range.

Using the same process to fit a table for Tamang males yields level 10 mortality in the "West" series for males. The expectation of life at birth for Timling's men is thus about the same as for women at 39.7 years. Implications of this for survivorship are such that about two out of three sons survive to inherit parental property while only one out of three sons survives to see all of his own surviving sons establish households of their own. While this chapter has established general survivorship probabilities for Timling's population, mortality will be discussed again in the next chapters in the context of its impact on the household.

7

Transitions: The Tamang Life Course and the Household Developmental Cycle in Timling

The accomplishments of this analysis thus far allow us to begin to examine the real operation of Timling's adaptation in the context of actual productive units in the village. Aggregate patterns of fertility and mortality have been determined, and the broadest physical and behavioral contours of Tamang life have been outlined. Given the discussion up to now, it would be possible to make some general comparisons with other populations in the Himalaya and throughout the world. Yet, to end here would be to ignore processes critical to our understanding of how these parameters interact with environment and society in Timling.

The impasse is simply put: No Tamang thinks of his or her life in these aggregate terms, and the fuller anthropological understanding of this mountain people must come to terms with the processes that have meaning to them. Even more, we must necessarily bring the analysis down to a level where variation between units has significance.

It is easy enough to find a unit in Nepali hill society that is large enough to incorporate the fairly abstract issues of production and reproduction, yet small enough to have meaning to the individual Tamang. Hardly an anthropologist who has worked in Nepal has failed to notice the special place of the household in village life. For the Gurung, the household is the primary "labour, ritual, commensal, and child-bearing group" (Macfarlane 1976:15). Further west, Magar family life centers around "farmstead-households," spatially and psychologically distinct from one another (Hitchcock 1966:35). The Tamang are like these other Tibeto-Burmese people in the meaning and function they attribute to the household.

This chapter will place the Tamang household into context by highlighting the links between individual life cycle events and the household developmental cycle. It illustrates the permeation of the central unit in Timling society by socially, culturally, and biologically determined events. The implications for household economy will also be dealt with here while the next chapter will go into the variation that occurs among these domestic units.

Talking about the Household

The literature on family and household processes straddles disciplines and is growing rapidly. A recent bibliography compiled by Peter Smith (1983), for example, includes selections from sociology and history in addition to anthropology, and the weight of listings clearly comes after the early 1970s. Many of these works have been devoted to shattering the myth of a rigid evolutionary sequence from large, extended family households in the past to the post-industrial nuclear family household of contemporary society (see, for example, Goody 1972; Laslett 1972; Wilk and Netting 1984). But while this rigid sequence is no longer credible, little consideration has been given to matters of definition. And where definition has been attempted (Bender 1967), the tendency has been to enter the arena with some kind of *a priori* idea of what a household is and then to append a set of functions to it.

Yanagisako's 1979 review clearly lays out the disadvantages of using such constructs for analysis across cultures. She suggests that a more appropriate focus would be on activities "central to the domestic relationships in each particular society," rather than on its domestic groups (1979:186). Wilk and Netting (1984) largely agree with her, offering a similar antidote: analysis must proceed from a focus on behavior—production, distribution, transmission, reproduction, and co-residence—and then must determine the overlapping actors in these behaviors.

As it happens, the concept of household organization favored by the Tamang agrees substantially with the traditional assumptions about peasant family and household; there are, however, differences. For the people of Timling, the household is best defined by the presence of a cooking hearth. Following the lead of Wilk and Netting and Yanagisako, we can begin by identifying those sets of activities that appear vital to social maintenance and see that the hearth retains its focal position throughout.

Beginning with the adaptive perspective, we consider those core activities typically assigned to the household: production, consumption, and reproduction. We have seen that Timling's subsistence economy is geared to extracting resources from a bounded local environment, within which land use rights are extended to the whole population. A subsidiary part of the adaptation has people leaving the village area for extended periods to work as porters, laborers, or soldiers in British and Indian Gurkha regiments. Looking at where the products of all these sectors go highlights the essential commonality of each of these productive activities.

With arable land, the produce goes to the very people who work it. Likewise, with the extraction of forest resources; those people who do the cutting will take the lumber to their own hearths. In both these cases, the units of production and consumption are identical even though the same people may not be involved in all aspects of production. Work is for the common good of those who share the hearth.

Agriculture dominates the Tamang economy, with some 62% of the average household's capital tied up in land. But other segments of Timling's subsistence pattern ratify the identification of hearth members as the essential group in village production. Livestock are owned by these same members and, even when their care is entrusted to others, milk, wool, and meat can be distributed only by the authority of these same people. Production in the case of the agricultural and pastoral sectors of the economy is always for the common benefit of these owners.

The transmission of property across generations further underscores the centrality of the hearth. At its most fundamental, the hearth group consists of a husband and wife, and new members are recruited by bearing children. It is sometime after marriage that a son will ask to establish his own hearth, in effect demanding the economic independence of his production and consumption unit. At the creation of a new hearth, the land held by the natal unit is divided, and separate stores of grain, potatoes, and timber are created.

Ritual emphasizes this separation. Each clan has its own *kulgi lha* (Tm. god of the hearth), to whom daily offerings must be made. Even when poverty forces the establishment of the new commensal unit to take the form of building a new firepit at one end of the same building, the *kulgi lha* must receive the first food cooked on the hearth each day. This offering is made by the household head to prevent the *kulgi lha* from harming other members of the domestic unit. Other ritual events also focus on the hearth: shamans and *lamas* are called periodically to cleanse a site of ghosts, and their ministrations always center around the hearth and are for the benefit of those who share it.

The Tamang household, so defined, bears a strong resemblance to Marshall Sahlins' idealized Domestic Mode of Production, the three major characteristics of which are:

> It is an economy of production for use.
>
> It is an economy of "concrete and limited objectives"—that is, it is penetrated with such "noneconomic" claims as ritual, ceremonial, and social diversions (1972:65).
>
> It is an economy in which households experience varying fortunes and this variation "notably including a substantial degree of domestic economic failure, is a constituted condition of primitive economy." (1972: 69)

The most important feature of this mode of production, however, is its organization around domestic groups, usually the family.

Although Sahlins begins from the bounded domestic group and proceeds to the question of what the group does, his conclusions are very similar to those here. The Tamang household is a unit producing for its own use, kinship relations are the important relations of production (Sahlins 1972:77), and the mode of production guarantees variation in the fortunes of households. Sahlins also introduces the issue of authority within the household. In Tamang society primary responsibility for household decisions inheres in the oldest adult male. It is he who decides what cooperative herding arrangements will be made; it is also he who decides the nature of the property division when a son claims his inheritance. And it is to him that wage earning individuals within the household are expected to surrender their money.

Variation among household fortunes is a function of factors both within and outside household control. In a setting where the primary means of recruiting new household members is through sexual reproduction, the household labor force is largely determined by the facts of birth and death. Some households will have many sons, others none at all. Further, the extent of property that the household begins its life with will be partially determined by the size of sibling groups within which land and other capital must be divided.

Even if every household followed exactly the same pattern of growth and dispersion, a cross-section of the village at a single time would reveal variation in composition and, hence, the labor potential of each productive unit. Fortes' seminal essay on the developmental cycle (1958) explicitly addresses the processes that determine this. The cycle through phases of expansion, dispersion, and replacement (1958:4–5) is the product of social and biological factors: life span, death, birth, marriage, and inheritance. It is at the level of the household that life processes are integrated with the village economy in the domestic mode of production.

Individual Time: Ethnographic Notes on the Life Course

All populations must undergo repetitive sequences of events that help determine their structure. I have already discussed two of these—childbirth and death—in demographic terms, but there are not only other events with significance in Tamang society but also other ways of talking about birth and death that convey more of their social meaning. In Timling, some transitional events have more to do with one sex than the other. In this section, I will follow the individual life course through its cycle and try to make clear the social significance of the occasion for Timling's people.

For the Tamang, life is a predictable process, with events marking changes in social status at more or less the same time for everybody. The important transitions after birth run without trauma through the first haircutting, receiving one's inheritance after marriage, establishing a new household, and eventually to death. Of all these transitions, death is given the greatest ritual attention and involves the largest number of people. The Tamang reckon a full share of life to be about six *legar,* or 72 years. A person becomes a productive household member eligible for the full funeral rites only after the first *legar.* By the midpoint of life, at three *legar,* the Tamang man should have established his household, taken his inheritance, and already have a child close to completion of his or her first *legar.*

Birth and Childhood

The names of children to be born are said to be written by god on the forehead of the woman who will bear them, and the barren women of Timling are described as those with no names on their foreheads. Miscarriage, on the other hand, is the result of mistaken conception. Although an unfortunate event, the spontaneous abortion is explained as the result of *"nge ngo a-re, shiji"* (Tm. "not on my forehead, so it died"). Births are avidly desired, and no woman in the village expressed any interest in medicine that would protect her from childbirth. Quite the opposite: women who had not yet borne children came to me asking if I had "the medicine that gives you children."

As with the Magar, Tamang children "are born into homes where they are much desired and liked" (Hitchcock 1966:48). An expectant mother continues her usual work right up to the time of birth. If labor begins when she is in the village, she returns to her household and waits in the darkness for her child to be born while she kneels on her hands and knees near the firepit. Otherwise, if she is on the trail or in the fields, she seeks a rock shelter or a protected place and sends somebody back to the village to inform her family of the birth. Later births are often unassisted, and nobody in the village specializes in midwifery. The first couple of births are usually assisted by an older woman, sister or husband's mother if they are present. Upon birth, the umbilical cord is tied off with string near the baby's stomach and cut with a *kukhri* (Np. a large curved knife); the afterbirth, called *ro* (Tm. the friend), is then taken by a woman and buried in "good" ground away from stinging nettles or ants so that the child will be without skin ailments. The new mother is not expected to be able to do any work for at least a week after childbirth.

A small number of inexpensive rituals mark the birth of a child after it has survived for at least three days. Before this time, the new baby is not considered a real human being and should it die it will be buried with only the mother and a few of her natal family members present. In a sense, a baby enters the world without a clan since it can only become part of the patriline after three days; to underscore this, male members of the household usually remain away from the child for three days after its birth.

When they return, they will bring a *bombo* and a member of the Ghale clan to help name the child and to offer rice *tormo* to the *kulgi lha*. Thread is tied around the baby's neck, wrist, and ankles to protect it, and water is then sprinkled on the mother and baby and around the room to purify the household.

The first years of life for the Tamang child are passed in near constant physical contact with household members. All older people in the family take turns carrying the baby around in a sling, and the mother nurses her child on demand if she is present. No major ritual such as first rice ceremony marks either the son's or daughter's first years. Solid food in the form of premasticated rice is introduced from an early age, but babies are offered their mother's breast at least until the birth of the next child.

The first important rite of passage is for boys only, and its timing varies with the boy's birth order and the relative wealth of the household. This is the *chewar*, or first haircutting ceremony. Any time after the age of two, a real or classificatory mother's brother is invited to perform the first haircutting to mark the time after which the boy can be considered something more than a baby. The mother's brother's duties, other than cutting the hair, include providing a new head-cloth, clothing, and a hat for the initiate at a cost of from 50 to 60 rupees, while the boy's family will have considerable expense of its own, especially for the first born son, whose *chewar* will be attended by most of the village.

A typical *chewar* will include the provisioning of guests with meat, beer and distilled liquor, rice imported from further south, and locally produced potatoes, corn, and greens. Guests are expected to follow the mother's brother's lead by placing a ghee *tika* on the boy's forehead and presenting a rupee or two to him. Still, it is a rare event when the expense of 600 to 700 rupees is even halfway matched by the value of these gifts. Whatever is given to the boy, however, makes its way to his parents. The expenses of a properly held *chewar* for the first son can delay the timing of this ritual for years in those few cases where households cannot easily afford them. Although it is unusual, it is not surprising to find Tamang boys in the village with their hair still uncut at the late age of 10 years.

Beyond the *chewar* there are no ritual events to mark Tamang transitions until marriage. Both boys and girls steadily increase their economic contribution to the household as they mature. At around eight to ten years of age girls begin with small tasks such as fetching water and caring for the younger siblings while boys do the same in their earlier years. As children near the end of their first *legar*, they begin to contribute work to the household in ways that they will continue and expand upon until they leave to set up their own hearths. Boys often accompany older male relatives to the pastures, and both sexes tend cattle close to the village. Young girls begin to join their mothers and older sisters in the fields from age eight.

Marriage

Toward the age of 20, the tempo of important rites of passage begins to pick up again. Marriage is a vital transition event through which virtually every Tamang must pass to be recognized as a complete member of the community. Such transitions as first menses that have important symbolic and social meaning in other Himalayan cultures pass without fanfare in Timling. Certain restrictions obtain: a menstruating woman should not cook or boil water for the men in her family, and she should sleep at a slight remove from others in the household, but there is no ritual seclusion and purification in a separate hut. The Tamang recognize first menses as the onset of fecundity, and a woman begins to be thought of as a potential sexual partner after her first period. Indeed, a few Tamang men told me that conception is achieved by mixing semen with menstrual blood within the woman's body, a belief that causes many to misinterpret menstruation as a time of high fecundity.

The Tamang may marry anytime after the first *legar* has passed although there is clearly tension between the conflicting desires to retain women in the household when they reach their full labor potential and the usefulness of marriage for extending reciprocity relationships with other households. Marriage in Timling is much more than the simple erotic union of two people; it ties whole households and clan segments into a web of mutually supportive relationships. No marriages took place in the village during my stay there except for the case when one already married man brought a second wife home from outside. He claimed that he had impregnated her and had no choice but to marry her, to the extreme annoyance of his first wife. While polygynous unions are acceptable in theory, first wives seldom relish the idea of sharing their hearth with another wife. The only really acceptable reason for such an arrangement is the inability of the first wife to produce sons. Lust for a younger woman is not regarded favorably by older wives. On the other hand, a man who is often out of the village for work in Bhutan would be thought justified in establishing a second household there complete with wife. Only one man in Timling availed himself of the option for having another wife nearby by taking a second in Lapdung where he held land, but a number of men spoke of their Bhutanese wives, married when they worked on road crews for the Indian government.

Marriages may be arranged by parents, asked for by the husband, or simply entered into by quietly choosing to live together. Although only the first two types involve ritual and some expense, the outlay is dwarfed by preparations for the more important rituals of death.

Even where wealth changes hands at marriage, the amount varies with each household. The direction of this form of property transfer is always toward the woman, a way for her to gain her inheritance when she leaves the household (cf. Macfarlane 1976:180–81). A woman's property is considered her own and cannot be alienated from her regardless of the success or failure of the marriage. The one exception occurs in cases where couples have not cohabited. Here money and goods of equivalent value to that given by the husband's family must be returned. This is an ambiguous situation, often requiring the mediation of village headmen, because the period of time between property transfers and agreed-upon cohabitation can be anywhere from a few days to years. Money may be spent or livestock may die in that time, and the true value of livestock must be determined before restitution can be made.

The woman's inheritance obtained in this way is called *pewa*. It includes cash, jewelry, small amounts of land for vegetable gardens (often originating from the *pewa* of a woman's mother), and clothing. In the case of a marriage between a relatively wealthy household's first son and the daughter of the Gompo Lama, the boy's father presented 1000 rupees in cash to the *lama,* who then used it to purchase a young buffalo, land, and jewelry for his daughter. Additional expense included six *pathi* of rice, five *pathi* of distilled liquor, and three *pathi* of potatoes in addition to a goat slaughtered for the wedding meal.

Ceremony is minimal. Negotiations are opened when the husband-to-be or his father visits the father of the desired woman with a flask of liquor. The proposition is put first and if the woman's father agrees, the men sit down together to drink and gossip. On the day of the wedding, the groom's family arrives to fetch the bride. A *tika* is placed first on the woman's forehead, then on the husband's, by the father of the bride, and a small amount of money is given to his daughter. Following this, the bride's whole family does the same, after which everybody returns to the husband's natal home to feast. The bride will very likely return to her own natal home afterward and will be expected to join her husband at a later date.

Technically, the wife-receivers have lower ritual status than the wife-givers, but the real effect of this is so small in Timling that one man exclaimed in disgust how these people are too *"pake"* (too much like rubes) to know any better.

Arranged marriages become problematic at this point. Far from being a passive victim in the dealings of men, the newly married bride can refuse to have anything to do with her new husband. She will signify an undesirable match by refusing to eat at the nuptial meal, not speaking with her husband, and showing extreme reluctance to move in with her husband's patriline after returning to her natal home. The pressure to cooperate with marriage arrangements, although strong (breaking a marriage at this point creates a rift between household heads who may already be good friends—the shunned household will feel obligated to retaliate by, for example, not attending the funeral rites of those in the woman's family), can be resisted. The likelihood of such resistance increases if the husband's household is in another village, and one solution for the unwilling bride is to take up residence with a local Tamang of her own choosing. The case of Setirani and Norgay is illustrative.

> Setirani is the second daughter of Norjang Ghale, one of the wealthiest men in the village and son of a man who was famous for the extent of his landholdings and herds that included yak, sheep, goats, and cattle. Although Norjang shared his inheritance with four other brothers, his share amounted to some 30 *hal,* or about 77 *ropani.* As a group, Norjang and his brothers followed the strategy of their father, arranging their children's marriages to suit practical ends. Thus, the patriline has kin links with villages throughout the seasonal migration route of its extensive herds.
>
> When Setirani was 19, she was given to a boy in Sertang. The boy's family was powerful in the politics of the dominant village in the *panchayat.* Setirani went along with her family to partake of the wedding feast in Sertang but refused to eat or even look at her new husband. Even though she was to stay in the village, she returned to Timling in three days and avoided the issue of staying married by moving to the Terai to live with her sister. Meanwhile, her husband went to Bhutan to work on road construction.
>
> Setirani eventually returned from Terai, and when her parents-in-law found out, they sent for her because they needed her help in the fields and with the cattle since their son was in Bhutan. She refused. At Dasain, Setirani's mother-in-law sent a portion of the feast to Timling for her to eat, but she declined, feeling that to eat it would be to acknowledge her marriage. A few months later, her husband returned to Sertang with gold earrings. Setirani was pressured into joining her husband at home, but not long after, he again left for Bhutan.
>
> She was not happy living in Sertang and one day met Norgay on the way to tending cattle. Norgay, who had been married twice before, knew Setirani from Timling and when she complained about her situation agreed to help her out of her marriage by taking her to his *goth* for a few days. After that, they moved to his father's house and he proclaimed their marriage. He was accused of wife stealing by Setirani's parents, who demanded that he return her to her rightful husband. The couple refused and lived without contact with Setirani's natal family for a while.

Setirani's parents eventually accepted her decision in spite of the relative poverty of Norgay's family, while Norgay went into debt to pay back part of the *pewa* that originated with his wife's first husband.

This case highlights a number of points. First, the extent to which arranged marriages are strategically made is hinted at by the pattern of marrying off daughters to places where kin relationships would be advantageous. Second, there is the ambiguity of who is responsible for paying back the husband's family expenses in a marriage. In this case, Norgay agreed to pay; if he hadn't, Setirani's family would have been held responsible since the marriage had never been properly consummated. Lastly, it is obvious here that a daughter's wishes can prevail in spite of the pressure to agree with her father's decision. The tenuous existence of arranged marriages has caused them to be out of favor with Timling's people. Although the material advantages are very tempting to household heads, there is an expressed feeling that couples should decide for themselves to avoid the bad feelings that accompany an unsuccessful match.

In spite of these negative feelings, 41.6% of 149 village marriages were reported to have been arranged. Unfortunately, I was unable to discover in all cases whether "arranged" referred to actual negotiations between two sets of fathers or to the more participatory act of requesting a father's permission through intermediaries. Thus, the most interesting statistic for changing notions of the "traditional" peasantry is that 58.4% of all marriages were reported to have been solely the spouses' choice.

A look at the distribution of age at marriage and cohabitation reveals a picture that diverges from much of the demographic literature for Nepal as a whole. Banister and Thapa, for example, report singulate mean ages at marriage for Nepali women at 17.5 (1981:43). In Timling, the average age is 19.8. There is an interesting parallel here with the Gurung, whose average female age at marriage is 19 (Macfarlane 1976:218–21). Table 7.1 displays the figures for ages at first marriage and cohabitation for Timling's women. These figures indicate a concentration of marriages for women between the ages of 17 and 20 but a slower rate than that reported in the Nepal Fertility Survey (Banister and Thapa 1981:44), where some 94% of women were married by age 24, compared to 87% in Timling. As a final note on the distributions, we can see that the rate of cohabitation at early ages is less than that of marriage. By the end of their 18th year 43.6% of the women of Timling had married, but only 37.5% of them had moved into their husband's patrilines. This might be explained by the tendency in early arranged marriages to wait longer to move. A woman gives her father's household the use of her labor for slightly longer while links of reciprocity are already established with other households.

Arranged and choice marriages differ along nearly every temporal measure. Table 7.2 highlights some of these variations. The consistently earlier ages at marriage and cohabitation for women with arranged marriages would suggest that these women have more children than the others. Other evidence indicates that the

Table 7.1. Distribution of Ages at First Marriage and First Cohabitation for 149 Tamang Women.

Age Group	1st Marriage N	1st Marriage %	1st Cohabitation N	1st Cohabitation %
10-14	11	7.4	7	4.7
15-16	20	13.4	16	10.7
17-18	34	22.8	33	22.1
19-20	29	19.5	32	21.5
21-22	21	14.1	24	16.1
23-24	15	10.1	18	12.1
25-26	11	7.4	11	7.4
27+	8	5.4	8	5.4
	$\bar{X}$......19.75		$\bar{X}$......20.18	
	SD......4.34		SD......4.13	

Source: Timling Marriage and Fertility History.

wealthier households are the most inclined to arrange marriages for reasons that include their ability to handle the expense and their desire to expand cooperative links with other households. At the same time, an equalizing factor, in the form of a greater rate of marital dissolution for arranged marriages, may cancel out this reproductive advantage. One way to explore this possibility is to compare the ages at which women begin their final union by type of first marital union. Here, the gap is substantially reduced, with women whose first marriages were arranged eventually settling on a partner at an average age of 22.10, compared to 22.72 for the other group. This measure must be taken as a rough indicator because it includes remarriages after both widowhood and divorce, but with the risk of widowhood roughly equal we can assume that the closing gap is a result of later remarriages after divorce for women whose first marriages were arranged.

Inheritance

The significance of marriage for women is that they must sever their relationships with their natal homes to become strangers in a new household. With the taking of her *pewa,* the Tamang woman has no new direct claims on her home of birth. For the male, the parallel event occurs when he claims his inheritance or share (*angsa*) to move away from his father and establish his own household. A son may claim his *angsa* any time after age 16 and his father is theoretically unable to refuse him. Once again, there is tension between the father's desire to keep his son in the household and the threat of the son's leaving. In practice, however, Tamang sons rarely claim their inheritance at an early age for a number of reasons: once they take their inheritance, they cannot make any additional claims on property added to the natal household after that time; leaving early would be a blow to the father's household labor force and may prejudice his desire to assist the son in the future; leaving too early could leave the son with an improper knowledge of subsistence techniques. Also, the father has some discretion in the land that he parts with, and an improvident leave-taking might incline him to part with less than choice parcels of land.

Thus the real impetus for a son to claim his inheritance comes with the arrival of his new wife who, as an outsider, is anxious to escape the subordinate status she has to other women in the household. In most cases, marriage and cohabitation are the prelude to household fission.

The items included in the *angsa* are carefully divided with consideration to the number of sons who will share in it and the continuing needs of the father and his wife. Typically, a father attempts to make some contribution to building an older son's new home by donating land, material, and labor. Poorer households can often afford to give little more than a gesture. In the case of Setirani and Norgay, the son claimed his *angsa* the same year he married Setirani. The decision to establish a new household was hastened by the destruction of his father's home by fire and the consequent move into a storage hut. Norgay had been anticipating

Table 7.2. Comparison of Means for Selected Marriage Variables (Tamang Women).

Variable		Marriage Type Arranged	Marriage Type Choice	Total
1st Marriage Age	$\bar{X}$	18.00	20.99	19.75
	SD	3.30	4.57	4.34
1st Cohabit Age	$\bar{X}$	19.00	21.02	20.18
	SD	3.09	4.56	4.12
Years between Marriage & Cohabitation	$\bar{X}$	1.00	0.03	0.44
	SD	1.68	0.24	1.19
Age Gap between Spouses (M-F)	$\bar{X}$	2.30	3.49	3.04
	SD	4.40	5.82	5.34

Source: Timing Marriage and Fertility History.

his move before the fire, however, and he had traveled to Bhutan to earn money and bring back necessary items.

A number of features of Norgay's transition will help make clear the inheritance process. To begin with, Norgay is a part of an inheritance unit that includes three generations of a single clan, all of whom have claim to the same land. Land division is incomplete since both his father and grandfather have retained some land for their own subsistence needs. Norgay's grandfather owned some 30 *hal* of land at his peak, including 3 *hal* of some of the best land in the lowest part of the valley. He had two sons who opted to remain in the household until long after their marriages. Norgay's father, being the eldest, would have had to build his own house had he decided to move out. He decided to stay until his own sons were old enough to contribute to his own household, and it wasn't until the relatively late age of 42 that he took his *angsa*. By this time he had three sons, two of them nearly full producers at ages 13 and 16. Since his father needed to retain land for his own use, his *angsa* consisted of 13 *hal* of land rather than 15. By the time Norgay was ready to claim his own *angsa* seven years later, he had to divide his share with his two brothers, subtracting the land retained by his father and grandfather. This left him with 3 *hal* and claims on the land that would become available when his grandfather and father died. Of the grandfather's land, Norgay can expect to receive a smaller portion since it will first have to be divided equally between his grandfather's two sons. This will bring his father's total up to 5 *hal*, which may not be split among Norgay and his brothers until his father dies.

Inheritance, then, is a continuous process that depends on the number of brothers born to each generation, marriage, and survival of older males in the patriline. In an ideal process, land will continue to enter the new household as it grows since deaths in ascending generations will free more for division. Norgay's situation is made somewhat more complicated because his father remarried a few years ago and his new wife bore a son, half-brother to Norgay, after the *angsa* was taken. This new claimant, Norgay insists, cannot legitimately demand any of the land already divided and must be content with a quarter share of his father's remaining property. This will leave him with an extremely small 1.25 *hal* unless Norgay's father can expand his holdings in the meantime.

Data on the timing of inheritance and the creation of new households were gathered in Timling through a non-random sampling of 50 household heads. This presents problems for generalizing to the village, but we can argue for the rough plausibility of the figures. Table 7.3 presents the average ages and standard deviations for alternate groupings of these households. The various groupings refer to average ages based on different criteria affecting those ages. The first category consists of all households, including those with only or youngest sons who received their *angsa* at the death of their fathers. Since our interest here is in the creation of new groups through household fission, I have excluded those cases of relatively seamless transition to form the second grouping.

Table 7.3. Average Age at Inheritance for Tamang Men.

Grouping	Average Age	SD	N
All Households	27.79	7.83	41
All Households Headed by Other than Only or Youngest Sons	28.79	8.10	28
All Households Overlapping LHM and Economic Survey	24.29	8.82	17
Households Overlapping LHM and Economic Survey Other than Only or Youngest Sons	27.10	7.17	10

Source: Life History Matrix.

The two "sample" categories are similar to the others except that they consist of households chosen for the economic survey when the information was available from the life histories. For both sets, we can see that the average age at which household heads come into *control* of the productive unit is actually younger than the average age that sons *establish* their own units.

It is difficult to make elaborate arguments from these data. I would argue that the age at which older sons choose to take their *angsa* is roughly 27; the standard deviations suggest much variation here and, hence, great potential for strategic decisions based on a whole range of economic and emotional factors. A Tamang male does not lightly separate from his natal home. He is constantly weighing the happiness of his wife in a home where she has no power, the size of his family, and the potential for his inheritance to grow from the continued acquisitions of his father and brothers. Using age 27 is not a completely arbitrary decision. From the point of view of parental households, it allows a conservative estimation of the potential labor contribution from sons. We can see from the data that average households have the labor of their sons for at least 10 years after they become full producers, a length of time that must more than make up for the minimal consumption requirements of sons in their earlier years.

Insofar as generalization can be accepted, we can say that households will begin the process of fission sometime after the oldest son reaches 27. If we assume that his age at marriage was about 23, his wife's about 20, and that the first child is born about three years later, then we begin to define a process of household development.

Having Children and the Nature of Paternity

Childbirth initiates a process that will increase the labor potential of each productive unit as well as tie it to others through potential marriages in the future. The Tamang are understandably concerned, given their inheritance system, with the paternity of each child in spite of relatively unrestricted sexual activity prior to marriage. While marriage is an ideal prelude to the beginning of childbearing for each woman, these events do not always fall into this sequence. In those cases where a woman becomes pregnant before marrying, she will be closely questioned about the identity of the child's father until she names him. Once named, a Tamang man is hard pressed to prove that he is other than the father. The word of the woman is rarely doubted, and most people have a fairly accurate idea of who is having sexual relations with whom. It could hardly be otherwise in a village where sexual encounters occur at all-night dances where couples are watched slipping off into the woods together and returning to the dance circle after a short period. Other occasions to arrange a liaison are even more noticeable. A young man steals into his partner's home late at night when he hopes that nobody will be awake. Shrouded by the darkness in a room packed with the sleeping bodies of the girl's parents and siblings, the couple try to have sex undetected until the early morning hours when the girl's lover sneaks out of the house. To continue this undetected would require superhuman powers, and the Tamang easily acknowledge and joke about such meetings. Should a pregnancy result and the male be unmarried, he will be strongly pressured to set up a household with the woman. He may already be married or adamantly refuse, however, in which case he is responsible for the upbringing of the child. If the child is a boy, he will inherit from his patriline even if he spends most of his early years in his mother's home. In practice, there are few refusals.

The Tamang do not consider bastards—called *pro* (Tm.), as opposed to *yangija* (Tm.) for a legitimate child—in any negative light. The only important issue is that the child's patrilineal clan be determined so that incest can be avoided and the material obligations of upbringing assigned. Consider the following case of adultery and childbirth:

> Kerimaya was born the only child in a Damrong household. When it became clear that no male heirs would be born to her parents, arrangements were made to have a Ghale from Lapdung marry her and take over the inheritance. Tarshen Ghale moved into the house and assumed all the rights and responsibilities of caring for Kerimaya's parents as if he were an only son. Over the years, the couple had two sons and a daughter. When the oldest son was 12 and able to do the household work of his father, Tarshen Ghale went to Bhutan with others to do road work. He remained in Bhutan for two and a half years.
>
> In that time Kerimaya became pregnant and a son was born shortly after her husband returned. Tarshen was not angry with his wife but wanted to know who the father of the boy was. He was told that his wife became pregnant when a *panchayat* official of the Gomtsa clan had visited from Sertang nine months before. Letters had already been written to him by Bumdi Ghale, a *panchayat* official from Timling who has learned to write and who took a special interest in a case involving a member of his own clan. But the man had denied paternity.
>
> After that, nothing much could be done. Letters continued to be written and the man continued to deny his responsibility in a case complicated by his already being married and having a family. The Gomtsa avoided the village for four years and took alternate trails to other settlements in the *panchayat* when business would have brought him through. Kerimaya and Tarshen had another son in that time, and Tarshen grew increasingly resentful of having to use his own resources to raise a Gomtsa when he had a Ghale son of his own. The issue of inheritance irked him as well, since with no man widely held to be the father, he might be expected to provide a small bit of land for the boy.
>
> In October 1981 a member of the district *panchayat*, a much loved Tamang from Borang, made a tour of the upper Ankhu Khola villages to talk to old friends and renew support for future elections. The man from Sertang was married to his sister and had no choice but to accompany him to Timling. An open meeting in front of the whole village progressed without interruption; Kerimaya and Tarshen were not present, the Gomtsa kept a low profile, and the issue of the child was in the distant past for most people. With the end of the meeting, the *panchayat* official moved on to Lapdung by horse while a number of Sertang residents prepared to return home. Among them was the Gomtsa, still unnoticed in the thinning crowd.
>
> Kerimaya looked down from the plot of land she was working just above the plaza and saw the Gomtsa. Wasting no time, she came bounding down before she could lose him again. She ran into the opening, grabbed the alleged father of the now four-year-old boy by the clothes on his chest, and began shouting: "Here he is! Here he is! The father of the boy, the man who ate at my hearth and never came back! Here he is!"

The word went quickly through the village, and Tamang men and women converged from all corners and surrounded the Gomtsa, blocking off any escape. His fellow Sertangis melted to the edge of the crowd while the Gomtsa simply resigned himself to the ordeal and crouched in his place.

This case illustrates beautifully a number of points that converge on the centrality of the household in Tamang social and economic life. First of all we can clearly see how the household must function as the means of provisioning and providing security for Tamang villagers. Kerimaya's parents are constrained by rules of inheritance that nevertheless flexibly allowed them to bring in a son-in-law for their old age. The land they own will end up in Ghale hands, but they will be taken care of as if they had sons of their own. Tarshen's resentment is far less a matter of jealously guarding the sexuality of his wife than of being sure his own sons have land to support themselves; his interest in settling the matter of paternity becomes urgent only when a third son of his own enters the household. All of the Tamang I spoke to sympathized with Tarshen's reluctance to raise the boy of another clan. More perplexing to them was the reluctance of the boy's actual father to own up to his paternity: it was, after all, a son and, hence, a useful addition to any family.

In the end, after some eight hours of harangue and complicated deliberation, the Gomtsa accepted his responsibility. Even this had to be accomplished through the adjudication of the national *panchayat* official because the case was too much for local channels and had to be brought before him in Lapdung. By accepting paternity, the Gomtsa accepted a new heir and acknowledged that the boy would eventually join him in Sertang even though everybody agreed that he should stay with his mother until older. Tarshen no longer needed to expend his own resources for the child's upbringing since the newly proclaimed father would be expected to send money to help pay for food and clothing. The resolution left everybody in Timling satisfied: household integrity was intact and clan responsibilities were satisfied.

Some husbands have less difficulty accepting a child not their own. In another Ghale household, a child widely regarded as the son of a village woman and a European involved in ecological research in the high pastures was born while the husband was also working in Bhutan—the boy is often called by the name Tar Ghale (Tm. white Ghale). This man, with only one other son, was pleased to accept the child as his own. He laughs at the joking about his *sahib* son, but insists that the boy is his.

Death

The rituals associated with death are the most important and expensive transition events in Tamang culture. In this they resemble the Gurung (Macfarlane

1976:181-82), although their ritual observances differ somewhat. Ceremonies associated with death dominate the life of the community throughout the year; their length and elaborateness will vary with household wealth although the effects of losing productive household members can be as devastating for the rich as for the poor. Because the impact of the household member's death will vary with her or his age and the point at which it occurs in the household developmental cycle, the complexity of ritual will also vary. Children below the age of 12 receive minimal ceremonies that usually involve only the immediate household (except in cases of neonatal death when a woman and her immediate patriline are the only ones involved). Any time after that, the number of people involved grows steadily with the age and connections of the dead person.

All Tamang desire elaborate funerals (*grel* or *ghewa*) and can guarantee them, in part, by having a large number of sons to share the expense and a large number of daughters to bring their affines. Done properly, the death memorial rites will last almost a whole year, with a massive three day ritual to mark the death itself, shorter *ghewa* at three month intervals (if they can be afforded), and a final ritual in early December or late November when the charred bones of the deceased are exhumed from the first funeral pyre, mixed with ghee and pulverized, and burned again. This last ceremony also lasts three days and culminates in the dead person being given his or her "*angsa*" in the form of a food offering. A prayer flag is erected on the ridge above the village, and the deceased no longer has a claim on the living.

The last ritual is nearly as expensive as the first. Even when relatives have intentions of carrying it out, they are often forced to wait, sometimes for years, before being able to do so. The ridge above Phyang, where households are poorer than those in Timling, is littered with the capped funeral pyres housing the bones of the dead because households cannot afford the last ritual. In one day of the first ritual of a series I witnessed, expenses approached 1000 rupees worth of cloth, grain for *tormo*, potatoes and grain for the mourners, and a goat. Total expenses for the full funeral cycle could easily reach 3000 rupees. It is not surprising that funerals can force families to use the full extent of their kin links with other households to feed the assembled mourners.

Death creates widows, men without wives, and households without fathers or mothers. Or death can take away only sons or daughters. I would not suggest that the Tamang calibrate their emotions to the economic implications of a relative's death—I have seen a man morose for weeks after the death of a sister's daughter placed into his care—but the significance of a person's death clearly varies with who the person is. In our own society we talk about "untimely deaths." Similarly, a man or woman's death in Timling can be an untimely interruption of the process of household-building. It can radically transform the prospects of a household from a successful to a failing domestic economy.

>Embi Ghale died during the monsoon season at the age of 39. His death was slow, painful, and expensive. A month before, he had taken his rifle to the forest above the village to go hunting

and had slipped off a rock and slammed the rifle butt into his face during the fall. He was carried back to the village and placed in his home by the fire. The pain was intense. In the weeks that he lingered, 9 goats and 16 chickens were slaughtered and offered to the gods of the forest and household gods. The week before he died, he was carried in desperation to a crippled *lama* of Sertang, reputed to have a very powerful mantra. Nothing worked and his family watched as "the god of the forest ate his flesh."

Embi was the grandson of the same legendary Ghale; his wife was brought to Timling from Kimtang near the village's winter pastures. When he died, he left two daughters, two sons, and a 35-year-old widow. Neither of his sons was old enough to do an adult's work, and his oldest daughter was only 12.

Embi Ghale's death interrupted the trajectory of his household's developmental cycle at a crucial time. What had been a successful and self-contained unit was now a household without the labor force to plough its own fields, cut wood, or work in the cash economy outside of the village. And with the oldest son only seven years old, there was no early prospect of it becoming relatively self-sufficient. Additionally, the timing and nature of Embi's death placed a severe strain on household resources. His wife stayed in the house with her husband most of the time and relied on Embi's family to help in the fields, but all of his brothers had little labor to spare and the harvest suffered. The goats and chickens for sacrifice came at first from Embi's own livestock, then his father's, and finally his brother's. These same people contributed to his *grel* after he died, but because they had already expended so much where the primary responsibility belongs to a man's sons, the *grel* was smaller than the status of his household warranted.

With two sons in the household, the land could not be reabsorbed by the closest Ghale relatives of Embi's generation. It would, however, have to be ploughed by them until his oldest son grew large enough to do that work. And other work normally done by adult males in the household would also need to be done by others. Embi's wife had the option of staying to raise her family in Timling, returning to her natal home in Kimtang, or remarrying in the village. She chose to remain in Timling for the time being and will probably not marry immediately since to do so would mean giving up the land of her husband.

Embi's death illustrates the potential that death holds for changing a household's fortunes. Where Embi had planned to acquire new land through purchases with money he earned every year outside of the village, the program of expansion was abruptly stopped and his sons' potential inheritance considerably reduced. At the same time, life for the household promised to be more difficult for the five to seven years it would take for the oldest son to grow into adult productivity.

The Household Developmental Cycle in Timling

The developmental cycle of domestic groups is a topic of considerable anthropological importance and is tied directly to fertility, mortality, migration, child spacing, age at marriage, and other demographic considerations. It provides a mechanism for connecting population processes with many broader social processes for which the form of the domestic units is a basic consideration—e.g., labor mobilization, land tenure practices, and socialization. (Foster 1978:415)

To glance at the cross-section of household types in Timling is to get a picture of a society in which the nuclear family is the dominant form. This is consistent with what we know from other peasant societies and elsewhere. Table 7.4 demonstrates the importance of the nuclear family household for Timling and two Gurung villages. Yet this cross-section can be misleading, especially when the Tamang life cycle implies a process of household formation and movement through definable transitions. In this section, I will explore the implications of this developmental cycle for Timling's adaptation.

I begin with the bare facts of individual life cycle events to construct a model of the household developmental cycle. Figure 7.1 takes a husband and wife and diagrams average ages for the important events. A man marries at age 23 and can expect to live until age 64 (assuming that he has already survived to have his last child at age 42). The household as a production unit defined by the authority of this man lasts some 37 years, in which time its character undergoes dramatic changes in its own composition and in its relationships with other households.

Although this figure provides a fair representation of the sequence of events that constitute the household cycle, it leaves us in the dark about the nature of the changing domestic labor force and the influence of changing household composition on individual events. Figure 7.2 makes up for these shortcomings by joining individual and household life cycle events into a single diagram. It is an idealized but very useful portrayal of the household developmental cycle along with its components. The following assumptions hold:

> Average ages for the whole population have been used to define the timing of events.
>
> The exception here is the age of death of men and women which have been set to the life table average for men and women who have survived until the birth of the fifth child.
>
> Women bear five children, slightly less than the actual figure but more useful as a model, and none of these children die.
>
> Units of production and consumption are as calculated in Macfarlane's research with the Gurung (Macfarlane 1976:114, 165).

Figure 7.2 graphically shows the importance of the time element to the household as a bounded economic unit containing most of its labor force and producing for itself. Household time is defined by the line furthest to the left while biological aging of individual members is represented by separate lines, husband and wife to the left and the separate children to the right. Recruitment to the domestic unit is almost entirely through biological reproduction except at the marriage of male children. At that time full female production units also join the household. The addition of spouses to the household is represented by a thickening of the lines for sons; as with their mothers, women are assumed to join their husbands at age 20. The household is then an entity largely affected by the biology of reproduction and aging, but with an important array of social facts affecting its composition, too. This is clear when we note that a household is *not* established immediately

Table 7.4. Household Structure in Timling and Two Gurung Villages.

HH Type	Timling N	Timling %	Thak* N	Thak* %	Mohoriya* N	Mohoriya* %
Nuclear	89	67.4	44	57.1	59	67.9
Stem	32	24.2	20	26.0	25	28.8
Joint/Extended	6	4.5	--	----	1	1.1
Other	5	3.8	13	16.9	2	2.2
Total	132	100.0	77	100.0	87	100.0

Sources: Timling Census and *Macfarlane 1976:17.

Figure 7.1. Sequence and Timing of Life Cycle Events in Timling.

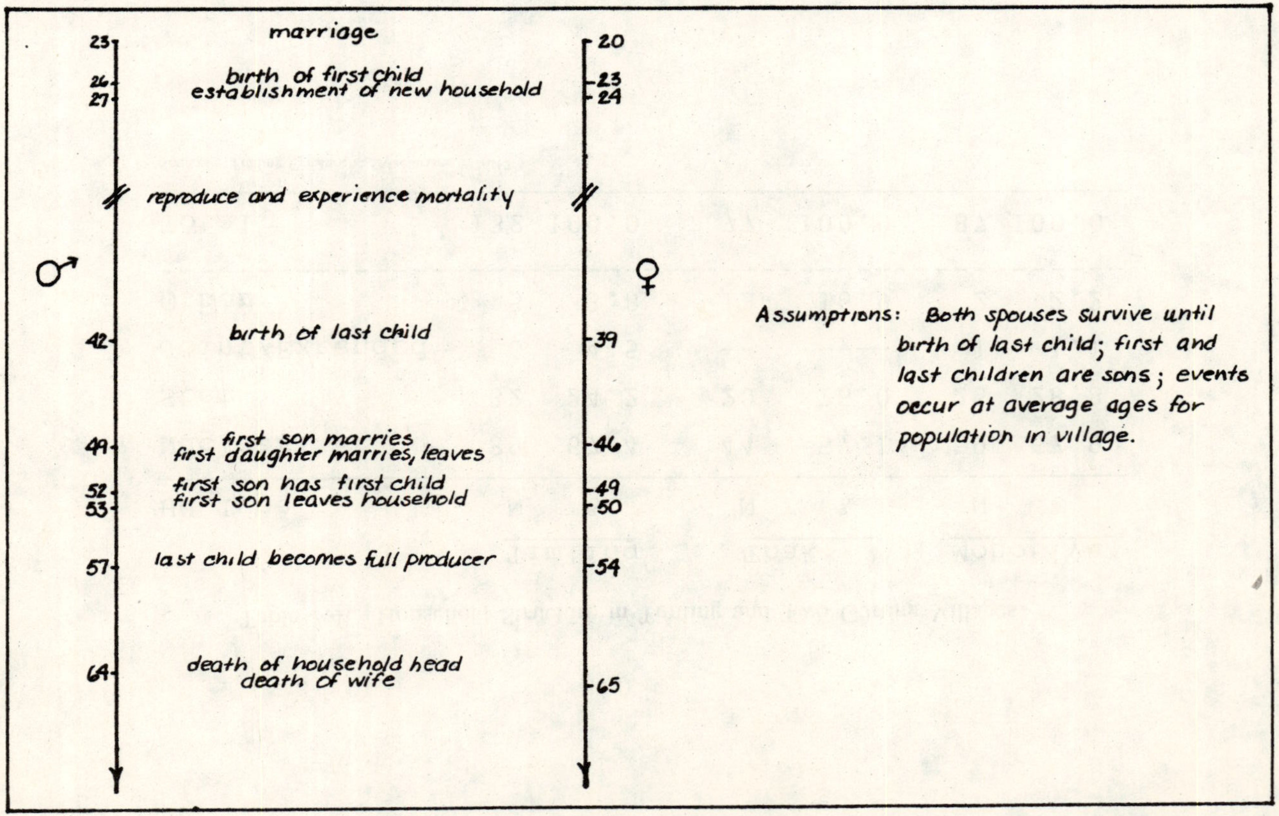

♂

Age	Event
23	marriage
26	birth of first child
27	establishment of new household
~	reproduce and experience mortality
42	birth of last child
49	first son marries / first daughter marries, leaves
52	first son has first child
53	first son leaves household
57	last child becomes full producer
64	death of household head / death of wife

♀

Age	
20	marriage
23	birth of first child
24	establishment of new household
39	birth of last child
46	first son marries / first daughter marries, leaves
49	first son has first child
50	first son leaves household
54	last child becomes full producer
65	death of household head / death of wife

Assumptions: Both spouses survive until birth of last child; first and last children are sons; events occur at average ages for population in village.

Figure 7.2. Tamang Household Growth Assuming No Children Die and Event Occurrences at Average Ages for Timling's Population.

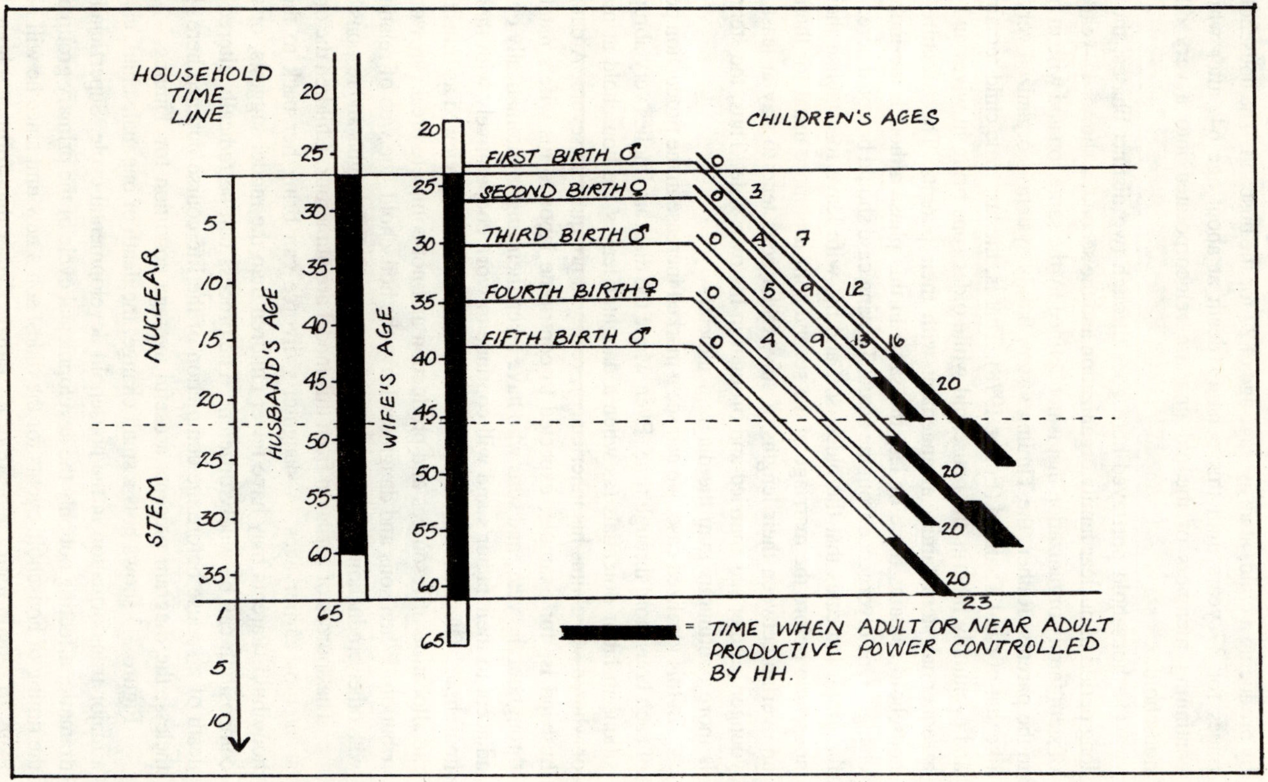

after marriage, or even after the birth of a first child. Rather, a son takes his inheritance from his father only after his soon-to-separate unit proves its viability by producing a child, at an average age of 27 for the husband. The household continues for 37 years until this person's death at about age 64, after which the continuing members of the old unit are reincorporated into a very different household.

The household portrayed here goes through two distinct phases, the first a long period of nuclear family organization and the second, a shorter 15-year period of stem family organization that is not defined by the same son and wife in relation to the parents. Rather, the Timling's stem family system is organized very much like that of rural Thailand (Foster 1978). That is, the last male child remains with and eventually inherits the household while older sons bring in wives and live in a sequential stem family arrangement with their parents. The structure of the household remains more or less the same in this phase although the individuals change. One divergence from the actual Tamang case should be noted here. Where the graph indicates that the oldest son and his wife leave to establish their own household before the marriage of the second son, it is more usual for there to be an overlap between their lengths of stay. Older sons tend to stay at least until a younger brother has married and brought in his own wife. Thus, the stem phase is more continuous than the diagram indicates.

In this idealized case, we can see a marked increase in the production potential of each household through time. Even where the diagram implies very abrupt transitions in labor potentials (as when a daughter leaves the household at marriage or when a son claims his inheritance), reality is not quite so severe. A daughter's husband is, for example, expected to contribute labor to his wife's natal home throughout the year, and sons who have taken their *angsa* automatically own land adjacent to their father's and will continue to work cooperatively with their natal household. These abrupt lines, then, are more accurately viewed as transitions in the allocation of resources and production and not complete breaks in work contribution. When sons and daughters leave the household, the web of relationships with other production units is extended into new reciprocal rights and responsibilities.

The sources of variation from this model are numerous. Children die or marry at later or earlier ages. A daughter's divorce can bring her back to the natal household. Parents may have fewer children than the model suggests, or the sex composition can be wildly different. The process can be radically altered by the death of a spouse before the completion of the life course outlined here. Nevertheless, the diagram presents a useful average condition for Timling.

Figure 7.3 shows how a small change, the death of one male child, can cause a major transformation in the household developmental cycle. Superficially, it is dramatic, affecting not only the developmental cycle of the primary group but also the timing of household events for the oldest son's new unit since he will be more likely to remain until the death of his father. Rather than forming a household at age 27, he waits until he is 38. As a direct consequence, the life of his own household

Figure 7.3. Tamang Household Growth Assuming One Male Child Dies and Event Occurrences at Average Ages for Timling's Population.

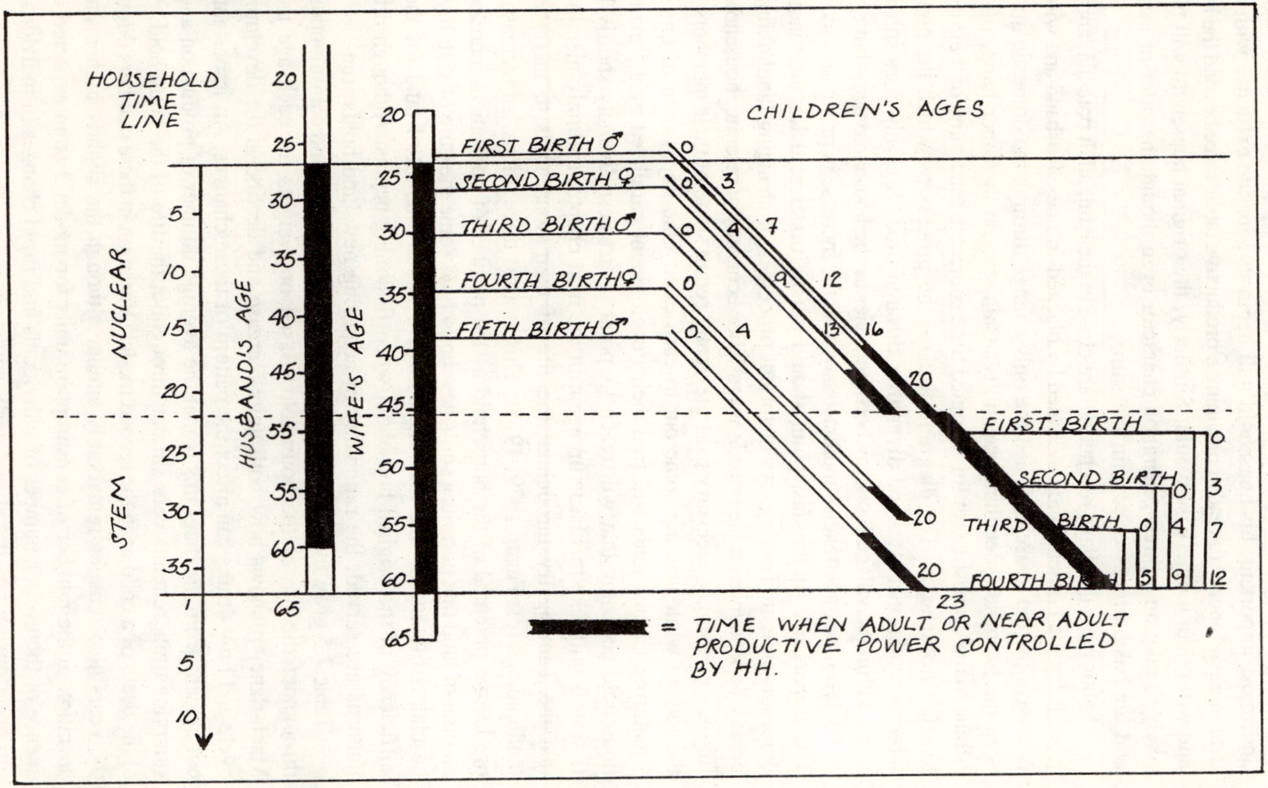

is considerably shortened, the stem phase will take up proportionately more time and, most important, his household will begin its separate existence with a great deal more autonomy (already containing a productive labor force beyond the husband and wife) than it otherwise would. Similarly, the original household will be more likely to take on a three-generation character even though the rules of formation and the basic processes remain the same.

Labor units that have reached or are close to their full adult potential and whose labor is for the household are indicated by blacked-in lines. Husband and wife labor is always for the household, and the only change through the domestic unit's life is in the husband's declining capability. Children, on the other hand, may contribute to the domestic unit for a limited time subject to the timing of their removal to other households. The diagram displays the process by which the household labor potential increases and diversifies through time. Not only does subsistence work within the village economy become easier as the household ages, but a variety of tasks can be undertaken simultaneously with the increase in productive members. The importance of this last point should not be underrated for the viability of domestic units in Timling. As historical processes of changing landholdings and greater dependence on the outside wage-labor economy accelerate, households will find it increasingly necessary to strategically retain some of their members within the village while sending some out to earn cash. One implication of this is that "maturing" households will find their development paralleled by a "maturing" household economy that will reach its point of greatest diversity shortly before fission. I will take this issue up again in the next chapter and only mention here that the Tamang try throughout the life of their households to increase their landholdings (cf. Fegan 1979, 1978). This assures three things: an increase in the productive potential of the household as the number of consumers increases, an amount of land that permits a son's new household some measure of viability when he claims his *angsa*, and the retention of a viable amount of land for the self-sufficiency of the original household when fissioning begins. Although different interests are served, the rationality of acquiring new land holds true.

Table 7.5 gives the changing composition of production and comsumption units throughout the life of the household. Based on weights for each age used by Macfarlane, it shows how both units increase and decline in the developmental cycle and how deaths can affect the pattern of these changes. An important point not evident from the diagrams is that the average number of production and consumption units remains very similar throughout the life of the household in spite of the death of a child as in the second model. Variation in these numbers throughout the years also remains remarkably similar although the slightly higher standard deviation in the number of consumption units for model 2 is an expected consequence of the greater number of individuals and rapid changes in individual consumption during childhood and early adolescence.

Table 7.5. Production and Consumption Units in the Life of a Tamang Household Using Two Assumptions of Developmental Cycle.

HH Age	1: No Deaths Production	1: No Deaths Consumption	2: 1 Child Dies Production	2: 1 Child Dies Consumption
1	1.80	2.00	1.80	2.00
2	1.80	2.25	1.80	2.25
3	1.80	2.25	1.80	2.25
4	1.80	2.25	1.80	2.25
5	1.80	2.50	1.80	2.50
6	1.80	2.50	1.80	2.50
7	1.80	2.50	1.80	2.50
8	2.00	2.50	2.00	2.50
9	2.20	3.00	2.20	2.75
10	2.20	3.00	2.20	2.75
11	2.20	3.25	2.20	3.00
12	2.20	3.25	2.20	3.00
13	2.60	3.25	2.60	3.00
14	2.60	4.00	2.60	3.00
15	3.00	4.00	2.80	3.00
16	3.20	4.25	3.00	3.75
17	3.20	4.50	3.00	4.00
18	3.40	5.00	3.20	4.50
19	3.60	5.75	3.00	5.25
20	3.60	5.75	3.00	5.25
21	3.60	5.75	3.00	5.25
22	4.20	5.75	3.40	5.25
23	4.60	5.75	3.80	4.75
24	4.60	5.75	3.80	4.75
25	4.60	5.75	3.80	4.75
26	5.00	6.75	4.00	5.75
27	3.40	4.25	4.20	5.50
28	3.40	4.25	4.20	5.50
29	4.00	4.25	3.80	5.50
30	4.80	6.00	4.80	7.25
31	4.80	6.00	4.80	7.50
32	4.00	5.00	5.00	6.50
33	4.00	5.00	5.00	6.50
34	2.20	3.00	4.00	6.00
35	2.20	3.00	4.40	6.00
36	2.20	3.00	4.40	6.00
37	2.20	3.00	4.40	6.00
Average	3.04	4.05	3.17	4.34
SD	1.06	1.40	1.07	1.63

In the next chapter I will examine the actual strategies households pursue as they progress through their developmental cycles. First, a summary of the points made here.

Production in Timling is organized around the household, a unit defined by a group of people whose labor is directed toward the provisioning and maintenance of a common hearth. The integrity of the household is buttressed by a combination of ritual, authority relationships, and concepts of ownership. Its members are recruited in the early years of the cycle through biological reproduction, supplemented in later years by the acquisition of non-family members. While a cross-sectional view of household types in the village shows a preponderance of nuclear families, a processual view establishes the centrality of stem family organization in the social system, with implications for the economic viability of units and the strategies they pursue during various phases of the cycle. From the evidence, we can posit a setting in which children will be desired for their contribution to the home economy within the village as well as for the diverse economic strategies they permit in later years for the maintenance of household viability and the well-being of older people within the domestic unit. All of this is consistent with a type of organization given theoretical shape elsewhere as the Domestic Mode of Production, the workings of which will be looked at more closely in the following discussion.

8

Variations in the Working of the Domestic Economy

Insofar as production is organized by domestic groups, it is established on a fragile and vulnerable base. The familial labor force is normally small and often sorely beset. In any "large enough community" the several households will show a considerable range in size and composition, range that may well leave some susceptible to disastrous mischance.

—Sahlins, *Stone Age Economics*

By its very nature, the Domestic Mode of Production must include variation in the fortunes of different households. Apart from overarching constraints affecting the whole population of Timling, individual household fortunes will differ with respect to the resources available at their inception and throughout their developmental cycles. We have already seen that stores of fertile, high quality land have become scarce within the traditional boundaries of the village and that younger households tend to begin their productive lives at a disadvantage compared to those households from which they have sprung. Other events in the form of different experiences of birth and death within the household also intrude on the relative success of productive units. Mere aggregation of total village experience conveys a useful picture of the underlying patterns of social and economic adjustment to the environment. Yet, when this "average condition" is taken as the norm, we risk being seriously misled about the workings of the domestic economy itself.

In its aggregate, the set of strategic behaviors that typify the village is organized for the survival of the group. The success of these behaviors has as its legacy the present population of Timling and its daughter villages. Yet the sources of variable success are ever-present and devolve on the experiences of each household. Every transition that affects household composition carries with it the potential of drastically altering the fortunes of the domestic unit. Thus, some of the critical sources of variation in Timling must include the timing of marriage and inheritance, the timing and sequence of childbirth, and the family's mortality experience.

This chapter will examine, first, material variation in household wealth and, second, the strategic activities that households engage in to ensure their survival in the face of these changing circumstances. The first part will be based on the 30 randomly sampled households in the economic survey, while the second part will examine the uses of children in selected cases of household development in Timling.

Timling is like other agro-pastoral societies in the extent to which an egalitarian ethic pervades social life; the Tamang's democratic spirit is apparent in the easy familiarity and the kinship forms of address that villagers extend to one another. Anthropologists in other parts of Nepal have suggested that these egalitarian societies grow out of the relatively equal access of all households to the means of production (Hitchcock 1966:108; Macfarlane 1976:192-200). In addition, a number of complex processes, including the operation of inheritance systems, have been shown to level differences among households (Wiegandt 1977; McGuire and Netting 1982). For Swiss Alpine peasants

> accumulation was limited not by community intervention or social claims to redistribution, but by limited resources, economic calculations that discouraged local investment beyond that necessary for a secure subsistence, and community credit facilities governed by an autonomous, representative communal body. (McGuire and Netting 1982:286)

And in another mountain society, in the Andes, the uneven distribution of land and labor among households is softened by a range of exchange mechanisms and reciprocal relationships that allow each household to survive (Brush 1977:133). Thus, we are encouraged to view the operation of the village economy in terms of both household property and strategic processes.

In Timling, variations in household economic status and production strategies are critical components of our understanding. The Tamang report that even in the best years the village is left very close to the margins and that one in three years they are left with a serious shortfall. The surplus production of one year is not stored for the next (cf. Macfarlane 1976:192), and there is no market for the grains grown in Timling; consequently, production is not easily converted into cash. Although very small fluctuations in harvests will affect the entire village in the form of "bad years," some households will fail to cover all their subsistence requirements in good years too. A number of redistributive mechanisms ensure that these families will not starve, but the chronic shortfall of grain places households in an undesirable relationship with their kin and neighbors.

Distribution of Wealth

Timling is an egalitarian society within a country where only 5% of the rural population is completely landless (Seddon et al. 1979:113). Even the least endowed family in the sample planted slightly more than two *hal* of land the year before my stay, and the Tamang are proud to point out that no household has less than that. In village meetings, the egalitarian life of the Tamang is manifested by the right of any adult to stand and speak on any issue. Powerful sentiments tend to moderate individual efforts to gain wealth in the village context. An overly enthusiastic quest for accumulating property will result in accusations of witchcraft and in general distrust. Accumulation may even be dangerous since a whole class of misfortunes, *syidi* (Tm.), is the result of envy. For example, poor people may inadvertently invest food with *syidi* by covetously looking at it. The person who eats this food is then stricken with attacks of vomiting and belching (Höfer 1981:21).

Some households are, nevertheless, materially better off than others in the village. Table 8.1 presents the distribution of total rupee value for cultivated land, livestock, household articles, and house structure for the 30 sample households. The range of variation is enormous by village standards although differences might not appear so impressive to us when they are converted into dollars. Between the low figure of 18,194 rupees ($2165) and the high of 82,888 rupees ($9864), the distribution is widely spread out.

A more refined way of looking at these values is to break them down by investment categories as in table 8.2. Here, we can see again that the largest investment category is in land, while the second largest is in livestock. But another interesting feature comes to light when we consider the ratio of minimum to maximum values across investment categories. Both land and livestock ratios are the same, at .101, while the proportional differences between minimum and maximum house values is much greater, with a ratio of .056. The difference between household item holdings is less, at .203. Since the ratio of minimum to maximum is highest when all investment categories are combined, the data suggest that households tend to equalize their relative wealth by different strategies of investment. Even further, differential investment in the two categories of livestock and land should reflect variant strategic behaviors for these households. If we take the ratio of lowest to highest values for the combined livestock and land categories, we can again see that the tendency is toward equalization; greater disparity exists in each of these categories separately than in their combined values. This suggests a tendency on the part of households to invest more in one category or the other rather than in both together.

The Gini index is another useful measure of wealth concentration that can be applied to the Timling data. Both the Gini index and the Lorenz curve on which it is based were designed to measure income concentration (Shryock and Siegel 1976:207-8), although they can be used to measure the concentration of any quantifiable variable in a population. Papers by Wiegandt (1977) and McGuire and Netting (1982) successfully applied the Lorenz curve and Gini index as indices of stratification in Alpine peasant villages. They will be used here to compare the Tamang with other groups as well as to cast further light on the degree of concentration in each investment category.

The Lorenz curve plots the cumulative proportion of one variable against another. In this case, figure 8.1 displays the curve for cumulative wealth and the cumulative proportion of households possessing it in Timling. In the sample, the lower 20% of the households owns 11% of the wealth; the lower 40% owns about 25%, and so on. The diagonal line represents a state of perfect equality, in which the cumulative percentages of X and Y are identical.

Table 8.1. Distribution of Total Wealth for 30 Timling Households.

Rupee Value	N	%	Cum. %
18,000-19,999	2	6.7	6.7
20,000-24,999	6	20.0	26.7
25,000-29,999	4	13.3	40.0
30,000-34,999	3	10.0	50.0
35,000-39,999	2	6.7	56.7
40,000-44,999	3	10.0	66.7
45,000-49,999	6	20.0	86.7
50,000+	4	13.3	100.0

Source: Timling Economic Survey.

Table 8.2. Value of Household Investment by Category (in Rupees).

	House	HH Items	Livestock	Land	Land+ Livestock	Total
Mean	4950	3049	5621	24340	29661	38025
S.D.	2702	1417	3229	12346	13814	15842
Min.	500	1291	1400	6686	13161	18194
Max.	9000	6373	13925	65872	72097	82888
Min/Max	.056	.203	.101	.101	.183	.220
Sum	148500	91476	168625	730206	898830	1140748
% Total	13.0	8.0	14.8	64.0	78.8	100.0

Source: Timling Economic Survey.

162   *Variations in Domestic Economy*

Figure 8.1.   Lorenz Curve for Distribution of Wealth in Timling and Thak Compared.

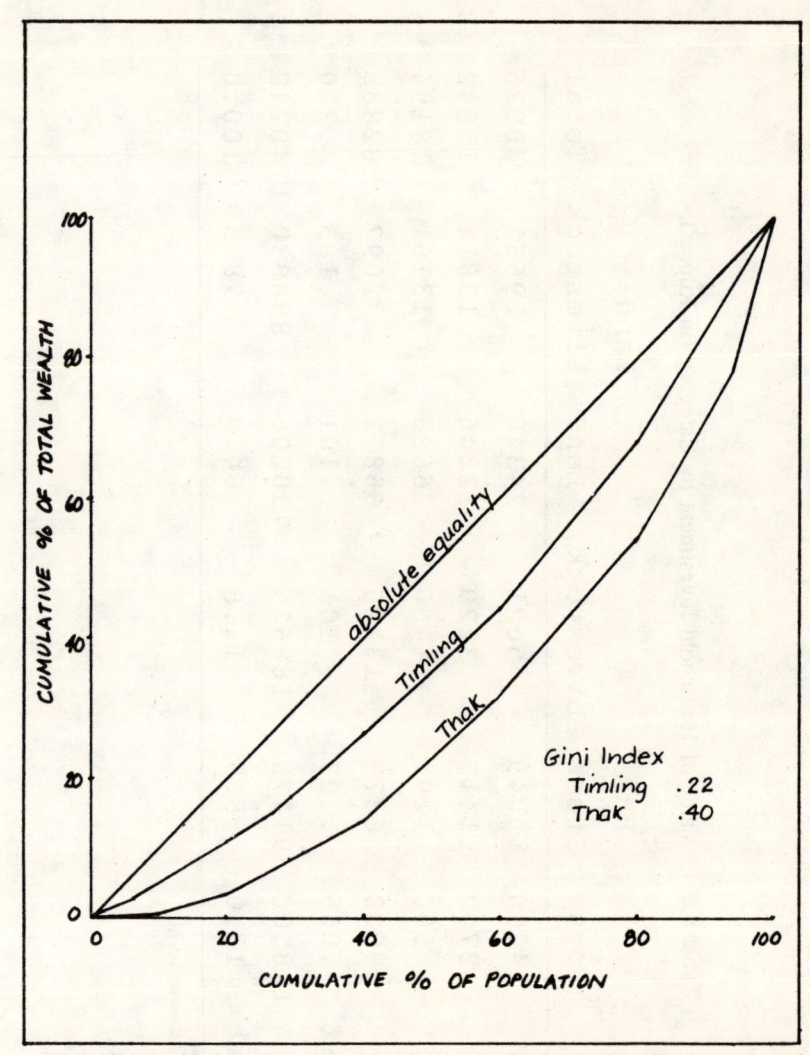

[Lorenz curve chart showing cumulative % of total wealth vs cumulative % of population, with curves labeled "absolute equality", "Timling", and "Thak". Gini Index: Timling .22, Thak .40]

The Gini coefficient is a measure of the area between the diagonal of perfect equality and the plotted curve. Gini values can vary between 0 and 1, with 1 being absolute inequality and 0 representing an absolutely equal distribution. Some indication of the reality reflected by the coefficient comes from knowing that the Gini index for the distribution of income before taxes in the United States of 1962 was .660, not a particularly egalitarian level (McGuire and Netting 1982:273).

Table 8.3 provides a comparison of Gini indices for the distribution of total wealth in Timling and in other selected groups. The Gini indices presented here are not strictly comparable because: (a) they measure different indicators of wealth, or (b) they apply only to the owners of a given resource rather than to the whole range of variation in wealth. In the case of (b), however, the indices would be even higher than they are, and we would find an even greater divergence from Timling's measure.

The Timling index is among the lowest in this selection, suggesting that the Tamang of this village merit the right to be called egalitarian as much as any other non-hunting and gathering group. The concentration of wealth in Timling is such that the top and bottom 20% of households control 32% and 11% of the wealth, while those 60% of the households in the middle control an almost proportionate 57% of the total.

It is especially interesting to compare indices for societies pursuing similar adaptations. Two societies for which we have data, Mase and Törbel (having in common with Timling a mountain environment and an agro-pastoral economy), lie at the lower range for this selection. The extent of wealth concentration for Timling is between that of these two villages but is closer to that of Mase, where the distribution is least unbalanced of any groups in the table.

A comparison with the people of Thak is even more interesting given the proximity of the Gurung and Tamang in Nepal, marked similarities in their cultures, and the possibility of a common ancestry in the south of Tibet (Höfer 1981:7). If comments by Macfarlane and Hitchcock about the relationship between land base and stratification are true, then Thak might be expected to show a higher concentration of wealth than Timling, if only because the circumscribed village of Thak must support its population on only 10 square miles of land, compared to the much larger area available to Timling. The limits of expansion may have been reached earlier in Thak, with the consequence that processes of intensification and land concentration are more advanced.

Gini indices for Thak were calculated using the table of wealth distribution provided by Macfarlane (1976:101). The coefficient for all 93 households is the highest, at .474, for any mountain population in table 8.3. Nor is it a particularly unstratified index when compared to all societies in the table. The presence of non-Gurung, including traditionally landless castes, within the sample somewhat confounds the comparison with the Tamang, however. When these households are excluded so that only Gurung count in the distribution, the Gini index falls to .403, much more in keeping with the kind of concentration found in the homogeneous Swiss villages. Nevertheless, the expectation that wealth is more unequally distributed in Thak than in Timling is supported.

As a final comment on the distribution of wealth in the village, we can consider the distribution of investment within each category. Here again we find support for the idea that households use differential investment in each category to make the total distribution of wealth more equal. Thus, the Gini indices for the different categories of investment—.304 for house, .248 for household items, .305

Table 8.3. Gini Indices for Timling and Selected Groups.

Society	Gini Index	Resource
Timling	.22	Total wealth
Mase, Swit.[a]	.16	Maximum wealth attained
Torbel, Swit.[b]	.40	Taxable property
Thak (whole sample)[c]	.47	Land, livestock, house
Thak (Gurung only)[c]	.40	Land, livestock, house
Tepotzlan[d]	.59	Total family wealth
Fulani[d]	.27	Household cattle
Navaho[d]	.50	Sheep per owner
Ganda[d]	.49	Household land
Andhra Pradesh[e]	.55	Land
Uttar Pradesh[e]	.39	Land

Sources: Timling Economic Survey, [a] Wiegandt (1977), [b] McGuire and Netting (1982), [c] calculated from Macfarlane (1976), [d] Henderson (1978), and [e] Cancian (1979).

for livestock, and .251 for land—are each higher than the index for the distribution of total wealth.

By noting the underlying equality of wealth distribution among Tamang households, I seem to be contradicting the opening remarks in this chapter. Where are the households that fail or are in danger of failing in Timling? Yet we know that some households do fail to reproduce themselves by virtue of a couple's inability to produce surviving sons or a series of catastrophic harvests that initiate a cycle of land sales and the dissolution of the productive base on which the household stands. For while the Tamang call attention to the fact that no household owns less than two *hal* of land, they conveniently ignore those cases where household sons have left and may never come back. One of the wealthiest households in the village, for example, includes as one of its members a distantly related man who never married and who eventually surrendered his small plots to the wealthy domestic unit in exchange for support until his death. Other household properties will be divided among brothers because their members have not given birth to heirs. And, finally, at least three households have listed on their census forms members who are presumed to have settled in Bhutan or the Terai and who have little incentive to return to claim their small inheritance.

Households do fail in Timling, but the data are necessarily confined to those that have succeeded until the present. The next section will examine the processes that contribute to the success and reproduction of domestic units by focusing on the actual histories of selected cases.

Organizing Work and Exchange in Timling

> I do not suggest that the household everywhere is an exclusive work group, and that production merely a domestic activity. Local techniques demand more or less cooperation, so production may be organized in diverse social forms, and sometimes at levels higher than the household. . . . Cooperation remains for the most part a technical fact, without independent social realization on the level of economic control. It does not compromise the autonomy of the household or its economic purpose, the domestic management of labor-power or the prevalence of domestic objectives across the social activities of work. (Sahlins 1972:77-78)

In spite of the relative autonomy of the Tamang household and the ideal of labor self-sufficiency that the people of Timling often express, it is frequently impossible for single domestic units to provide all their labor needs internally. Even in cases where the labor power exists, matters of convenience or the desire for company will bring people from separate households together for work. Sahlins makes the point that the household exists as a kind of mini-state in its internal relations but that no such coordination of authority and dominance organizes the relations among households in the Domestic Mode of Production (1972:95). This is certainly true in Timling, where there is substantial equality among households and no group has institutionalized authority within the whole village except by agreement of the assembled clans. Yet people join together to work on projects as varied as cutting wood, ploughing fields, shucking corn, and building trailside resting places to gain religious merit.

Work in Timling is organized at several levels. Within the household people share their labor and production without keeping accounts. Ideally, everything is freely shared and goes for the common good of those who sit around the same hearth. The reciprocity is "open-ended, and the return for any given service is unspecified in terms of kind, amount, and time" (Brush 1977:104). This type of exchange extends outward from the domestic unit to include close relatives such as fathers and brothers who have their own households, but once the bounds of a person's own domestic unit have been crossed, some kind of calculation of just how much labor or how many goods can be shared is weighed against one's own household requirements. When working for other households without expectation of return, a Tamang is performing *sayog* (Np.) labor or *sayog laba* (Tm. to do *sayog* labor). Such tasks as hauling wood for a funeral pyre and donating labor for house building can fall into this category. In such cases, kinship is an effective organizing principle for knowing the people from whom *sayog* may be requested (*sayog ripa:* Tm. to ask for help). The constellation of people from whom *sayog* can be expected extends outward in concentric circles from those who have once lived in the same household. Thus, the first people one would ask include parents and brothers, followed by a father's parents and brothers.

Within the household, there is no need even to ask for help. Tasks are loosely assigned by sex and age, and there is usually a general understanding of the work to be done so that the intervention of the household head in the manner of a shop foreman is rarely required. A woman will informally decide to work in a given plot for the morning or to weave on her porch. Sons stay with the cattle and herd them where they choose depending on the time of year. Special tasks or the direction of wealth flows from wage labor, however, make it clear that authority inheres in the oldest adult male in the household. Rejection of this authority can lead to unusual divergence from the expected pattern of inheritance, as the following case nicely shows.

> Embi Damrong is an ambitious man by village standards. He runs the closest thing to a shop in Timling, packing in such items as *bidi*s, cloth and soap from Trisuli Bazaar and selling them in the village from his house. Embi, more than any other Tamang in the area, identifies closely with the national Nepali culture and prefers to be known by the Nepali name, Krishna Bahadur. He is wealthy, a ready source of loans which he will give out at high interest and with land or livestock as collateral. The villagers call him *lobi* (Np. greedy), a *naramro manche* (Np. bad man) who will not do his own work but finds ways to have others do it for him.
>
> As the youngest son, Embi would have been expected to inherit his father's house. Instead, he took his *angsa* the year I was in the village and built a new house on land purchased by his father. His older brother, a much more traditional Tamang with little Nepali at his command, remained with his parents.
>
> Stories about why this happened abound in the village, but all agree that the main reason was his withholding the money that he owed from work in Bhutan. It is said that he returned with 7,000 rupees from selling the scent glands of musk deer and gave his father only a few

hundred along with a few bolts of cloth for his mother and sisters. Embi himself complains that his father demanded too much work at home and in the *goth* when he had more lucrative prospects.

Whatever the reason, Embi is distrusted by the villagers; he is spoken of with thinly disguised contempt and his wife is considered a witch. His violation of the rules of sharing in the household and consequent establishment of his own household are used as the icon of his meanness.

Other forms of labor in Timling are non-reciprocal and either are subject to calculation or are owed because of traditional relationships. In this last category, the labor owed by a husband to his wife's natal household is a good example. Earlier, I gave the case of a Tamang male who married a woman against her parents' wishes. Once the terms of the new marriage had been settled and her parents had become reconciled to it, the new husband entered into the household labor pool of his wife's family. In practice, his labor is demanded about seven times a year by his own report, but in some cases the commitment of time can be substantial—as when he was expected to accompany his wife's brothers to Trisuli Bazaar to help carry rice back to the village. The total time for such a trip is over a week, yet he was expected to comply without question. In this case, he was unable to make the journey himself but satisfied his responsibility when his brother went in his stead, thus using generalized reciprocity to satisfy a non-reciprocal labor requirement.

The forms of labor exchange I have discussed up to now involve some form of kinship relation, affinal or otherwise. In the last category, labor may also be given to unrelated households for payment in the form of money or goods or to work off a debt. A day's work in Timling is worth about 10 rupees, but payment can be translated into goods or a mixture of goods and money too. The value of work is also calibrated to the task and the person carrying it out so that while 10 rupees a day is considered fair price for ploughing or helping to build a house, working in the fields at weeding is paid only three rupees a day since it is not considered particularly onerous and adult males rarely do this work.

A task can be performed by individuals working in different relationships with the household for which the work is being done. For example, Embi Damrong used a combination of *sayog* and paid labor when he had his house built. Those who were paid received different kinds of payment for the same work. Some took home goods, others cash, and others worked off debts. Using a combination of wealth and family relationships, Embi was able to expand his work force from himself and one 14-year-old son to 13 men; his two-story house was finished in one month. Another house in the village is still far from complete after a year with only two stone walls. The household head commands only his own labor and the occasional *sayog* of his brother and father and cannot pay others in money or goods.

Informal cooperative work groups perform tasks on the basis of sharing the same kind of work for different households in the village. Thus, people join together whether related or not to cut wood, plough, weed, or anything else made easier and more pleasant with more participants. Ploughing is more likely to be shared by related men for the simple reason that brothers are more likely to have adjoining fields and to herd their plough animals together. Even in these cases, however, seed for the individual plots will come from the household stores and not be saved.

A last important kind of labor not involving relatives needs to be briefly mentioned. Most Tamang households have *jajmani* (Np.) relationships with particular Kami households from the metalworker settlement near Timling. These metalworkers are specialists who repair and make tools, jewelry, and household utensils for the families with whom they have this relationship. Their clients pay them not with money or work, but with a share of each harvest. The Kami own a little land and raise some livestock themselves, but by far the greater part of their subsistence comes from the client households whose tools they maintain. In effect, the Kami are additional consumption and production units shared by a number of Tamang households.

The exchange of goods in Timling follows a logic similar to the exchange of labor with the exception of commodities from Trisuli Bazaar—cooking oil, soap, cloth, and *bidi*s or cigarettes—which are meant to be sold and are not generally given freely to the same people that *sayog* labor would be given to. Within the household all goods are expected to be shared without calculation by its members. As we have seen, the cases where this rule is violated will alter other cultural expectations. As one moves away from the household to widening circles of kin, casual sharing becomes less frequent. The cutoff between generalized and reciprocal exchange is, however, not always easy to determine. Embi Damrong, for instance, is less inclined to share anything outside his own household circle, while the head of one Ghale household freely donated a *hal* of land for the use of two of his sons-in-law. Outside of the household circle, cooked food tends to be shared with anybody. Raw materials, land, cattle, grain, and commodities are generally kept account of and either traded or sold. Cash is most important for the purchase of items that have moved up from the bazaars, but it also buys grain from villages outside of Timling's traditional territory and is likely to be used as a medium of exchange with unrelated households within the village. For unrelated households, grain and potatoes are easily bartered while other exchanges are governed by cash reckoning. With related households—parents', brothers', and affinally linked households—the exchange of goods is likely to be considerably more fluid.

The discussion of labor and goods exchange highlights the value of kinship within Timling's economy. Kinship binds households and individuals into reciprocal and cooperative units in an economy where cash has not yet become dominant; it counteracts what Sahlins calls the anarchic tendencies of the Domestic Mode of Production (1972:95-99) and ensures the survival of marginal households to a point beyond their own productive capacity. Kinship establishes the "gift community" within which transactions are qualitatively unique (Hyde 1983). We can see from this how the organization of the village economy encourages couples to bear as many children as they can. Even beyond the truth of actual household membership in which household labor is enhanced by large families (Mamdani

1972), the logic of the domestic economy suggests that advantages continue after children leave the hearth. Fathers acquire the labor of sons-in-law when daughters marry; sons continue to share labor with their father's household even after they claim their *angsa*. And more than labor passes through permeable household boundaries; tools, food, and other goods are also shared when the kin link is close enough.

This last detail is important. The Tamang are organized into patrilineal clans, the members of which acknowledge a common ancestor. If kinship defined as clan membership were the only consideration, we would expect each clan to form its own network within which labor and goods were shared in balanced reciprocity. Each household then could count on the support of the sum of households within the clan plus affinally linked households brought into its orbit by the marriage of daughters. In fact, this is not the case. A point is reached at which a Ghale will not share labor and goods with another Ghale simply by virtue of having a common ancestor. The strongest and most reliable kin links in Timling are those most consistent with the nuclear family. Another round of relationships is reached when kinship is through the ascending generation, a father's brothers and his sons, and the bonds grow progressively weaker as the links become more distant—a process of differentiation that has been called the "segmentary lineage" (Keesing 1975:29-31; Evans-Pritchard 1940:192-248) or "expansionist" (Sahlins 1961). In effect, the household must produce its own allies with each new generation since leaving this up to the clan as a whole would eventually isolate the domestic unit from the possibility of its closest links. The logic of the system is such that sons who fail to reproduce or who reproduce sparingly are in a precarious position relative to those who do.

Household Time and the Expansion of the Domestic Economy

Our discussion of Timling's economic organization through kinship must take us back to the household developmental cycle since, if the set of labor and exchange relationships extends outward from the hearth, it follows that changes in family and household composition must affect the nature of the domestic economy. In fact, the household developmental cycle from nuclear to stem family household is exactly paralleled by changes in the economic potential of the household and the relationships it holds with other productive units. As a household moves through its developmental cycle, it changes from a unit whose primary exchange relationships are directed toward other units—owing labor to the wife's natal household and being more likely to assist the husband's father's household at tasks than to be assisted. As a household matures, however, and some of its own members pod off into other units, it too becomes the focus of an expanding network of kin links through which it can command the labor of others. Changes in productive relations are of two types: (1) those that occur within the household itself as its members mature and become productive and (2) those that expand its network of kin-based links with other households. In both cases, the strength of a domestic production unit is based on the number of offspring a couple can bear.

Chayanov (1966:53-60) was one of the first to recognize the importance of changing family composition to household economy. Starting from a recognition that peasant production was organized for low intensities of labor use and production, he made a number of assumptions about peasant economy to explain how it worked. Several of these assumptions make it hard to apply his exact model to Timling—it is even possible that they were wrong for the Russian peasantry of his time (cf. Harrison 1975)—but some elements of his theory provide a starting place for this discussion of Tamang economic cycles.

Hunt (1979:248-49) stresses that the Chayanov model is based on a household economy in which consumption and production are interdependent and wages are not paid out. A further assumption is that resources, usually in the form of land, are always available to each household (Chayanov 1966:112) so that the household is never in the position of not being able to fulfill its own needs because it can't control enough land for its crops. Chayanov's other points follow from these constraints, operating in tandem with production for use value rather than for market exchange and a desire for a constant standard of living on the part of peasants (Barlett 1980:558). It follows from this that the labor intensity is proportional to the consumer/worker ratio; that is, as households increase in size, their members are able to work less even when landholdings may have increased to satisfy growing consumption requirements (Brush 1977:124-25).

The situation in Timling does not duplicate these assumptions for reasons mentioned throughout this discussion. We know, for example, that Tamang households employ not only wage labor but also other sources of labor outside the nuclear family. Additionally, while new land may still be available within the traditional boundaries of Timling, that which can be opened is of inferior quality and does not give the yields of established plots at the lower elevations. Finally, the case of Embi Damrong indicates that some households have production goals that go beyond mere use values even though these goals violate strongly held cultural prescriptions to the contrary. We might suggest that Timling more nearly approached the model at some time in the past but that recent changes are moving it further from the ideal Chayanovian peasant economy.

In spite of these divergences from the model, we find evidence from the economic survey of 30 households that family size and the total value of household capital are positively correlated in Timling. Table 8.4 presents Pearson's correlation coefficients and their level of significance for family size, consumption units, and production units in relation to each investment category and the sum of total investment for each household. Chayanov himself supplies correlation coefficients for the relationship between farm income and the number of workers. These coefficients of .42 and .64 for two different locations show a connection between family size and economic activity but are ambiguous about the direction of causality: is

Table 8.4. Pearson's r for the Relationship between HH Size Variables and Value of Investment.

Investment	HH Size r	HH Size p	Production Units r	Production Units p	Consumption Units r	Consumption Units p
House value	.213	.129	.198	.147	.241	.100
HH item value	.295	.057	.374	.021	.349	.029
Livestock value	.223	.118	.295	.057	.289	.061
Land value	.341	.033	.460	.005	.422	.010
Total wealth	.375	.021	.487	.003	.461	.005

Sources: Timling Economic Survey and Timling Census.

farm size determined by family size, or is it the other way around (Chayanov 1966:64)? For Chayanov, the real relationship becomes clear with a look at time series data:

> We see that a considerable part of the farms that sowed small areas gradually acquired a labor force as family age and size increased, and by expanding their sown area passed into the higher groups, thus also expanding the volume of their economic activity. Conversely, former large farms passed into lower groups, corresponding to the small families created after division. This shows us that the demographic processes of growth and family distribution by size also determine to a considerable extent the distribution of farms by size of sown area and numbers of livestock. (1966:67)

But Chayanov is cautious in assigning too much causal weight to the household developmental cycle:

> in order to avoid incorrect treatment of our conclusions we ought to stress that at any particular moment the family *is not the sole determinant of the size of a particular farm,* and determines its size only in a general way. The comparatively high correlation coefficients established between these figures are, nevertheless, far from 1.00. This alone indicates the existence of parallel factors which in their turn exert a pressure on the figure being studied. (1966:69; Chayanov's emphasis)

If we turn to the correlation coefficients for Timling, we find strong support for the relationship between family size and wealth. Even better, the highest and most significant coefficients are for correlations between production units and the various investment categories (with the exception of house value, a different kind of investment since the house is usually built before the family matures). This is as we would expect from Chayanov's theory since size alone is less important than the labor value of household members.

Our problem is similar to Chayanov's when confronted with his early evidence: while the relationship between family size factors and wealth is fairly obvious, we are unable to determine the actual processes at work from these figures. We are faced with two distinct explanations and a third that is a combination of these. First, the positive relationship between, say, land value and the number of production units could very well be the result of increases in household size leading to increases in household capital and the consequent ability to buy more land. Evidence from other parts of Nepal would support this interpretation. For example, Macfarlane (1976:63) gives the case of Gurung sons in the British army using their wages to increase household lands. Similarly, Hitchcock (1966:16-19) writes that land in Banyan Hill may be acquired, although rarely, by outright purchase or by financing a loan. Older households would be in a better position to accomplish both of these by virtue of having sons in the army or receiving pensions from the household head's earlier army service (Hitchcock 1961:19). Gorer (1967:87) tells us that Lepcha households in Sikkim were in a favorable position for land acquisition according to the number of working adults they included. Caplan's (1970) work with the Limbu tells the same story.

But another possibility is that land holdings in Timling are simply becoming smaller through the process of partible inheritance, and older households, naturally larger than new ones, have more only because their holdings were assigned at an earlier date. The Tamang themselves explain some of the wealth differentials in these terms, pointing out that the sons of comparatively rich men will have much less when they claim their *angsa*.

A combination of both these processes is a likely explanation in Timling. As available land becomes ever more limited, individuals in each new generation will inherit smaller amounts. At the same time, processes of land acquisition through purchase and the collection of loans are augmented by household growth since the household head not only controls the labor of his sons and daughters but should rightfully receive the wages they earn while working outside of the village. Even the smallest earnings should be turned over to the household, as I discovered when I paid a 15-year-old Ghale from one of the wealthier families 10 rupees for a day's work cutting wood. Two days after paying him, I asked him what he had done with the money. He replied that he had turned it over to his father.

Turning to another of Chayanov's points, that the intensity of labor declines with an increase in the number of workers, we can look at agricultural labor requirements in Timling. Agriculture has been shown to be the primary component of Tamang subsistence in the village, and the logic of increasing household land is tied into this value. Yet we find that the greater the amount of land a household possesses, the greater the labor surplus, available beyond agricultural labor requirements, a household has to invest in other activities. In Timling, the correlation coefficient between the number of production units in a household and the amount of land at its disposal is a reasonably high .460. Larger households have more land. But when we look at the correlation between production units and surplus labor beyond agricultural requirements, we find a coefficient of .956, significant at the .001 level. This means that households in Timling do not increase their holdings proportional to the size of their workforce—that some kind of cutoff exists beyond which investment in land is no longer strategic to household subsistence. The question of whether households do not acquire new land because it is not available or because they stop at the satisifaction of needs is still open, however. Chayanov and Sahlins would explain the relationship with reference to self-imposed household constraints: if people don't need land to maintain a constant standard of living, they will not try to get it. The free time bought with an increase in labor capacity can then be invested in other pursuits—elaboration of ritual, gossip, and storytelling in "the original affluent society" (Sahlins 1972:1–40), wage labor in others (cf. Macfarlane 1976:140–52 for a discussion of surplus labor). My impressions from Timling are that time not invested in agriculture and other local subsistence pursuits is invested in a variety of other activities—including gossip, ritual, and storytelling, but also the quest for wage labor outside of the village. We can look at the issues raised by this discussion through illustrative cases of lineage expansion and labor use.

Lineage Expansion: The Ghale of Ganglememe

The Ghale of Ganglememe live in neatly lined two-story houses in the northeastern corner of Timling. Widely regarded in the village as the wealthiest patriline, members of the clan who live there also tend to be more traditional in the sense of following Ghale dietary practices and placing great store in the traditional relationships among kin. It may not have always been so since most people in the village tell dark stories of how they came upon their wealth by stealing Damrong land some three generations ago. The man responsible for the theft has been dead since 1953, but his legacy includes 14 households headed by his sons and grandsons and at least 70 living descendants. His oldest son was 72 years old in 1981, which would place the older man's year of birth at close to 1890 and possibly earlier.

Figure 8.2 displays the lineage chart for this Ghale patriarch and his descendants and helps us to detect a number of trends in the processes of lineage expansion. The Ganglememe patriarch's father (G1) had at least three sons and a daughter who married a Damrong from the village. Descendants of his two brothers still live in Timling but within far smaller networks of close kin. Thus, the older brother had one surviving son who had three sons, two of whom died before producing sons of their own. He is represented by one household in Timling. Likewise, the youngest brother is presently represented by a single household in the village although another of his sons moved his household to Lapdung and has descendants there.

The father (G1) of these three brothers left about 110 *ropani* (14.3 acres) to be divided at his death, and the *angsa* of two brothers has been passed down fairly intact across the generations with some additions through purchase. The Ganglememe patriarch (G2), however, took his *angsa* of about 37 *ropani* and turned it into close to 400 *ropani* (52 acres) by the time of his death. This is a phenomenal figure by village standards, where the average holding amounts to only 24 *ropani* and the largest single holding in Timling (belonging to this man's son) is about 83 *ropani*.

A change of this magnitude in Timling's economy calls for some skepticism, yet allowing for the rough estimates these numbers represent and moving backward from verifiable inheritance at the younger generations, this is the figure we arrive at. One of the patriarch's sons (G3), all of whom were literate, firmly reported his *angsa* as 80 *ropani*. Assuming that all *angsa* were about the same, we arrive at the 400 *ropani* figure. As a check on this generation, we can move down to two brothers (G4, G5) of a younger generation from whom data were independently gathered. Figuring from the economic survey, the two brothers were assigned remarkably similar amounts of land—22.5 and 21.2 *ropani*. Since the set of male siblings included four people, we arrive at a figure very close to the 80 *ropani* inheritance of their father; any amount over this can easily be accounted for as land acquisition after the father took his *angsa*. A similar method of reconstruc-

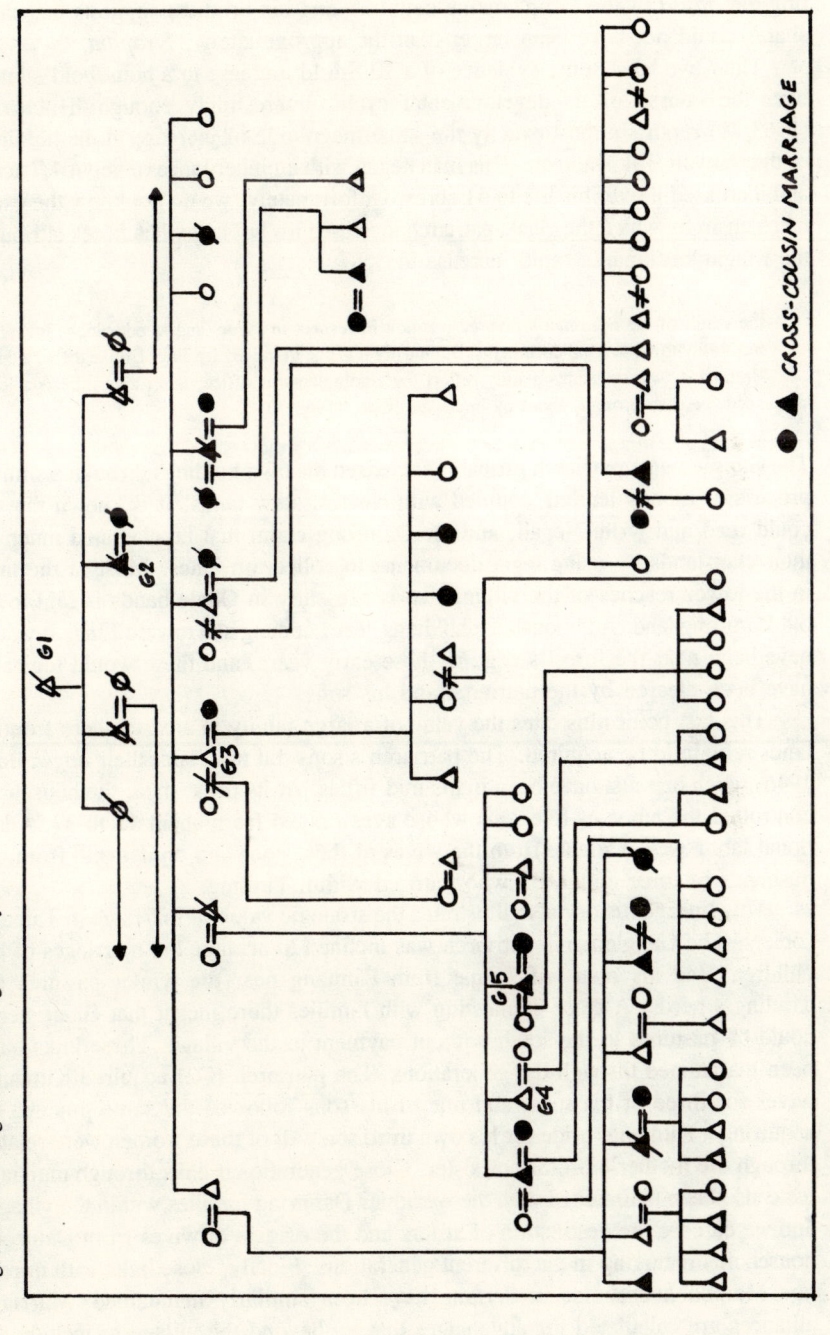

Figure 8.2. Ganglememe Lineage History.

ting the *angsa* of the Ganglememe patriarch and his brothers suggests that their shares could not have been larger than the approximately 37 *ropani*.

Thus, we have some evidence of a 10.8-fold increase in a household's lands over the course of its developmental cycle. Interestingly enough, Hitchcock (1963:70) reports almost exactly the same magnitude of increase in the holdings of the Banyan Hill headman. This man began with an inheritance of about 4.7 acres and increased it over his life to 51 acres. Unfortunately, we do not know the exact mechanism by which the Ghale patriarch increased his holdings. Hitchcock attributes the Magar headman's rapid increase to:

> the result of the headman's favored position in respect to labor, and to education, including the ability to write legal documents. But mostly it is due to money lending. Unlike the wealthiest Brahmans, whose estates mainly reflect the emoluments of office, this estate reflects a local need for cash brought about by increased trade. (1963:70)

The Ganglememe patriarch probably increased his own holdings through a similar process of money lending coupled with clearing new lands. It is known that he could read and write Nepali, and the Damrong claim that he alienated much of their clan lands by using legal documents to collect on loans. Most of the land in the lower reaches of the village that is presently in Ghale hands is said to be old Damrong land. Additional landholdings near Lapdung and toward Lingjyo would have been near the forest's edge in those early years, and these would logically have been cleared by the patriarch and his sons.

This last point illustrates the value of a large family in a case where frontier lands remain to be acquired. The patriarch's sons did not claim their *angsa* until 1946, when he must have been in his mid-fifties. At its peak, then, the household controlled the labor of five sons whose ages ranged from about 15 to 37. Additional labor was available from the wives of these sons and on demand from the husbands of three daughters who married within Timling.

This lineage history also illustrates the strategic value of marriage in Tamang society. The Ganglememe patriarch was inclined to arrange the marriages of his children, and his own wife came from Kimtang near the winter pastures for Timling's herds. A close connection with families there meant that Ghale herds could be pastured to the south without payment to the village. These links have been maintained through the generations. The patriarch (G2) acquired Kimtangi wives for three of his sons, and one of his sons followed the same practice by acquiring a Kimtangi bride for his own third son. All of these women were related through the mother's brother or sister. Close generational links through marriage have also been maintained with the wealthier Damrong families within the village, and we can see the destination of sisters and the origins of wives from Damrong households recurring in the different generations. Finally, close links with important Mamba households in Sertang have been similarly maintained. Marriage alliances are calculated for advantages that go beyond the village to include the entire region in which resources are exploited.

The reconstruction of *angsa* and land acquisition across generations suggests drastic change in the availability of land within the area, too. While landholdings in the earliest generations seem to have grown, in part, as a function of family size, later generations appear to be unable to increase their holdings to the same magnitude. This can only be the result of the growing pressure on the size of holdings brought about by population increase, a movement from a frontier adaptation where new land is abundant to a "limited good" adaptation where the resource pie is finite (Foster 1967). This process will be taken up in the final discussion; here I would note that the change from abundant to scarce land resources implies the need for new strategies for household survival and land acquisition. None of the Ganglememe patriarch's sons reported going outside of the village for wage labor before 1953, when he died. Yet, opportunities to do so certainly existed. The earliest reported journey to Bhutan was in 1952, but other opportunities to earn wages existed in the form of portering jobs (at very low wages) and the British and Indian armies. Sirman Ghale, of another descent group, joined a Gurkha regiment in 1943. Although this patriarch's growing landholdings were due, in part, to money lending, it seems that the greater portion may have been related to the clearing of new land. More recent land histories bespeak a different kind of process.

Another Way of Getting Rich: A Damrong Family History

A good example of becoming wealthy by way of other strategies will be illustrated through the case of Embi Damrong, who was discussed earlier in this chapter. The path to riches followed by this family differs considerably from that of the Ghale example and is arguably the result of combined strategies that make effective use of Tamang norms in combination with opportunities not formerly available to the people of Timling.

When I was in the village, Embi Damrong claimed his *angsa* for reasons already mentioned. His share of *ropani* amounted to 35 because his father divided the household land three ways, keeping a full share for himself until his death; thus, the total landholding of his father was about 105 *ropani* (13.65 acres). Yet Embi's father (D1) began his household with very little land, perhaps six *ropani*. An only son, ne is said to have been so poor in his early years that Nyemsar Ghale allowed him to live in the lower part of his house in exchange for labor. Although part of his rise to wealth must be attributed to having a large family, land acquisition was accomplished by gaining control of other people's land rather than by opening new plots from the forest.

Embi's father married the daughter of the Ganglememe patriarch against the wishes of her father and brothers. Opposition was so intense that he was beaten and left Timling for a number of years, some say for Pokhara. When he returned, he had the capital to extend loans at high interest and began the process of alienating people from their land. With increasing wealth in his household, the Ghale became reconciled to the marriage, and relations between the two lineages were further consolidated with the arranged marriages of all three of his sons and one of his

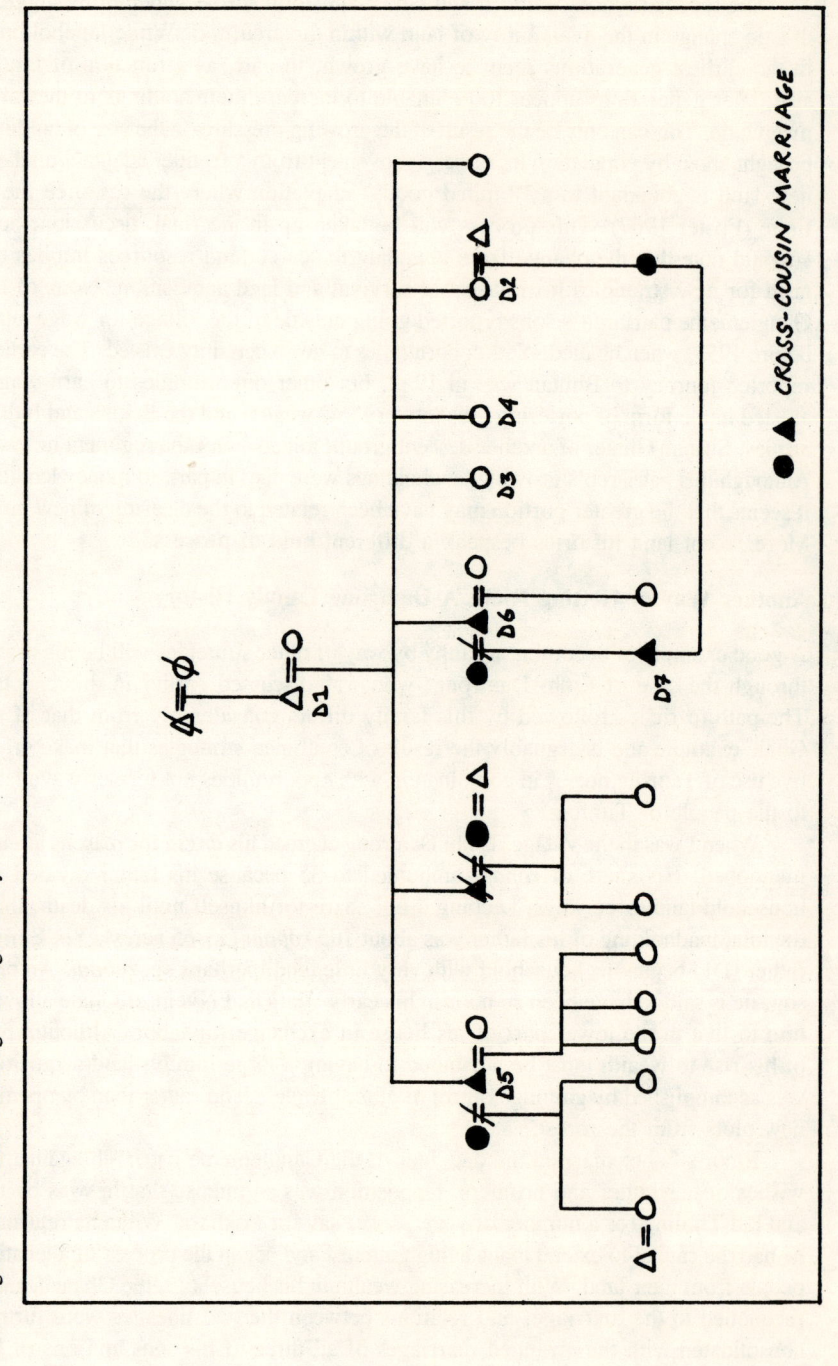

Figure 8.3. Embi Damrong's Lineage History.

daughters to Ganglememe Ghale. Another of his daughters (D2) married the Gompo Lama, also a Ghale, by her own choice, and two other daughters (D3, D4) were married to Lapdung Ghale who were descended from the Ganglememe patriline.

Embi's father used his sons to enrich the household but concentrated on their value as wage earners in addition to domestic labor. He sent his oldest son (D5) to work in Bhutan in 1961, keeping two sons, aged 23 and 15, behind to work for the household. This son returned three years later, and Embi was sent in 1971. Their objective in Bhutan was not so much to work on road crews for three rupees a day but to deal in the illegal trade in musk deer. With the capital from his son's wages and his earnings from loans, Embi's father bought land and opened a small store from his house.

Embi's older brother began to concentrate on maintaining the subsistence end of the household economy, preferring to stay in the high pastures and studying to be a *lama* when he was in the village, but Embi (D6) actively sought opportunities to increase his monetary wealth. He became a *panchayat* official and used his connections with his office and with his affines in Lapdung to get wage work with the Indian mining company in Lari, Timling's high pasture. Shortly after his last trip to Bhutan, in which he made money and refused to turn it over to his father, he became a salaried worker making at least 400 rupees a month as a messenger and supplier for the mining company. The tension between his father and himself increased because of his new refusal to turn his salary over to the household. A year later, Embi moved into his own household, where he relocated his store, bringing with him a man from the Kami settlement who remains indentured to him for his inability to pay off a debt. His 15-year-old son and the Kami helper take care of the herding and ploughing chores while Embi uses his frequent trips as a messenger to Trisuli Bazaar to keep the store supplied.

Embi has continued the new alliance with the Gompo Lama's family by arranging that the *lama*'s daughter should marry his son. But this gamble may not pay off since his son's new wife refuses to sleep with the boy and does not speak to him when he returns from the pastures.

The brief account of this Damrong history highlights a different kind of strategy less dependent on self-contained labor. Where the Ghale lineage we examined commanded abundant labor reserves at crucial times in its development, expanding wealth for the Damrong was based on a combination of family and capital. Embi, in particular, is less reliant on the labor reserves of his own domestic unit than other households examined and shows a capacity for expanding his landholdings through the cash economy at a time when Chayanov's model would place his household at a disadvantage in the ability to command labor and wealth. His success has not been without costs, however, since he clearly weighed the relative advantages of adhering to traditional expectations in the household economy of his father versus relying on the new opportunities of the cash economy. His denial of tradition has won him notoriety and envy which a household more dependent on the nexus of kin could ill afford.

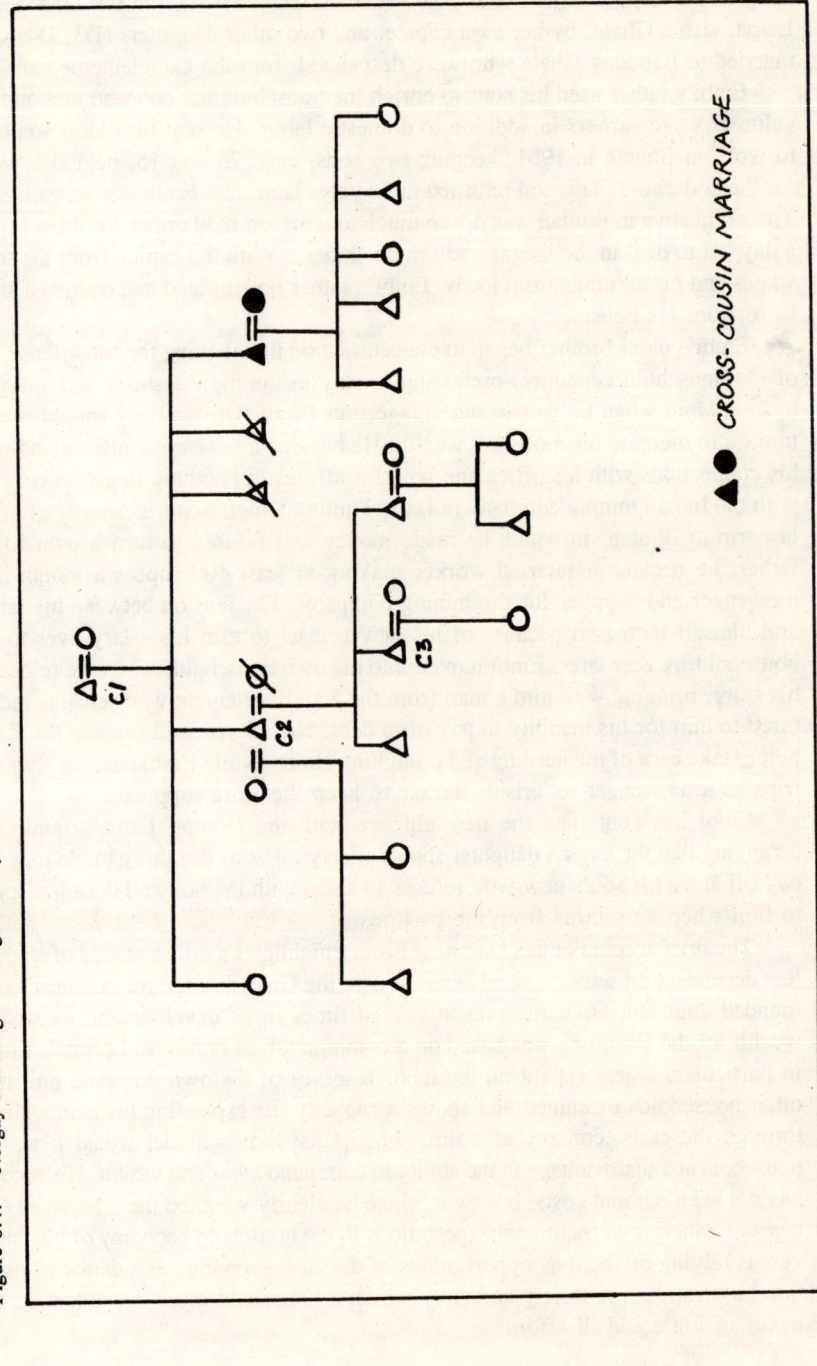

Figure 8.4. Norgay Damrong's Lineage History.

Variations in Domestic Economy   181

Households in Decline: Another Damrong Lineage

Figure 8.4 presents the lineage history of Norgay Damrong, the same man who married Setirani of the Ganglememe Ghale. Norgay (C3) controls about 19.5 *ropani* of land, having purchased and received the use of some in addition to his *angsa*, which he claimed in 1977. Yet his grandfather (C1) controlled close to 110 *ropani* (14.3 acres) at his peak. The example of Norgay's lineage illustrates the complexity of inheritance and relative decline in status in a family where three generations control a once unified amount of land.

Norgay's grandfather had four sons and a daughter but two sons died before marrying and producing heirs of their own. As a consequence, the *angsa* of Norgay's father (C2) remained relatively substantial even though his father kept an equal share for his own use until his death. In spite of the promise of 36 *ropani* (4.68 acres) for his immediate *angsa,* Norgay's father (C2) elected to remain in his father's household until 1970, after his brother's second son was born and he was already 51 years old with sons old enough to marry. He worked this land for seven years until Norgay claimed his inheritance. The land was divided then among three brothers and the father. His father kept control of one brother's land in addition to his own since the son was in Bhutan.

Much of this case has already been discussed in the last chapter. The point to be raised here is that inheritance is not only a complex process, but that individuals in the household time the point of division to suit their own strategic interests. Thus, Norgay took his inheritance before the birth of his father's son by a younger second wife to circumvent the lessening of his share. His father's marrying a second wife still in her fecund years represented an economic threat to Norgay and his brothers. We can also see from the diagram that inheritance can be drastically affected by such events as death. In Norgay's father's generation, the death of two brothers made for a larger inheritance than would otherwise have been possible, while the death of Norgay's actual mother created new risk for Norgay's own inheritance when he might otherwise have reasonably predicted the size of his *angsa*.

Finally, as with the Ghale, it is unlikely that younger generation households will be able to increase their lands to the extent of their grandfathers' holdings. It is possible that the first generation on this diagram was able to do so well, again, because of the extent of new land available from the forests. The expansion of Norgay's father's holdings was contingent on the remittances of his sons, and Norgay himself has been able to expand his own holdings through the largess of his wife's father, who lent, rather than gave, land for him to farm. Where Embi Damrong started his household with cash at his disposal, Norgay has no cash reserves, cannot read or write, and cannot command the labor to free him from the village for lengthy stretches of wage labor outside. More land will inevitably come to Norgay and his brothers when his grandfather and father die, but these amounts will already be divided and reduced. Assuming that his father has no more sons, Norgay can expect an additional 6.75 *ropani* to come his way not long before any sons he might have can claim their own *angsa*. Norgay's half-brother faces an even grimmer situation since, without older brothers actively contributing to the household land, this 6.75 *ropani* will constitute his *angsa* unless he is able to bring back money before then.

The Struggle to Break Even: Chamdi Ghale

As a final example of family processes, I will take the case of Chamdi Ghale, a Gurkha soldier in the Indian army until his retirement in 1980 after 21 years. Chamdi is the youngest son out of four; his inheritance was divided with his brothers in 1960, shortly after he enlisted, and he relied on these brothers to cultivate the 18 *ropani* and take care of his wife while he was away. His service allowed him to return to Timling for two months out of every 24, and these infrequent visits may partially explain the low fertility of his wife, who bore only two daughters, aged 12 and 6 in 1981.

Chamdi's military pay and the retirement checks of about 400 rupees a month would normally put him in a good position to expand his holdings and, indeed, he purchased half a *hal* of land soon after his return from India this last time. His major problem, however, is lack of a household labor force and rapidly declining hopes of acquiring family labor since his wife is 37 years old and has not borne a child since 1975. As a consequence, Chamdi is rarely in the village—both he and his wife are in constant movement between plots and the cattle pastures in the summer months. His daughters free him occasionally, but he will risk leaving them with the herds for a day or two at the most. In a household already 20 years old, when the normal course of events allows a degree of relaxation with sons maturing and beginning to bring daughters-in-law into the household, Chamdi is unable to lessen his attention to the agro-pastoral economy of Timling and can scarcely consider expanding much more unless he wishes to hire workers for his land. His options include taking in a second wife to have sons, one that he isn't ready to consider since he is genuinely attached to his present wife, or trying to bring in a son-in-law when his oldest daughter marries. Barring either of these, the advantages of new property are few for his household.

Overview of Household Processes in Timling

Taken together, these cases illustrate processes and constraints vital to the experience of particular households through time. The critical variable in a household's development is the size of the household through time, and the major impetus for increasing the size of households is the desire to have control over labor. Control over labor insures the future security of aging parents as well as decreasing the drudgery of work for parents in the short term. The Tamang explicitly say as much when asked about the value of children. Answers to questions about the worth of children were impressively uniform. The common response to why a couple would want children was to enumerate the kinds of work that contributed to survival:

Parents without children have a life of sorrow. They do all the work themselves. Who goes to Trisuli to haul salt for them? When they are old who will care for them? And when they die, their brothers will eat their land—their brothers who have done nothing for them. (Sankyathapa Damrong, male, age 23)

I want as many children as come . . . one to send outside the village to work, another to cut wood, yet another to plough. If one dies, there will always be another around to work. (Ibid.)

Children are necessary. Some might die but having as many as possible means there will always be others. One can be a *lama*, another a shaman; others can watch sheep and cattle and cut wood. . . . I want to send one to school, too, to learn to be rich. (Surti Mepa, *lama*, age 32)

Having many children divides the work and makes sure there are more if some die. Parents will be taken care of. Children tie us to other households. They teach each other their skills. (Tiksarani Ghale, Surti's wife, age 32)

People without children have a harder time at working. And who will do their death rituals? Who will care for them? (Selzawati Mamba, female, age 60)

Although the desire for help and security is powerful motivation for having children, the early years of childhood create work for people. Chayanov's model (1966:58-59) makes much of this, suggesting that drudgery for the early years of household development would increase. But the assumptions of his basic model of peasant family development are so abstract as to have little bearing on Timling's reality. For one thing, he assumes that the household is formed at a couple's marriage when we have seen that the Tamang tend to wait until after the birth of their first child. Secondly, his rigid succession of births at three-year intervals without intervening deaths must overestimate the numbers of consumers and producers to join the average household through its development. In Timling, too, child care is easily shared by all sexes and among households. I would suggest, therefore, that the measure of consumption units has no value as a measure of drudgery and has most application to the discussion of food and land requirements. The consumer/worker ratio has no meaning as a constraint since adult producers can fairly easily produce additional food for more than one person. The important variable for looking at household economy is the number of producers; barring sickness or invalid status, the number of consumers must increase along with this since the value of both progresses with age. Even in Chayanov's model, the consumer/worker ratio changes from only 1.00 to 1.94 at its peak, and the first born child is already 13 years old by then. In the model for Timling presented in the last chapter, the ratio peaks at 1.60 and 1.75 for the differing assumptions; the average ratios and standard deviations are small for all models, as table 8.5 shows. If we modify Chayanov's table to approximate more nearly the situation in Timling (five children per household and consumption and production values based on Macfarlane's), we arrive at a peak of 1.70, an average ratio of 1.37, and a standard deviation of 0.16 over the developmental cycle. The consumer/worker ratio is a significant variable only if we assume, as Chayanov does, that labor inputs are closely calibrated to the consumption requirements of the household. Even here we would need to

Table 8.5. Average Consumer/Worker Ratio throughout Household Cycle, Chayanov and Timling.

Chayanov	Mean = 1.46	S.D. = 0.17
Timling Model 1	Mean = 1.35	S.D. = 0.12
Timling Model 2	Mean = 1.34	S.D. = 0.16

know the actual number of consumption units to predict household production. In cases like Timling, where most households do not have extravagant holdings relative to their needs, households would be expected to produce as much as they can given their land and technology; the goal of production is to grow enough food for subsistence, and to attempt to grow more than the basic minimum can be construed as a strategy of averting risks from crop failure and other disasters (cf. Ortiz 1973).

If the first factor of critical importance to the household is the ability to produce children, especially sons who will stay longer than daughters and who increase the household's labor options, then the second most important variable is that of timing. We have seen that Chamdi Ghale's options are restricted by his failure to have sons early on.

From the point of view of an established household head, it is desirable to keep his sons in the household as long as possible. Their labor potential is only realized when they have passed their mid-teens. After this, they become useful for diversifying the household economy in addition to their earlier realized values in reducing the drudgery of necessary labor. Timling's mountain adaptation is one grounded in diversifying risks and, by extension, the secure household is one that can obtain its livelihood from the widest range of activities. The early years of a typical household force its members to focus their activities on the traditional elements of Tamang subsistence. Assuming that they have adequate land and herds to begin with, the few productive members of the young household have fairly heavy labor requirements within the village to keep them occupied. In addition, they must direct part of their labor to the demands of other households—parents, wife's parents, brothers—whom they are expected to help. The maturing household eventually loses its obligations to others as these ascending generations die and brothers become increasingly self-reliant. At the same time, having sons and daughters of one's own begins to bear fruit as daughters marry and secure the labor obligations of their spouses and sons bring in wives. Not only is labor potential increased but the aging household itself becomes a new center of the obligation network. Finally, when sons reach an age close to 15, the household head can begin to diversify his economy to include wage labor. Either he or his son will be free to leave for Bhutan to work on roads, or they can seek wage work elsewhere in Nepal. Before the decline in new lands for agriculture, this phase of diversification would have seen an expansion of the local adaptation through opening new plots. The focus on wage labor is something new in Timling, and we can expect it to become more critical to the adaptation for reasons to be dealt with in the concluding chapter. None of the Ganglememe's children was sent abroad to work for money although there is good evidence that they traveled frequently through the mountains of Nepal. Yet, younger households constantly speak of the need to have children to bring money into the household.

The labor power of sons encourages the household head to want to retain control over them. Yet, sons are free to leave their father's home at any time. From the point of view of the son, a time must come when he begins thinking as the potential head of his own household rather than as a member of his father's. At that time, effectively around age 20, he must begin weighing the relative merits of remaining or demanding his *angsa*. The variation in timing of household formation and dissolution is a function of this decision. Norgay's leave-taking was a result of this kind of calculation while the advantages of remaining in their fathers' homes outweighed the disadvantages for extraordinarily long periods of time for the son of the Ganglememe patriarch and Embi Damrong's brother. Embi himself made a momentous decision, taking the risk of alienating himself from much of the village by so pointedly denying the Tamang way.

The calculation that goes into this decision must be based on a range of factors, from the likelihood of acquiring more land for one's *angsa* through the contribution of siblings to the domestic economy, to the advantages of staying in the parental home until one's first child is old enough to make a labor contribution of his or her own, to the more prosaic concern of how well one gets along with a stepmother. Norjang Ghale may have felt that the Ganglememe patriarch's ability to acquire land was a good reason to remain in the household until he was 36 and already had a son aged 14 years. Embi Damrong left at the late age of 39, when it was clear to him that he commanded enough resources to be the primary agent of any future land acquisition for his household.

Finally, we should note that a large household is not simply secure in its diversified economy. It is also in a strong position to expand its holdings. There are many reasons to expand; a basic one is simply to increase the subsistence base of a growing household, as Chayanov points out. Another is to insure that the *angsa* of household sons will be large enough for their own subsistence and anticipated growth. This explains the average household's desire for land and is one reason that Chamdi Ghale is more concerned with reducing his drudgery than increasing his resources base. Without sons there is no need to. But it leaves only partially answered the phenomenon of the Ganglememe patriarch.

To attempt a solution requires that we acknowledge the links that Timling's local economy has with the world outside the village. At the time of the patriarch's most intensive land acquisition the economy of the village was barely monetized. Nepal was a closed country held as a kind of feudal estate by the Rana rulers in Kathmandu. It is unlikely that these rulers had any interest in their remoter mountain subjects since their wealth came from production at the more hospitable elevations. Timling's was an economy geared toward subsistence and intimately connected with the salt trade from Tibet. All of the sons of the patriarch have made frequent trips to Kyerong, and the ridges above Timling were yearly visited by Tibetans who traded yak, sheep, and goats for grain and mustard from the village below. The Ganglememe patriarch obviously needed to expand his holdings to provide for his large family and their *angsa,* but there is also good evidence that he used his rich labor resources to become heavily involved in trade with Kyerong. Of all people in the village, members of Ghale households are the most likely to be seen with Tibetan jewelry and utensils. The large family of this particular Ghale lineage placed them in a good position to operate as middlemen in the salt trade on behalf of the rest of the village and possibly for other points south. The patriarch is remembered as having large herds of yak and yak-hybrids; these herds ceased to be maintained shortly after the closing of the border with Tibet, and the last yak owned in the village was sold in the mid-1960s, since the primary use for yak in addition to their milk was as beasts of burden in trans-Himalayan trade. With the border closed, the labor intensity of herding yak was too great to justify keeping them only for dairy products, and they were gotten rid of. On the evidence, therefore, we can suggest that the holdings were expanded to such a great extent in order to produce grain for barter in an economy whose era is past. Indeed, most of the sons have increased their *angsa* only slightly, suggesting not only the growing scarcity of land but also their perception that they do not need more land.

9

Timling in a Changing World: Implications for Theory

Enough said? Nothing is more tiresome than an anthropology "among-the" book: among the Arunta this, among the Kariera that. Nor is anything scientifically proven by the endless multiplication of examples—except that anthropology can be boring.

—Sahlins, *Stone Age Economics*

The continuing survival of Timling's people amid the special constraints and opportunities of this Himalayan environment is testimony to the human ability to adjust behavior. Their solutions to the problems of obtaining a livelihood within this complex world are suitably rich when examined in detail; they nevertheless retain an elegance that allows us to outline their logic. But the workings of this economy have implications that go beyond the village. After examining this single case in detail, we are in a position to comment on processes occurring throughout the Himalayan landscape and elsewhere. At the same time, each isolated case brings its own contribution to social theory, bolstering some conclusions and modifying others.

I began research in Timling with the goal of describing the village economy and its implications for population processes. This study has been organized from the point of view of cultural ecology; the focus is on the people's adaptation, the continuing survival of a population. Data have been presented for a range of economic and demographic variables with a view to showing the logic and effects of having children in a particular environment, and we have taken up the different issues of adaptation more or less separately. The first part of this chapter will recapitulate much of what has been said, but from the point of view of an integrated mountain adaptation. I will consider the three components of Timling's adaptation using the concepts of spatial demographic, techno-economic, and socio-economic adaptation enumerated by Brush (1977:154–57).

This consideration of a Tamang adaptation introduces a paradox, however. We find in Timling a mountain peasantry successfully organized for survival, yet contained within that organization are the seeds of its own change. The people of Timling are not, nor have they ever been, in a homeostatic relationship with their environment. As Bennett (1969:14) puts it, the study of a people's adaptation must focus on movement. We may look at adaptive strategies—those apparently regular behaviors formed by many separate adjustments of problem-solving individuals—and arrive at the illusion of static adjustment, but adaptive processes, those long-term changes, are contained in the logic of the former. Following Boserup (1965) and Cohen (1977), I take population growth as the key variable in explaining change up to the present.

Kunstadter (1972:348) writes:

> Primitive societies (and prehistoric populations) are often assumed to have been in homeostasis—they would have to have been, it is argued, in order to have survived so long. The assumption must be correct, in the long run, for the human species as a whole, but it seems unlikely to have been even a good approximation in the short run, and for particular communities, except under special circumstances. I have suggested in this paper, following Malthus, that population growth is the normal condition of mankind.

We can examine why this is so in Timling as an example and explicate the means of coping with it. Even more, our knowledge of resources currently available and likely to become available to Timling in the near future places us in a good position to project future alternatives and choices that these Tamang will shortly be facing.

Timling stands on the threshold of crisis, the nature of which is paralleled by the crisis facing Nepal as a nation (Blaikie 1981; Blaikie et al. 1979; Seddon et al. 1979). The components of this national crisis include massive deforestation and erosion (Eckholm 1976; Calkins 1981) and population growth beyond the ability of Nepal's infrastructure to sustain (World Bank 1979:35–48; Poffenberger 1980). Some of these problems are embedded in the organization of power and wealth flows, but the Tamang case given here suggests that in the absence of exploitive caste relationships a good part of the explanation must include adaptive processes themselves.

Finally, the logic of high fertility in Timling stems from the organization of production and consumption at the household level. Our understanding of the relationships working in this village will allow us to comment on broader issues of population and development theory.

Timling's Adaptations: Spatial and Economic

Our first synthesis of the Tamang adaptation is to take the slice out of time, that brief period when I was resident in Timling, and describe the workings of the economy and its context as though these were enduring patterns. The Tamang exploit a wide range of micro-environments within their traditional territory but focus their subsistence activities on the lower, agriculturally productive areas. Hence, Timling lies within easy reach of its upper and lower landholdings, and no household is more than an hour's walk from its major field even though subsidiary holdings may be as far as three hours away. In cases where investments of time require absence from the village, as in those times of year when household herds are in the forest or high pasture, members of the household will live in dispersed temporary shelters and have frequent contact with the village as they bring grain and milk back and forth.

Neighborhoods are organized along kinship lines. Living close together helps to maintain clan solidarity and ratify cultural values of generalized reciprocity among kin. This reliance on kin permeates all other adaptive strategies in Timling, and the relationship among space, cooperation at work, and kinship distance is so integrated that one can be used to predict the other in the village. The patriline ties households together within neighborhoods, but the village is bound together by marriage between clans and the cooperative links established in this way.

Timling's adaptation is structured to take advantage of the widest number of resource opportunities within the local environment. Although mountain environments are often considered impoverished by people from urban industrial societies, it is useful to think of the Tamang environment as one that offers diverse openings for the satisfaction of subsistence needs. This environment becomes marginal or constraining only when the whole set of resources is strained by scarcity, and even though this becomes increasingly true, needs are being satisfied in the current situation. No single use zone will fulfill all of a household's requirements, however. Thus, the logic of survival is such that Tamang spread their production activities and their risks as broadly as possible. The Tamang economy is an economy of diversity.

Within the agricultural zone, we have seen that this diversity takes the form of three subdivisions, based on the kinds of crops that are suitable to particular altitudes and soils. The Tamang take this diversification even further by maintaining widely spaced plots within each subdivision, a rational strategy of risk avoidance given the unpredictable nature of weather patterns in mountain environments. This diversity, then, is predicated not only on the physical nature of the environment but on a perceived need to spread investments of time and labor across all components of the economy. The logic carries over into the expanding cash economy, in which wage labor represents yet another resource to insure a family's subsistence, either by making it possible to buy grain outright in bad years or by allowing households to expand their lands.

Village economy is directed toward subsistence ends, but there has probably never been a time when Timling was self-sufficient. At the very least, the Tamang have always been involved in the trans-Himalayan salt trade, and the village could have always found a ready market for its grain surplus by trading with Tibetan pastoralists to the north. With this in mind, the increasing importance of wage labor since the 1950s is not a radical transformation of a pristine, self-sustaining tribal economy—regional links have always been important to the Tamang for trade and the seasonal movement of animals. What differs now, though, is the nature of the commodity being marketed. Trade with the north involved the barter of finished subsistence goods—the product of labor—for other subsistence goods. The relationship between parties in the transaction, who were often connected as ritual friends (Np. *mit*), was essentially equal. Conversely, Timling does not produce enough as a village to market a surplus, and there is no demand in the south for grains that the people of Timling can grow. Their consistently marketable products, then, are no longer subsistence goods exchanged for different subsistence goods of the same value. Rather, the people of Timling must sell their labor in a market where supply is high, and they are tied to non-Tamang regions in fundamentally subordinate relationships. Timling retains kin-based regional relationships with other Tamang villages to the South only where there is an equality of need. This is notably true for affinal links with Kimtang; the two villages share the same pastures in the seasonal movement of sheep and goats, and households bound by marriage are exempt from the tax that villages levy for the use of their lands.

If kinship can be thought of as the organizing principle for exchange in Timling, the basic unit of organization is the household. Tamang households are the key landholding and animal owning segments of society. Members of the household produce for their own use, working in whatever part of the diversified village economy—wage labor, work in the fields, cutting wood, and tending herds are all directed toward provisioning the people who share the same hearth. Similarly, labor and goods are exchanged among households where the degree of calculation changes with kin relation while exchanges within the domestic group are ideally carried out free of expectation. There is room for violating this ideal, but the resulting disharmony underscores the expectation.

In spite of the more generalized reciprocity within the household, kinship, sex, and age establish a modest hierarchy of expected roles. The oldest adult male, usually the father or grandfather of younger males, makes strategic decisions affecting the domestic unit. Women and daughters are expected to fulfill functions specific to their sex. Sons begin to chafe at the demands and control of their labor by the household head as they grow older and become potential householders themselves.

The organization of Timling's economy—household as the primary economic unit, kinship as the nexus of exchange, diversified pursuits as the key to survival and avoiding risks—reinforces the desire to have as many children as possible. Village studies conducted elsewhere (for example, T. Hull 1975; Cain 1977; Nag et al. 1978) have all concluded that children make important contributions to the household economy, especially in the extent of their time investments. In this sense, they reduce the drudgery of work. There is good reason to believe they do the same in Timling as they grow older, and strenuous tasks can be shared by many hands. But children's value goes beyond simply contribution to a finite set of household labor requirements when, after age 15 or so, they become important resources in themselves for expanding and diversifying the domestic economy. In earlier years, this took the form of actually opening new land for cultivation. The present adaptation encourages their use as wage labor or as workers at home that free older members of the household to seek wage work outside of the village. In times of scarcity, their incomes can save household land by making it unnecessary to take loans from wealthier households, using the land as collateral. Their time away from the village also reduces the number of mouths to feed around the hearth while the domestic unit, nevertheless, receives the hoped for money. In times of relative self-sufficiency, cash can be saved to purchase new land or put into jewelry and other commodities against future shortfalls.

Children expand the net of kinship. They marry and bring the households of other clans into affinal relationships. When sons marry and build their own hearths, their households are caught in the orbit of the parental domestic unit. Thus, the nature of the domestic mode of production itself creates the need for children as a strategy for risk aversion and support.

Decision-Making, Adaptive Strategies, Adaptive Processes

The structure of a people's adaptation tells us how they extract their livelihood from the environment at a given time. Yet we know that some mechanism for a flexible adjustment to changing circumstances needs to be included in the system, or the dangers of extinction are compounded. Bennett's model of cultural ecology (1969, 1976) gives us the concepts to talk about these processes. I have already mentioned adaptive strategies and processes as two components of his model. The pivot on which social change rests is contained in the third component: individual decision-making. Here, I will begin with a description of the two major cycles in Timling's strategic adjustment to the Himalayan environment.

For the Tamang, two sets of recurrent behaviors define their adaptation. They move together like interlocking wheels of different sizes, and the points at which they touch circumscribe the range of strategic behaviors from which household members may choose. The first of these is the annual subsistence cycle, a fairly rigid set of activities constrained by the requirements of crops and animals on which survival depends. This cycle will have the people of Timling working at agriculture from March until December of each year. Periods of greatest labor intensity fall in the earlier and later phases, when the villagers must plough their fields and harvest their crops. The care of livestock meshes with this cycle in the annual movement from the village to the pastures at higher elevations and to the south in winter months. Each of these basic subsistence activities has its own labor requirements, the cyclic intensity of which permits or forbids investing time in other work during different times of year. Thus, the months of March and April and from September until the first weeks of December are those when work is most singlemindedly devoted to the agro-pastoral part of the economy. The lulls in this cycle permit greater attention to other categories of work: household maintenance, cutting and storing wood, seeking wage labor, or performing elaborate and necessary rituals.

A second important pattern that recurs in the Tamang adaptation moves much more slowly and is imperceptible to the short-term observer. This is the household developmental cycle, that pattern of formation, growth, and fission in the domestic group that takes an average of 37 years to complete. The household developmental cycle is far less rigid than the subsistence round, being subject to extreme variations based on the timing of important life cycle events such as marriage and cohabitation, births and deaths within the household, and the age at which sons claim their inheritance. Thus, the nature of the cycle is determined by a combination of unpredictable biological events and the decisions of household members, which can be anticipated but not wholly known.

A household's status, its ability to expand the resource base and diversify its economy, is determined by its particular developmental trajectory and the timing of the annual subsistence calendar. Households in the early phases of their developmental cycle are more severely constrained by the requirements of the agro-pastoral economy than are mature households which control the labor of three or four adults. The former are forced by the subsistence round to seek supplementary wage work only at those times of year when agricultural and pastoral demands are least pressing, even when labor exchange through the kin network can be used to give them more leeway. Not only is reciprocity outside of the household less secure than within, but the early years when a household is smallest are also the time when the most work is owed to other households. Thus, it is at the later stages of development that households will send members away from Timling for long stretches.

The role of decision-making within this system becomes crucial where the alternatives are most numerous. The range of these is determined by the set of cultural expectations together with the needs of provisioning the household. Agricultural and pastoral techniques are relatively invariant although there is room for choice in the organization of work and in the selection of which cooperative links should be strengthened and which allowed to wither. From the point of view of Timling's overall adaptation, the most important choices have to do with marriage and the timing of inheritance.

For the woman's family, marriage establishes vital links with other households and thereby expands the circle of kin who can help the family in times of need. Or, advantageous exchanges in shared pasture can be set up, as we have seen with the Ganglememe lineage. For the domestic units that are yet to be formed, age at marriage and cohabitation are the single most important variables influencing family size and, hence, domestic labor potential and diversity. Powerful households are more inclined to control their daughter's marital options because they can afford the risk of an unsuccessful match—more than one person is making a decision here, and a strong-willed daughter can veto her father's decision at almost any point before moving into her husband's home.

The timing of inheritance is almost entirely the decision of the son after about age 16. In making the choice, he must weigh the viability of the new domestic unit (land and labor requirements), the risk of alienating related households (leaving too soon may earn the non-cooperation of fathers and brothers), and the potential of an expanding inheritance from the contributions of other siblings to his natal household. In practice, the average age for this leave-taking is around 27, but wealthier households may keep the first sons much longer, as in two of the most successful lineages where they stayed until nearly 40 years old. On the average, a Tamang household can expect to control more than two adult or near-adult labor units after about 15 years when it enters its stage of greatest flexibility and growth potential.

In the absence of detailed historical information we can only infer the long-term adaptive processes that have characterized Timling's adaptation. Nevertheless, we know some of the changes that have taken place, and we can show how the organization of the economy itself has demanded those changes. I have written that Timling lies on the threshold of crisis; our sketchy knowledge of its past indicates that it has been at a number of such crises in its history and that it is only the particular details and available options that differ now.

The logic of Timling's economy has been shown to encourage women to bear as many children as possible—this would be the case in any economy that approximates the Domestic Mode of Production as laid out by Sahlins (1972). In a natural fertility population, of which these Tamang are an example, the number of children that a woman bears is limited almost entirely by exposure to the risk of becoming pregnant. I have shown, using the Bongaarts model (1978, 1975), that the most important factors limiting the fertility of Timling women are time spent in marital unions (cohabitation) and the length of breastfeeding. These fertility reducing effects are extreme, helping to reduce average fertility from a potential of nearly 14 births per woman to just slightly over 5. But even given the very high mortality, in which over 25% of these ever-born children die before age five, enough children survive to more than replace their parents each generation. The intrinsic rate of natural increase implied by the figures I have collected in Timling is 1.2% annually, much lower than the 2.1% rate for Nepal as a whole (Banister and Thapa 1981:25) but one that indicates a doubling time of about 60 years.

Even in the absence of these figures, the growing population of Timling is manifest in the lineage histories I have presented and in the expansion of the original Timling settlement into its daughter villages. All of these villages occupy formerly forested lands, indicating one of the most significant effects of population growth in the subsistence economy: increasing scarcity of resources.

The movement of Tamang ancestors into Timling's area some 15 generations ago can be attributed to the search for new resource frontiers. Since their arrival, the Tamang have not only expanded into all parts of the territory containing arable land, but have also modified their agriculture toward greater diversity and intensity of production. It is likely that the original settlers in Timling practiced slash and burn agriculture in conjunction with heavier reliance on the pastoral economy than the present population. The people of Timling always speak wistfully of a past in which their grandfathers herded massive numbers of sheep, goats, and yak in the high pastures. Individual households are said to have herded 100 to 200 sheep and goats. Brian Hodgson's manuscripts from the mid-nineteenth century include references to agriculture by a Tamang informant.

> After two years we cultivate another field because the soil of it is wasted. And in two years time that field becomes jungle and again after 2 years we cultivate the same field. (The field) which is close to our house we always cultivate. After two years we burn the jungle of the same field and dig it & the ashes becomes manure and as much jungle we can cut down we cultivate it. . . . We sow Mokae (maize) corn twice in a year (one sort small) and in that field any other corn cannot grow—except Mokae, but some times we sow kodae (millet) in it. The field on which potato grows no corn can grow in it—the same potato seed remains for nine years. Corn&c is yearle sown. . . . First we plough the field then throw the manure over it & sow the mokai & Kodoe, Thori, Phapur: these are sown only once in a year and suker Kund is produced three times in a year. . . . The field that produces strongly is not changed—& other fields are changed after 3 or 4 years. (cited in Macfarlane 1976:29; errors in original)

This kind of agriculture once characterized the entire hill region of Nepal but is now found only in those few areas where arable land is still relatively abundant. In addition to the move toward intense agriculture, Tamang farmers in Timling introduced the potato, one of the most important staples in their subsistence, sometime after the middle of the last century.

The result of these changes is a massive reorientation of the Tamang economy even though they must have occurred incrementally. Other indications of changing fortunes are less obviously tied to the economy. Older residents of the village report, for example, that certain days of the year used to be devoted to communal work projects, especially maintenance of the trails in and out of the village. These projects are rarely carried out now because most households will not relinquish the labor. Similarly, the village ceased to offer goats to one of the important deities a few years ago, and older Tamang attribute to this sin of omission a string of bad harvests from too much rain. The process of which these changes are a part relates to the organization of the economy in which the household holds primary responsibility for its own survival. In trying to cope with a new reorientation in Timling's adaptation, household heads are choosing to invest their workforce in subsistence or wage labor activities more directly relevant to the survival of the domestic group.

Timling's changing adaptation moves in a close relationship with its growing population, which is, in its turn, the result of the economy's domestic organization. Constraining Timling's adaptation at any time has been a moving set of resource frontiers. Early on, these frontiers were defined by the forest's edge which, when rolled back, created new arable land. Later resource frontiers involved the addition of new crops such as potatoes and new techniques such as double cropping. In the process of altering their adaptive strategies, the Tamang have moved from a pattern of actually expanding into new land to one of expanding the production on a finite amount of land. At one time, these processes depended almost entirely on the capacity of the local ecosystem, and Timling's people were able to pursue their livelihood largely unencumbered by non-reciprocal relationships with outside groups. Until recently, the path of intensification and expansion has followed the process outlined by Ester Boserup (1965).

More recently, however, the technology and strategies of farming have not changed, and land quality has begun to decline; the possibilities for exploiting new resource frontiers within Timling's bounded environment have been exhausted. Additionally, political events beyond the control of the village have closed the potential for intensifying trade and other relationships to the north. Thus, the latest resource frontier for each household is the cash economy in which labor can be sold. For the first time in their history, these Tamang must choose to expand into a frontier where they are inherently disadvantaged. Their inability to speak and read standard Nepali and lack of experience in the national Nepali culture combine with the long-lived prejudices of dominant peoples to make them losers in the competition for scarce employment opportunities. The majority of Tamang are guaranteed assignment to the most menial and unpleasant work in their efforts to find jobs outside of the village. Those few employment opportunities in salaried positions such as the messenger job for the new mine create a new kind of competition among households within the village. Households can be at a disadvantage for reasons beyond the number and ages of their members' simple labor potential; a new yardstick of security in the form of education and degree of integration into Nepali versus Tamang culture has been introduced. A Tamang who dilutes the hold of traditional village relationships to assume a Nepali identity has the advantage. Today, the people of Timling are faced with the dilemma of accepting either a declining standard of living based on local adaptations or a debased status relative to other groups outside of the village.

Implications for Theory

Anthropology is, among other things, the science of the specific case. Each village study contributes to the process of theory-building by bringing paradigms to bear on empirical reality in an attempt to bring order and understanding to the apparent randomness of events. The process is dialectic; theory informs research and the village study often modifies theory. Yet, we need make no apology if our research only confirms our expectations since this is itself a kind of contribution. We need to ask ourselves now what implications the case of Timling has for broader disciplinary issues.

Anthropology, Demography, and Social Change

This research has amply illustrated the potential for solid demographic field research in anthropology. In spite of the trying conditions of fieldwork, extremely detailed information on marriage and fertility was collected from each village woman, all of whom were illiterate and entirely unacquainted with survey research. The demographic analysis here is gratifyingly consistent and has shown that analysis designed for much larger populations or samples (e.g., Bongaarts 1978) can be successfully applied to village data and, importantly, to small populations still minimally affected by processes outside their own setting.

In terms of anthropological theory, this analysis has shown that the ecological perspective advanced by John Bennett can provide a satisfying organization for the study of a people's adaptation. The incorporation of individual decision-making into a model of adaptive processes enables us to describe the functioning of a society in its environment while simultaneously identifying the components of change. And by allowing the individual level decisions to be constrained by other levels of organization (the household, the village), we can see how rational decisions at one level necessitate changes in a system.

One implication of this work follows from this. The case of Timling suggests that Sahlins' Domestic Mode of Production, in which the greatest production and consumption autonomy is given to the household, is an organization unknowingly constituted for change. Sahlins (1961) has called the segmentary lineage an organization for predatory expansion. Timling's history demonstrates that the real organization for expansion is the domestic economy, which must depend for its long-term survival on growing resource frontiers. In its early stages when land is abundant, it preys on unoccupied territory. Where land is scarce, people organized in this fashion have the choice of intensifying their production or pushing other populations off their territory. In Nepal, where the state intervenes to make the last choice impractical, the people of Timling are being forced by the logic of their economy into dependent relationships with the outside world. All of this is related to the responsibility of the household to provision itself and to fortify its security through diversification.

While the economy's logic encourages an expanding population, it simultaneously dampens the rate of growth. The need for security creates the desire to expand relationships by having children; this is balanced by the more immediate household labor requirements, which create the desire to hold children in the household, to delay their age at marriage and, hence, decrease their fertility.

A second implication of this analysis has to do with the definition of peasantries. Nearly all features of Timling's organization would satisfy Macfarlane's criteria (1979:18-32), yet others (cf. Faith 1980) might argue that these Tamang are not peasants since they control their own land. Added to this is the problem of change in the organization of the economy—indicated by household movement into monetized relations that override more traditional kin relationships. Any categorical definition has the problem of what exceptions to include in a type. Basing the definition of peasantries on the limited experience of a single geographical region is no solution since it adds little comparative advantage outside the region. But a definition culled from societies throughout the world is too broad to be useful.

Discussions of peasantry invariably converge on the familial nature of production, however. This study suggests that the more operable research focus must be on the organization of the economy and the processes that define it. Thus, we have a continuum from the Domestic Mode of Production to a monetized economy, and each society's place along that line can change through time without needing to pinpoint that moment when it ceases to be peasant. This follows Caldwell's view of the familial mode of production and supports Orlove's and Yanagiasako's stress on process.

Cultural ecology encourages us to examine the provisioning of society and the processes related to it. In societies at one extreme of this continuum, of which Timling is an example, we see that demographic events have a major determining role in the trajectory of basic economic units. The processual view implies historical depth; we see that change has always characterized Timling's past but that past processes never so directly threatened the mode of production based on kinship until the nature of resources was transformed.

The case of Timling implies a method that: (1) identifies the fundamental unit of production and consumption; (2) isolates the systems giving this unit its particular structure in a population—demographic processes, cultural rules, the individual life cycle, and the household developmental cycle; (3) examines the organization that links these units within a population; and (4) identifies the constraints that channel the flow of cyclic and long-range processes—relations with the outside world, local ecology, and the resource base.

Theories of Population

This brings us to Timling's implications for population theory. We have seen the convergence of more strictly policy-oriented research objectives and the aims of anthropological research in the work of Caldwell (Caldwell et al. 1982; Caldwell 1981) and Cain (1982, 1981, 1977) and in the research programs of the Population Council (1981). Work in Timling suggests that the emphasis on examining the sociocultural context of fertility behavior is far from misplaced. McNicoll's suggestions that research focus on the institutional constraints and alternatives that bound the decision-making process (1980:442-43) are especially relevant here. The Timling data show that the demand for children is intimately connected to the organization of the economy and the specific set of responsibilities that characterize the kinship relations in the village. Children are valuable for reasons that go beyond their labor contribution. They are a logical extension of a mountain economy based on diversification. But more than this, children are the glue that gives Tamang society its cohesiveness by contravening the "centripetal" nature of the domestic mode of production, as Sahlins has put it. Children bind household to household through marriage and shared labor. In the one drastic case of a Tamang household that has ceased to rely heavily on traditional kinship expectations, we have found the example of social anarchy that Sahlins attributes to the domestic mode of production left unregulated. The denial of kinship is a prerequisite for an economy in which Tamang exploits Tamang, and even Embi Damrong straddles a line between traditional values and complete reliance on the monetized economy.

This research has further contributions to make, but first we need to understand how Timling differs from most of the societies in which similar work has been done. Apart from the obviously extreme nature of the physical setting, I wish to argue that the most important difference is in the degree to which Tamang relationships have *not* been monetized and class relationships within the village have *not* been formalized. This is not to say that variation in household fortunes doesn't exist. Evidence from lineage histories shows that there are wide variations in the trajectories of domestic groups, sometimes extending across generations. But the egalitarian ethos has been maintained, and the Gini coefficients I have discussed demonstrate the fundamentally equal distribution of material wealth when Timling is compared with other cases.

The lack of stratification that characterizes the village today is the result of the relative wealth in land that characterized Timling's environment until the latter part of this century. In such a situation, the only constraint on a family's success was the amount of labor it controlled and experience has shown that the largest families were also the most successful in terms relevant to the Tamang: their household economies were the most diversified (security), and their members had the most free time (lack of drudgery). In addition, the net of kinship ensured that older household members could look forward to an easy future. No resident of Timling is unaware of the Ganglememe patriarch's phenomenal success, and even Embi Damrong's father, who relied on cash at the beginning of his household developmental cycle, eventually headed one of the biggest households in the village. Conversely, no Tamang desires to be in Chamdi Ghale's situation with his stores of money and no sons.

Furthermore, in a society where primary resources for survival are abundant and labor is organized as in Timling, there are virtually no costs in having children. Time costs in childcare are not important since children are easily placed in the care of other households in the kin network when both parents need to be elsewhere. Opportunity costs are non-existent since the economy is geared to more or less the same pattern of activities for each household; there is almost no alternative to being a mother and member of the household labor force in the traditional economy. The increased consumption requirements of the household economy are probably negligible for as long as a child is a non-producer, and the advantages that children bring would far outweigh these costs.

In Timling, the ethos of abundance carries over even now. Respondents were quick to list the advantages of having children but could think of disadvantages, if then, only when they were pressed and always in terms of the growing awareness of sudden land scarcity. Even then, they simply transferred the idea of children as a resource to the new resource frontiers of the cash economy. Tacked on to the long list of ploughing, cutting wood, herding animals, carrying water, and whatever other chore was important in the traditional economy was earning money.

Caldwell's theory of wealth flows and the diffusion of western ideology (1978) may need slight changes in emphasis on the basis of the Tamang case. The implications are that security and avoidance of risk can be the dominant reasons for desiring children in some settings, as Cain argues (1982). Cain places his modifications of Caldwell into a context of environmental risk—where it is high, the security value of children will be high (1982:167). The whole organization of the Tamang economy supports this, with children another opportunity to expand the household economy.

Hajnal (1982) has identified two major household formation systems and related them to the same end of provisioning society. Two extremes are identified: the northwest European system with its late age at marriage, neolocal residence, and circulation of young people as servants and the joint household system with low ages at marriage and the presence of two or more married couples in a house. He consciously excludes the stem family system from his discussion, yet its existence in widely separated regions (Berkner 1972; Foster 1978) and in the Himalaya demands attention. Timling's stem family system, along with Thailand's and peasant Austria's, suggests an intermediate formation system that may be based on resource availability and partible inheritance in a family-centered economy. Other possibilities, such as the contrast between rates of population growth in stem and joint family systems, also need exploration.

Finally, the case of Timling has relevance to how we define Nepal's population experience. We have seen consistent differences between Timling's vital rates and those for Nepal as a whole. Rather than casting doubt on the accuracy of estimates for Timling, they suggest that generalizations based on national survey data for a country so diverse must be used cautiously. Rarely are large surveys conducted in the remoter regions; the Nepal Fertility Survey, for example, may not have adequately sampled villages more than a two-day walk from land strips or roadheads, accessibility being one of the characteristics of sampled villages (NFS 1976). These data have been used to report mean ages of marriage at 16 for Nepali women (Hajnal 1982:488), but neither Timling nor Thak shows such low mean ages for villages inhabited by two of Nepal's major ethnic groups. A research program that incorporates the experience of these remoter areas is thus suggested.

Timling's Future

What can we say about Timling's future from all of this? Most of the processes I have described have been commented on by researchers in villages throughout Nepal—Bishop (1978) for the extreme northwest, Hitchcock (1966, 1963) for the Magar, Macfarlane (1976) for the Gurung, and Hoffpauir for another Tamang village closer to Trisuli (1978). Hitchcock (1963:70) provides the earliest documentation for a case in which cash was the most significant component of land acquisition. He writes in a later work (1966):

> With increasing pressures on the land due to the growth in population, the emergent money economy, and intensification of trade, have come new patterns for the concentration of wealth.... (p. 104)

> The disappearance of vacant, cultivable land, combined with increased population has pushed more and more farms below the level of marginal productivity. In Banyan Hill, land partition

among sons has made an increasing number of farms too small to meet subsistence needs. The most common reason for borrowing is simply to meet the need for food. Given such a situation, great advantage lies with the person . . . who has means and ability to lend money. Land and money both flow in his direction. (p. 105)

Similarly, for the Gurung, Macfarlane writes:

The mechanism whereby certain families are forced down and others up is the budgetary surplus or deficit. A combination of favorable conditions has led the Gurungs to expect a higher standard of living over the last twenty years. . . . Yet such expenditure demands an income which many families do not have. They are forced to sell capital, gold and land, or go into debt. At the same time the reserves of good new land have come to an end and each generation sees the present fields subdivided between an increasing number of children. . . . The problem has also been delayed by army money; the poorer households have remade their fortunes by sending a son abroad. Yet the problem is likely to grow. Such deficits are the way in which an increasing split between a class of small peasant proprietors and a landless group comprising up to half of the village could occur during the next twenty years. (1976:199)

Sadly, there is no reason to suspect that Timling's experience will be any different. The best land is gone and the newest resource frontier is the first in history in which households are differently advantaged based on factors other than their age and sex composition. It is unlikely that the people of Timling will alter their perception of the value of children since their economy will continue to rely on diversity within the domestic mode of production. In many ways, the Tamang face a harsher future than either the Magar or Gurung since not only is their environment in Timling harsher, but their opportunities are more severely constrained by prejudice.

The people of Timling place great faith in the road making its way from Trisuli to the mine in their high pastures. Some hope to plant fruit trees to be able to market the produce in Kathmandu. Others see it and the mine as the source of new jobs. More likely, a variety of short-term labor positions will come to some households and the near future will bring increasing inequality in the village distribution of wealth, as some households gain the ability to supplement their lands and others begin the downward spiral to landlessness. Embi Damrong's strategy of playing the cash economy off traditional kin links promises to become the wave of the future for those households that are currently the most wealthy; failed households will join the new Nepali landless class or be siphoned off on that road to the squatter settlements of Kathmandu and the Terai.

Appendix 1

Inventory of Tamang Material Goods

Item	Tamang Name	Life	Value (rp)
Men's clothing			
Turban			
homespun	bajaro	2 yrs	30
bought	ga yen	3 yrs	70
Wool jacket			
brown	mlang gey	2-3 yrs	250
white	tar gey	2-3 yrs	250
Short jacket	shelpo gey	2 yrs	120
Main garment			
homespun	shelpo yen	2 yrs	***
bought	koda yen	1 year	28
Waist cloth	khepkikhey	5 yrs	40
Loincloth	toti	1-2 yrs	2
Women's clothing			
Skirt	shama	2 yrs	65
Upper garment			
red	ola jah	2 yrs	90
white	goda jah	2 yrs	65
Shirt	cholo	5 yrs	110
Waist cloth			
white	tar rumal	1 yr	10
blue	ping rumal	1 yr	10
Half blouse	tunde chola	1 yr	30-35
Household/Storage			
Wooden box			
20 pathi	murnang	lifetime	200
10 pathi	chibyang	lifetime	100
5 pathi	pathinga	lifetime	50
Salt box	dom	lifetime	12-13

Appendix 1

Item	Tamang Name	Life	Value (rp)
Grain basket			
small	jita dalo	10 yrs	***
large	ghanta dalo	10 yrs	***
Hearth rack	'khe	3-4 yrs	***
Net bag	pare	4-5 yrs	30
Potato basket	domsong	1-2 yrs	***
Carrying baskets			
small	dembe	2 yrs	5
large	daga	2 yrs	10
Sitting pad	chakari	3-4 yrs	10
Cooking tripod	jangu	lifetime	10
Handmill	renda	lifetime	30
Tray	nakhle	3-4 yrs	10
Sifter	chizhi	3-4 yrs	10
Skin mat	nayang	2 yrs	10
Plant basket	perengu	2 yrs	***
Wooden bowl	sho	lifetime	***
Wok	janga	8-9 yrs	22
Tongs	'khop	1 yr	***
Mortar/pestle	lang	10 yrs	***
Trough			
wood	'kho	8 yrs	20
chicken	naggai 'kho	lifetime	***
dog	niggi 'kho	2 yrs	***
Steps	li	8-9 yrs	***
Wool blanket	rari	5-6 yrs	250-300
Cane fence	mira	1-2 yrs	***
Agricultural			
Plough	gor	2 yrs	10
Plough tip	pala	1 yr	10
Sickle	wari	3-4 yrs	4-8
Cane walls	chapdel	2 yrs	20
Poles for goth	'khum	3-4 yrs	***
Hayrick	tangho	4-5 yrs	***
Bee hive	sindur dong	8-12 yrs	***
Plough pole	goriung	8-9 yrs	6
Yoke	'khum	4-5 yrs	***

Item	Tamang Name	Life	Value (rp)
"	chesingh	4-5 yrs	***
"	chetcho	4-5 yrs	***
Grain husker	kutalon	15 yrs	***
Churn	shangdong	lifetime	***
Digging tool	'komo	1 yr	10
Miscellaneous			
Loom	tara	lifetime	***
Backstrap	peda	lifetime	***
Kukhri	gotcha	lifetime	25-30
Scabbard	'khusup	2-3 yrs	***
Small knife	kartha	lifetime	5
Rifle	banduk	lifetime	200-500
Rain shield	charku	1 yr	30
Wool cap	ruri tibi	4-5 yrs	30
Stirring rod	yodo	2 months	***
Stirring rod	chapa	1 yr	***

***Indicates an item for which no price can be given, either because the manufacture of the object is considered to be a part of each household's basic repertoire or because the item is too trivial and easily made.

Appendix 2

Household Inventory for 30 Sample Households in Timling

Article	Number in Sample	Rupee Value
cane stool	2	10
bedstead	1	--
sleeping/sitting mat	9	30
wooden chair	-	--
blankets	64	250
brass bowl	5	10
plates	141	8
knife	5	30
ladle	43	5
cauldron	41	370
tripod	43	30
grain baskets	95	30
wooden box	75	200
tin box	9	130
water pot	36	310
wooden flask	49	10
bag	13	10
lantern	1	40
wick lamp	2	3
lock	33	10
mirror	10	3
razor	2	5
spinning wheel	1	25
loom	27	--
spindle	15	--
plough	31	30
ax	30	30
drying mat	89	6
winnowing tray	31	10
grinding stone	27	30
rifle	8	1000
radio	1	300
thermos	-	--
watch	2	150
photos	10	25
pens/pencils	7	5
scissors	4	5
kerosene	2 mana	3
jewelry item	60	250 (av.)

Total value for 30 HH   92,950 rupees (7811 $US)

Average value per household   3,098 rupees (260 $US)

Glossary

I have tried to minimize resorting to Nepali and Tamang words in the text of this study although a number of terms are unavoidable. In spelling Nepali words, I have followed the convention of Macfarlane (1976) in transliterating the *devanagari* script in which Nepali is written. The Tamang language, however, is not a written tongue in the village in which I did fieldwork, and pronunciation is often different from other villages, even those within the same region. My convention has been, therefore, to spell Tamang words as I heard them and without diacritical marks that would only be confusing to most readers. Following are words that appear in the text with some frequency:

aba (Tm.)—father
ama (Tm.)—mother
angsa (Np.)—a male's inheritance, taken when he leaves his father's home
bajaro (Tm.)—a turban worn by western Tamang men
Bhote (Np.)—a word used to refer to Tibetans and related peoples; considered derogatory
bidi (Np.)—a small leaf-rolled cigarette popular in Nepal and India
bompo (Tm.)—Tamang shaman
chewar (Np.)—first haircutting ritual for boys
gompo (Tm.)—Buddhist temple found in most Tamang villages
goth (Np.)—cattle shelters, whether temporary or permanent
grel (Tm.)—one of the major Buddhist mortuary rituals for Tamang
hal (Np.)—a unit of land equal to that which can be ploughed by a team of oxen in a day; roughly three ropani
jajmani (Np.)—institutionalized work relationship in which particular members of a lower caste work for another group for standard payments at harvest time
kulgi lha (Tm.)—god of the hearth; a clan deity worshipped in each household
lama (Tm.)—principal religious specialist for Buddhist religion
lambu (Tm.)—religious specialist in charge of clan lore and special rites for earth deities

Glossary

legar (Tm.)—a 12-year cycle in the Tibetan calendar

lho (Tm.)—animal symbol associated with a particular year in the calendrical cycle

lobi (Np.)—greedy

mani (Tm.)—stupa; a stone cairn erected over the remains of powerful lamas or wealthy men

mani'khilba (Tm.)—to do the death rituals

mle (Tm.)—cock; the vulgar word for penis

naramro manche (Np.)—bad man

panchayat (Np.)—the basic administrative unit in the Nepali national government

pathi (Np.)—a unit of volume equal to roughly eight pints

pengayen (Tm.)—adult male clothing; a blanket tied at the shoulders

pewa (Np.)—a woman's inheritance, usually given at marriage

pradhan panch (Np.)—the elected head of the panchayat

ropani (Np.)—a unit of land not used in Timling but equal to about .333 hal or .13 acres

sayog (Np.)—help

sayog laba (Tm.)—to do work for free

sayog ripa (Tm.)—to ask for help

syidi (Tm.)—a category of affliction based on envy

thangka (Tm.)—religious iconography in Tibetan Buddhism

tika (Np.)—an auspicious mark placed on the forehead

timnyu (Tm.)—monkey; Timling's name comes from timnyu + ling, place of monkeys

tormo (Tm.)—representations of deities made from a thick porridge

Yambu (Tm.)—Kathmandu

Bibliography

Alirol, Philippe
    1976   Animal husbandry in the Ganesh Himal region: an essay in ecological synthesis. *Contributions to Nepalese Studies* 3(1): 47–61.
    1977   Modelisation d'un complexe de'ecosystemes: exemple du Nepal central. *Himalaya: Ecologie-Ethnologie*. Paris: Centre National de la Recherche Scientifique, pp. 521–38.

Arnold, Fred, et al.
    1975   *The Value of Children: A Cross-National Study*. Honolulu: East-West Population Institute.

Banister, Judith and Shyam Thapa
    1981   The population dynamics of Nepal. Papers of the East-West Population Institute No. 78. Honolulu: East-West Population Institute.

Barlett, Peggy
    1980   Adaptive strategies in peasant agricultural production. *Annual Review of Anthropology* 9: 545–73.

Barth, Fredrik
    1967   On the study of social change. *American Anthropologist* 69: 661–69.

Becker, Gary S.
    1960   An economic analysis of fertility. *Demographic and Economic Change in Developed Countries*. Princeton: Princeton University Press.

Bender, D. R.
    1967   A refinement of the concept of household: families, co-residence, and domestic functions. *American Anthropologist* 69: 493–504.

Bennett, John W.
    1969   *Northern Plainsmen: Adaptive Strategy and Agrarian Life*. Chicago: Aldine.
    1976a   Anticipation, adaptation, and the concept of culture in anthropology. *Science* 192: 847–53.
    1976b   *The Ecological Transition: Cultural Anthropology and Human Adaptation*. New York: Pergamon.

Berelson, Bernard
    1976   Social science research on population: a review. *Population and Development Review* 2(2): 219–66.

Berger, John
    1979   *Pig Earth*. New York: Pantheon.

Berkner, Lutz
    1972   The stem family and the developmental cycle of the peasant household: an eighteenth century Austrian example. *The American Historical Review* 77(2): 398–418.

Bishop, Barry C.
    1978   The changing ecology of Karnali Zone, Western Nepal Himalaya: a case of stress. *Arctic and Alpine Research* 10(2): 531-43.

Blaikie, Piers
    1981   Nepal: the crisis of regional planning in a double dependent periphery. W. B. Stohr and D. R. Fraser Taylor (eds.), *Development from Above or Below?* New York: John Wiley and Sons.

Blaikie, Piers, John Cameron, and David Seddon
    1978   *Nepal in Crisis: Growth and Stagnation at the Periphery.* New Dehli: Vikas Publishing House.

Bongaarts, John
    1975   Why high birth rates are so low. *Population and Development Review* 1(2): 289-96.
    1976   Intermediate fertility variables and marital fertility rates. *Population Studies* 30(2): 227-41.
    1978   A framework for analyzing the proximate determinants of fertility. *Population and Development Review* 4(1): 105-32.

Boserup, Ester
    1965   *The Conditions of Agricultural Growth: The Economics of Agrarian Change under Population Pressure.* Chicago: Aldine.

Brush, Stephen B.
    1976a   Cultural adaptations to mountain ecosystems, introduction. *Human Ecology* 4(2): 125-33.
    1976b   Man's use of an Andean ecosystem. *Human Ecology* 4(2): 147-66.
    1977   *Mountain, Field and Family: The Economy and Human Ecology of an Andean Valley.* Philadelphia: University of Pennsylvania Press.

Buchanan, Francis H.
    1971   *An Account of the Kingdom of Nepal and of the Territories Annexed to this Dominion by the House of Gorkha.* New Delhi: Manjusri Publishing House. [Original 1819]

Bulatao, Rudolfo A.
    1979   Further evidence of the transition in the value of children. Papers of the East-West Population Institute No. 60-B. Honolulu: East-West Population Institute.

Cain, Mead
    1977   The economic activities of children in a village in Bangladesh. *Population and Development Review* 3(3): 201-27.
    1978   The household life cycle and economic mobility in a village in Bangladesh. *Population and Development Review* 4(3): 421-38.
    1981   Risk and insurance: perspectives on fertility and agrarian change in India and Bangladesh. *Population and Development Review* 7(3): 435-74.
    1982   Perspectives on family and fertility in developing countries. *Population Studies* 36(2): 159-75.

Caldwell, John C.
    1976   Toward a restatement of demographic transition theory. *Population and Development Review* 2(3): 321-66.
    1978   A theory of fertility: from high plateau to destabilization. *Population and Development Review* 4(4): 553-77.
    1981   The mechanisms of demographic change in historical perspective. *Population Studies* 35(1): 5-27.

Caldwell, John C., P.H. Reddy, and Pat Caldwell
    1982   The causes of demographic change in South India: a micro-approach. *Population and Development Review* 8(4): 689-727.
    n.d.   The micro approach in demographic investigation: toward a methodology. Unpublished manuscript. Australian National University.

Calkins, Peter H.
  1981   Silent slopes: environmental economics for the Nepalese hills. *Human Ecology* 9(4): 495-501.
Cancian, Frank
  1979   *The Innovator's Situation: Upper Middle-Class Conservatism in Agricultural Communities.* Stanford: Stanford University Press.
Caplan, Lionel
  1970   *Land and Social Change in East Nepal: A Study of Hindu-Tribal Relations.* Berkeley: University of California Press.
Carr-Saunders, Alexander M.
  1922   *The Population Problem: A Study in Human Evolution.* Oxford: Clarendon Press.
Carroll, Vern
  1975   The demography of communities. In Vern Carroll (ed.), *Pacific Atoll Populations.* Honolulu: University of Hawaii Press and East-West Population Intitute, pp. 3-19.
Chayanov, A. V.
  1966   *The Theory of Peasant Economy.* Homewood, Ill.: Richard D. Irwin for the American Economic Association.
Clark, Colin and Margaret Haswell
  1970   *The Economics of Subsistence Agriculture.* New York: St. Martin's Press.
Coale, Ansley and Paul Demeny
  1966   *Regional Model Life Tables and Stable Populations.* Princeton: Princeton University Press.
Cohen, Mark Nathan
  1977   *The Food Crisis in Prehistory: Overpopulation and the Origins of Agriculture.* New Haven: Yale University Press.
Dahal, Dilli Ram
  1983   Poverty or plenty: innovative responses to population pressure in an Eastern Nepalese hill community. Ph.D. dissertation in Anthropology. University of Hawaii, Manoa.
Davis, Kingsley and Judith Blake
  1956   Social structure and fertility: an analytic framework. *Economic Development and Cultural Change* 4(3): 211-35.
Dobremez, J. F. and C. Jest
  1976   *Manaslu: Hommes et milieux des vallées du Nepal central.* Paris: Centre National de la Recherche Scientifique.
Dunnell, Robert C.
  1980   Evolutionary theory and archaeology. *Advances in Archaeological Method and Theory* 3: 35-99. New York: Academic Press.
Easterlin, Richard A., George Alter and Gretchen A. Condran
  1978   Farms and farm families in old and new areas: the northern states in 1860. In Tamara K. Hareven and Maris A. Vinovskis (eds.), *Family and Population in Nineteenth-Century America.* Princeton: Princeton University Press, pp. 22-84.
Eckholm, Eric P.
  1976   *Losing Ground: Environmental Stress and World Food Prospects.* New York: Norton.
Elder, Glen H., Jr.
  1981   History and the family: the discovery of complexity. *Journal of Marriage and the Family* 43(3): 489-519.
Evans-Pritchard, E.
  1940   *The Nuer: A Description of the Modes of Livelihood and Political Institutions of a Nilotic People.* London: Oxford University Press.
Faith, Rosamond
  1980   Review of Alan Macfarlane, *The Origins of English Individualism: The Family, Private Property and Social Transition. Journal of Peasant Studies* 7(3): 384-89.

Fawcett, James T. (ed.)
  1972 *The Satisfactions and Costs of Children: Theories, Concepts, Methods.* Honolulu: East-West Population Institute, pp. 20–63.

Feeney, Griffith
  1975 Demographic concepts and techniques for the study of small populations. In Vern Carroll (ed.), *Pacific Atoll Populations.* Honolulu: University of Hawaii Press and East-West Population Institute, pp. 20–63.

Fegan, Brian
  1978 Establishment fund, population increase and changing class structures in Central Luzon. *Canberra Anthropology* 1(3): 24–43.
  1979 Folk-capitalism: economic strategies of peasants in a Philippines wet-rice village. Ph.D. dissertation in Anthropology. Yale University.

Fix, Alan G.
  1977 The demography of the Semai Senoi. Anthropological Papers of the Museum of Anthropology, University of Michigan, No. 62.

Flannery, Kent V.
  1972 The cultural evolution of civilizations. *Annual Review of Ecology and Systematics* 3: 399–425.

Ford, Clellan S.
  1945 *A Comparative Study of Human Reproduction.* New Haven: Yale University Press.

Fortes, Meyer
  1958 Introduction. In Jack Goody (ed.), *The Developmental Cycle in Domestic Groups.* Cambridge: Cambridge University Press, pp. 1–14.

Foster, Brian L.
  1975 Continuity and change in rural Thai family structure. *Journal of Anthropological Research* 31(1): 34–50.

Foster, George M.
  1967 *Tzintzuntzan: Mexican Peasants in a Changing World.* Boston: Little, Brown.
  1978 Domestic developmental cycles as a link between population processes and other social processes. *Journal of Anthropological Research* 34(3): 415–41.

Freedman, Ronald
  1975 *The Sociology of Human Fertility: An Annotated Bibliography.* New York: Irvington Publishers.
  1979 Theories of fertility decline: a reappraisal. *Social Forces* 58(1): 1–17.

Friedman, Jonathan
  1974 Marxism, structuralism, and vulgar materialism. *Man, N.S.*, 9(3): 444–69.

Fürer-Haimendorf, Cristoph von
  1956 Ethnographic notes on the Tamangs of Nepal. *Eastern Anthropologist* 9(3–4): 166–77.
  1964 *The Sherpas of Nepal: Buddhist Highlanders.* Berkeley: University of California Press.

Geertz, Clifford
  1961 Studies in peasant life: community and society. *Biennial Review of Anthropology*, pp. 1–41.
  1963 *Agricultural Involution: The Process of Ecological Change in Indonesia.* Berkeley: University of California Press.

Godelier, Maurice
  1977 *Perspectives in Marxist Anthropology.* Cambridge Studies in Social Anthropology No. 18. Cambridge: Cambridge University Press.

Goldman, Noreen, Ansley J. Coale, and M. Weinstein
  1979 The quality of data in the Nepal Fertility Survey. Scientific Report No. 6. London: World Fertility Survey.

Goldstein, Melvyn C.
  1976   Fraternal polyandry and fertility in a high Himalayan valley in northwest Nepal. *Human Ecology* 4(2): 223–33.
  1977   Culture, population, ecology and development: a view from NW Nepal. In *Himalaya: Ecologie-Ethnologie.* Paris: Centre National de la Recherche Scientifique, pp. 481–89.
Goldstein, Melvyn C., and Donald Messerschmidt
  1980   The significance of latitudinality in Himalayan mountain ecosystems. *Human Ecology* 8(2): 117–34.
Goody, Jack
  1972   The evolution of the family. In Peter Laslett and R. Wall (eds.), *Household and Family in Past Time.* Cambridge: Cambridge University Press, pp. 103–24.
———. (ed.)
  1958   *The Developmental Cycle in Domestic Groups.* Cambridge: Cambridge University Press
Gorer, Geoffrey
  1967   *Himalayan Village: An Account of the Lepchas of Sikkim.* London: Thomas Nelson and Sons, Ltd. [Original 1938]
Gorz, Andre
  1980   *Ecology as Politics.* Boston: South End Press.
Greenfield, Sidney M. and Arnold Strickon
  1981   A new paradigm for the study of entrepreneurship and social change. *Economic Development and Cultural Change* 29(3): 467–99.
Greenwood, Davydd J.
  1974   Political economy and adaptive processes: a framework for the study of peasant states. *Peasant Studies* 3(3): 1–10.
Gudeman, Stephen
  1978   *The Demise of a Rural Economy: From Subsistence to Capitalism in a Latin American Village.* London: Routledge and Kegan Paul.
Guillet, David
  1981   Land tenure, ecological zone, and agricultural regime in the Central Andes. *American Ethnologist* 8(1): 139–56.
  1983   Toward a cultural ecology of mountains: the Central Andes and the Himalayas compared. *Current Anthropology* 24(5): 561–74.
Hagen, Toni
  1961   *Nepal: The Kingdom in the Himalayas.* Berne: Kummerly and Frey.
Hajnal, John
  1982   Two kinds of preindustrial household formation system. *Population and Development Review* 8(3): 449–94.
Halperin, Rhoda
  1977   The substantive economy in peasant societies. In Rhoda Halperin and James Dow (eds.), *Peasant Livelihood.* New York: St. Martin's Press, pp. 1–16.
Hareven, Tamara
  1974   The family process: the historical study of the family cycle. *Journal of Social History* 7(3): 322–29.
  1977   Family time and historical time. *Daedulus* 106(2): 57–70.
  1978   Cycles, courses and cohorts: reflections on theoretical and methodological approaches for the study of family development. *Journal of Social History* 12(1): 97–109.
Harris, Marvin
  1968   *The Rise of Anthropological Theory.* New York: Crowell.
  1979   *Cultural Materialism.* New York: Random House.

Harrison, M.
- 1975 Chayanov and the economics of the Russian peasantry. *Journal of Peasant Studies* 2(4): 389–417.

Henderson, Eric
- 1978 Social stratification, social change, and the community. MS. Department of Anthropology, University of Arizona. [Cited in McGuire and Netting 1982]

Hitchcock, John T.
- 1961 A Nepalese hill village and Indian employment. *Asian Survey* 1(9): 15–20.
- 1963 Some effects of recent change in rural Nepal. *Human Organization* 22(1): 75–82.
- 1966 *The Magars of Banyan Hill.* New York: Holt, Rinehart, and Winston.
- 1973 Ecologically related differences between communities in West Central Nepal. Paper presented at American Anthropological Association Meetings, New Orleans.
- 1977 Buying time: population, trees, Liebig's "law," and two Himalayan adaptive strategies. In *Himalaya: Ecologie-Ethnologie.* Paris: Centre National de la Recherche Scientifique, pp. 443–51.
- 1980 *A Mountain Village in Nepal.* New York: Holt, Rinehart, and Winston.

Hodgson, Brian
- 1874 *Essays on the Languages, Literature, and Religion of Nepal and Tibet together with further Papers on the Geography, Ethnology, and Commerce of those Countries.* London: Trubner and Company.

Höfer, András
- 1969 Preliminary report on a field research in a western Tamang group, Nepal. *Bulletin of the International Committee on Urgent Anthropological and Ethnological Research* 11: 17–31.
- 1978 A new rural elite in Central Nepal. In James Fisher (ed.), *Himalayan Anthropology.* The Hague: Mouton, pp. 179–86.
- 1981 *Tamang Ritual Texts I: Preliminary Studies in the Folk Religion of an Ethnic Minority in Nepal.* Wiesbaden: Franz Steiner Verlag.

Hoffpauir, Robert
- 1978 Subsistence strategy and its ecological consequences in the Nepal Himalaya. *Anthropos* 73(1–2): 215–52.

Holmberg, David
- 1983 Shamanic soundings: femaleness in the Tamang ritual structure. *Signs: Journal of Women in Culture and Society* 9(1): 40–58.
- 1984 Ritual paradoxes in Nepal: comparative perspectives on Tamang religion. *Journal of Asian Studies* 63(4): 697–722.

Howell, Nancy
- 1974 The feasibility of demographic studies in "anthropological" populations. In M. Crawford and R. Workman (eds.), *Method and Theory in Anthropological Genetics.* Albuquerque: University of New Mexico Press, pp. 249–62.
- 1976a Toward a uniformitarian theory of human paleodemography. In R. H. Ward and K. M. Weiss (eds.), *The Demographic Evolution of Human Populations.* New York: Academic Press, pp. 25–40.
- 1976b Notes on collection and analysis of demographic field data. In John F. Marshall and Steven Polgar (eds.), *Culture, Natality and Family Planning.* Chapel Hill: Carolina Population Center, pp. 221–40.
- 1979 *Demography of the Dobe !Kung.* New York: Academic Press.

Hull, Terence H.
- 1975 Each child brings its own fortune: an inquiry into the value of children in a Javanese village. Ph.D. dissertation, Australian National University.

Hull, Valerie
 1975 Fertility, socioeconomic status, and the position of women in a Javenese village. Ph.D. dissertation, Australian National University.
 1980 Intermediate variables in the explanation of differential fertility: results of a village study in rural Java. *Human Ecology* 8(3): 213-43.
Hunt, Diana
 1979 Chayanov's model of peasant household resource allocation. *Journal of Peasant Studies* 6(3): 247-85.
Hyde, Lewis
 1983 *The Gift: Imagination and the Erotic Life of Property*. New York: Vintage Books.
Jackson, Darrell
 1977 Paradigms and perspectives: a cross-cultural approach to population growth and rural poverty. In T. Scarlett Epstein and Darrell Jackson (eds.), *The Feasibility of Fertility Planning: Micro-Perspectives*. New York: Pergamon, pp. 3-20.
Jochim, Michael A.
 1981 *Strategies for Survival: Cultural Behavior in an Ecological Context*. New York: Academic Press.
Johnson, Allen
 1982 Reductionism in cultural ecology: the Amazon case. *Current Anthropology* 23(4): 413-28.
Jones, Rex and Shirley Jones
 1976 *The Himalayan Woman: A Study of Limbu Women in Marriage and Divorce*. Palo Alto: Mayfield Publishing Company.
Kantner, John F.
 1982 Review of David S. Kleinman, *Human Adaptation and Population Growth: A Non-Malthusian Perspective*. *Population and Development Review* 8(2): 398-400.
Keesing, Roger M.
 1974 Theories of culture. *Annual Review of Anthropology* 3: 73-97.
 1975 *Kin Groups and Social Structure*. New York: Holt, Rinehart, and Winston.
Kirch, Patrick V.
 1980 The archaeological study of adaptation: theoretical and methodological issues. M. B. Schiffer (ed.), *Advances in Archaeological Method and Theory*. New York: Academic Press, Vol. 3: 101-56.
Kleinman, David S.
 1980 *Human Adaptation and Population Growth: A Non-Malthusian Perspective*. Montclair, New Jersey: Allanheld, Osmun and Co. and New York: Universe Books.
Knodel, John and Susan De Vos
 1980 Preferences for the sex of offspring in eighteenth and nineteenth century Germany: an examination of evidence from village genealogies. *Journal of Family History* 5(2): 145-66.
Kroeber, Alfred L.
 1939 *Cultural and Natural Areas of Native North America*. Berkeley: University of California Press.
Kuhn, Thomas S.
 1962 *The Structure of Scientific Revolutions*. Chicago: University of Chicago Press.
Kunstadter, Peter
 1972 Demography, ecology, social structure and settlement patterns. In G. A. Harrison and A. J. Boyce (eds.), *The Structure of Human Populations*. London: Oxford University Press, pp. 313-51.
Lama, Santibir
 1981 *Tamba Kaiten Hvai Rimtim*. Kathmandu: Ratna Pustak Bhandar.

216   Bibliography

Landan, Perceval
    1976   *Nepal.* Kathmandu: Ratna Pustak Bhandar. [Original 1928]

Lappé, Frances M., Joseph Collins and David Kinley
    1980   *Aid as Obstacle.* San Francisco: Institute for Food and Development Policy.

Laslett, Peter
    1972   Introduction: the history of the family. In Laslett and Wall, *Household and Family,* pp. 1-89.

Laslett, Peter and R. Wall (eds.)
    1972   *Household and Family in Past Time.* Cambridge: Cambridge University Press.

Lauro, Don
    1979   The demography of a Thai village: methodological considerations and substantive conclusions from field study in a Central Plains community. Ph.D. dissertation, Australian National University.

Lee, Richard B.
    1972   Population growth and the beginnings of sedentary life among the !Kung Bushmen. In Spooner (ed.), *Population Growth,* pp. 329-42.

Leone, Mark P.
    1972   Issues in anthropological archaeology. In Mark Leone (ed.), *Contemporary Archaeology: A Guide to Theory and Contributions.* Carbondale: Southern Illinois University Press, pp. 14-27.

Leridon, Henri
    1977   *Human Fertility: The Basic Components.* Chicago: University of Chicago Press.

Lingner, Joan W.
    1974   *A Handbook for Populations Analysts, Vols. 1-2.* Chapel Hill: The Carolina Population Center.

Lorimer, Frank
    1954   *Culture and Human Fertility.* Paris: UNESCO.

Lotka, Alfred J.
    1907   Relation between birth rates and death rates. *Science* 26: 21-22.

Macdonald, Alexander W.
    1975   The Tamang as seen by one of themselves. In Alexander Macdonald (ed.), *Essays on the Ethnology of Nepal and South Asia.* Kathmandu: Ratna Pustak Bhandar, pp. 129-67.

Macfarlane, Alan
    1968   Population crisis: anthropology's failure. *New Society* 10 October, 1968.
    1976   *Resources and Population: A Study of the Gurungs of Nepal.* Cambridge: Cambridge University Press.
    1978a   Modes of reproduction. *Journal of Development Studies* 14(4): 100-128.
    1978b   Demographic anthropology. *Reviews in Anthropology* 5(1): 45-51.
    1979   *The Origins of English Individualism: The Family, Property and Social Transition.* New York: Cambridge University Press.

McGuire, Randall and Robert McC. Netting
    1982   Leveling peasants? The maintenance of equality in a Swiss Alpine community. *American Ethnologist* 9(2): 269-90.

McNicoll, Geoffrey
    1975   Community-level population policy: an exploration. *Population and Development Review* 1(1): 1-21.
    1978   On fertility policy research. *Population and Development Review* 4(4): 681-93.
    1980   Institutional determinants of fertility change. *Population and Development Review* 6(3): 441-62.

Mamdani, Mahmood
   1972   *The Myth of Population Control: Family, Caste, and Class in an Indian Village.* New York: Monthly Review Press.

Mani, M. S.
   1978   *Ecology and Phytogeography of High Altitude Plants of the Northwest Himalaya.* New Dehli: Oxford and IBH Publishing Co.

March, Kathryn
   1983   Weaving, writing, and gender: metaphors of continuity and exchange. *Man (N. S.)* 18(4): 729-44.

Martin, Paul S.
   1972   The revolution in archaeology. In Mark Leone (ed.), *Contemporary Archaeology: A Guide to Theory and Contributions.* Carbondale: Southern Illinois University Press, pp. 5-13.

Mayr, Ernst
   1959   Darwin and evolutionary theory in biology. Betty Meggers (ed.), *Evolution and Anthropology: A Centennial Appraisal.* Washington, D.C.: The Anthropological Association of Washington, pp. 1-10.
   1970   *Populations, Species, and Evolution.* Cambridge: Harvard University Press.

Mazaudon, Martine
   1973   *Phonologie Tamang: Etude Phonologique du Dialecte Tamang du Risiangku.* Paris: Société D'Etudes Linguistiques et Anthropologiques de France.

Meillassoux, Claude
   1981   *Maidens, Meal, and Money: Capitalism and the Domestic Community.* Cambridge: Cambridge University Press.

Messerschmidt, Donald A.
   1974   Gurung shepherds of Lamjung Himal. *Objets et Mondes* 14(4): 307-16.
   1976a   Ecological change and adaptation among the Gurungs of the Nepal Himalaya. *Human Ecology* 4(2): 167-85.
   1976b   *The Gurungs of Nepal: Conflict and Change in a Village Society.* Warminster: Aris and Phillips, Ltd.

Miller, Barbara D.
   1981   *The Endangered Sex: Neglect of Female Children in Rural North India.* Ithaca: Cornell University Press.

Mintz, Sidney
   1973   A note on the definition of peasantries. *Journal of Peasant Studies* 1(1): 91-106.

Molnar, Augusta
   1978   Marital patterns and women's economic independence: a study of Kham Magar women. Kirtipur, Nepal: *Contributions to Nepalese Studies* 6(1): 15-29.
   1982   Women and politics: case of the Kham Magar of western Nepal. *American Ethnologist* 9(3): 485-502.

Mueller, Eva
   1976   The economic value of children in peasant agriculture. In Ronald Ridker (ed.), *Population and Development: The Search for Selective Interventions.* Baltimore: Johns Hopkins University Press, pp. 98-153.

Murra, John V.
   1972   El 'control vertical' de un maximo de pisos ecologicos en economia de las sociedades Andinas. In Inigo Ortiz de Zuniga (ed.), *Visita de la Provincia de Leon de Huanuco.* Huanuco, Peru: Universidad Nacional Hermilio Valdizan, pp. 429-76.

Nag, Moni
   1962   *Factors Affecting Human Fertility: A Cross-Cultural Study.* New Haven: Yale University Press.

218 Bibliography

    1978   Economic values and costs of children in relation to human fertility. Center for Policy Studies Working Paper No. 36. New York: The Population Council.

Nag, Moni, Benjamin White, and R. Creighton Peet
    1978   An anthropological approach to the study of the economic value of children in Java and Nepal. *Current Anthropology* 19(2): 293–306.

Nardi, Bonnie Anna
    1981   Models of explanation in anthropological population theory: biological determinism vs. self-regulation in studies of population growth in Third World countries. *American Anthropologist* 83(1): 28–56.

Neel, James V., and Kenneth M. Weiss
    1975   The genetic structure of a tribal population: the Yanomama Indians. *American Journal of Physical Anthropology* 42(1): 25–51.

Nepal Fertility Survey
    1976   *Nepal Fertility Survey 1976.* Kathmandu: Nepal Ministry of Health and Nepal Family Planning and Maternal Child Health Project.

Netting, Robert McC.
    1972   Of men and meadows: strategies of alpine land use. *Anthropological Quarterly* 45(3): 132–44.
    1977   *Cultural Ecology.* Menlo Park, CA: Cummings Publishing Co.
    1981   *Balancing on an Alp: Ecological Change and Continuity in a Swiss Mountain Community.* Cambridge: Cambridge University Press.

Netting, Robert McC. and Walter S. Elias
    1980   Balancing on an Alp: population stability and change in a Swiss peasant village. In Priscilla C. Reining and Barbara Lenkerd (eds.), *Village Viability in Contemporary Society.* American Association for the Advancement of Science Selected Symposia Series No. 34.

New Internationalist
    1979   Population: Fiction and Fact. September, 1979, 79: 5–7.

Nisbet, Robert A.
    1969   *Social Change and History: Aspects of the Western Theory of Development.* New York: Oxford University Press.

Norboo, Samten
    1981   Migration of the Tamang tribe from Tibet. *The Tibet Journal* 6(1): 39–42.

Northey, William B.
    1937   *The Land of the Gurkhas: Or, the Himalayan Kingdom of Nepal.* Cambridge: W. Heffer.

Odell, Mary E.
    1982   The domestic context of production and reproduction in a Guatemalan community. *Human Ecology* 10(1): 47–69.

Orlove, Benjamin
    1977   Against a definition of peasantries: agrarian production in Andean Peru. In Rhoda Halperin and James Dow (eds.), *Peasant Livelihood.* New York: St. Martin's Press, pp. 22–35.
    1980   Ecological anthropology. *Annual Review of Anthropology* 9: 235–73.

Orlove, Benjamin and David Guillet
    1985   Theoretical and methodological considerations on the study of mountain peoples: Reflections on the idea of subsistence type and the role of history in human ecology. *Mountain Research and Development* 5(1): 3–18.

Ortiz, Sutti
    1973   *Uncertainties in Peasant Farming: A Columbian Case.* New York: Humanities Press.

Pant, S. D.
    1935   *The Social Economy of the Himalayas.* London: Allen and Unwin.

Pawson, I. G. and Corneille Jest
  1978   The high altitude areas of the world and their cultures. In Paul T. Baker (ed.), *The Biology of High Altitude Peoples*. London: Cambridge University Press, pp. 17-45.
Peattie, Roderick
  1936   *Mountain Geography: A Critique and Field Study*. Cambridge: Harvard University Press.
Peters, Larry G.
  1978   Psychotherapy in Tamang shamanism. *Ethos: Journal of the Society for Psychological Anthropology* 6(2): 63-91.
  1981   *Ecstasy and Healing in Nepal: An Ethnopsychiatric Study of Tamang Shamanism*. Malibu, CA: Undena Publications.
  1982   Trance, initiation, and psycho-therapy in Tamang shamanism. *American Ethnologist* 9(1): 21-46.
Pignede, Bernard
  1966   *Les Gurungs: Une Population himalayenne du Nepal*. Paris: Mouton and Co.
Poffenberger, Mark
  1980   *Patterns of Change in the Nepal Himalaya*. Delhi: Macmillan Company of India, Ltd.
Polgar, Steven
  1972   Population history and population policies from an anthropological perspective. *Current Anthropology* 13(2): 203-11.
  1975b   Population, evolution and theoretical paradigms. In Steven Polgar (ed.), pp. 1-25.
  _____. (ed.)
  1975a   *Population, Ecology, and Social Evolution*. The Hague: Mouton.
Population Council
  1978   *The Population Council: A Chronicle of the First Twenty-five Years, 1952-1977*. New York: The Population Council.
  1981   Research on the determinants of fertility: a note on priorities. *Population and Development Review* 7(2): 311-24.
Price, Larry W.
  1981   *Mountains and Man: A Study of Process and Environment*. Berkeley: University of California Press.
Rappaport, Roy A.
  1968   *Pigs for the Ancestors: Ritual in the Ecology of a New Guinea People*. New Haven: Yale University Press.
Regmi, M. C.
  1963-65   *Land Tenure and Taxation in Nepal, Vols. 1-3*. Berkeley: University of California Press.
Rhoades, Robert E. and Stephen I. Thompson
  1975   Adaptive strategies in alpine environments: beyond ecological particularism. *American Ethnologist* 2(2): 535-51.
Richerson, Peter J.
  1977   Ecology and human ecology: a comparison of theories in the biological and social sciences. *American Ethnologist* 4(1): 1-26.
Ross, Eric B.
  1982   Comment on Allen Johnson, Reductionism in cultural ecology. *Current Anthropology* 23(4): 423.
Ross, James L.
  1981   Hindu and Tibetan reproduction and fertility in Northwestern Nepal: a study of population, ecology and economics. Ph. D. dissertation, Department of Anthropology, Case Western Reserve University.
Roth, Eric A.
  1981   Sedentism and changing fertility patterns in a Northern Athapascan isolate. *Journal of Human Evolution* 10: 413-25.

Sacherer, J.
    1977   The Sherpas of Rolwaling: a hundred years of economic change. In *Himalaya: Ecologie-Ethnologie*. Paris: Centre National de la Recherche Scientifique, pp. 289-93.
Sahlins, Marshall
    1961   The segmentary lineage: an organization of predatory expansion. *American Anthropologist* 63(3): 322-45.
    1972   *Stone Age Economics*. Chicago: Aldine Publishing Company.
Salisbury, Richard F.
    1975   Non-equilibrium models in New Guinea ecology: possibilities of cultural extrapolation. *Anthropologica* 17(2): 127-48.
Sanders, William T. and Barbara Price
    1968   *Mesoamerica: The Evolution of a Civilization*. New York: Random House.
Sanderson, Warren C.
    1976   On two schools of the economics of fertility. *Population and Development Review* 2(3-4): 469-77.
Scott, James C.
    1976   *The Moral Economy of the Peasant*. New Haven: Yale University Press.
Scrimshaw, Susan
    1978   Infant mortality and behavior in the regulation of family size. *Population and Development Review* 4(3): 383-403.
Seddon, David, Piers Blaikie and John Cameron (eds.)
    1979   *Peasants and Workers in Nepal*. New Dehli: Vikas Publishing Co.
Shakabpa, Tsepon W. D.
    1967   *Tibet: A Political History*. New Haven: Yale University Press.
Shanin, Teodor
    1973   Peasantry: delineation of a sociological concept and a field of study. *Peasant Studies* 2(1): 1-8.
Shryock, Henry S. and Jacob S. Siegel
    1976   *The Methods and Materials of Demography*. New York: Academic Press.
Silverman, Sydel
    1979   The peasant concept in anthropology. *Journal of Peasant Studies* 7(1): 49-69.
Simmons, George B., et al.
    1982   Post neo-natal mortality in rural India: implications of an economic model. *Demography* 19(3): 371-89.
Smith, Peter C.
    1983   Societal change, family process, and the individual: a selective review pertinent to research on Asia. MS. Presented at the Conference on Family Research in Asia, July 25-29, East-West Population Institute, Honolulu, Hawaii.
Smith, Peter C. and Dee Chapon
    1978   Instructions for completing and coding the life history matrix. Asian Marriage Survey Note 2. East-West Population Institute.
Spooner, Brian (ed.)
    1972   *Population Growth: Anthropological Implications*. Cambridge: MIT Press.
Spooner, Brian and Robert McC. Netting
    1972   Boserup in the context of anthropology. *Peasant Studies Newsletter* 1(2): 54-59.
Steward, Julian H.
    1938   *Basin-Plateau Aboriginal Sociopolitical Groups*. Smithsonian Institution, Bureau of American Ethnology Bulletin No. 120.
    1955   *Theory of Culture Change*. Urbana: University of Illinois Press.
Stocking, George W.
    1968   *Race, Culture and Evolution*. New York: Free Press.

Taylor, Doreen, F. Everitt and Karna Bahadur Tamang
  1972   *A Vocabulary of the Tamang Language*. Kirtipur, Nepal: Summer Institute of Linguistics.
Thadani, Veena N.
  1978   The logic of sentiment: the family and social change. *Population and Development Review* 4(3): 457–99.
Thadani, Veena N.
  1980   Property and progeny: an exploration of intergenerational relations. Center for Policy Studies Working Paper No. 62. New York: The Population Council.
Thapa, Shyam and Robert D. Retherford
  1982   Infant mortality estimates based on the 1976 Nepal Fertility Survey. *Population Studies* 36(1): 61–80.
Thomas, R. Brooke
  1979   Effects of change on high mountain adaptive patterns. In Patrick Webber (ed.), *High Altitude Geoecology*. AAAS Selected Symposia Series No. 12, pp. 139–88.
Thouret, J. C.
  1977   Etagement des rythmes thermiques et leurs deformations saisonnieres dans les heuts pays sous-himalayens (Nepal, Centre-Ouest). In *Himalaya: Ecologie-Ethnologie*. Paris: Centre National de la Recherche Scientifique, pp. 59–68.
Toffin, Gerard
  1976a   The people of the upper Ankhu Khola valley. *Contributions to Nepalese Studies* (Kirtipur, Nepal) 3(1): 34–46.
  1976b   The phenomenon of migration in a Himalayan valley in central Nepal. In *Mountain Environment and Development*. Kathmandu: Swiss Association for Technical Assistance in Nepal.
United Nations
  1955   *Age and Sex Patterns of Mortality; Model Life Tables for Underdeveloped Countries, Series A*. Population Studies No. 35.
Vayda, Andrew P. and Bonnie J. McCay
  1975   New directions in ecology and ecological anthropology. *Annual Review of Anthropology* 4: 293–306.
Ware, Helen
  1978   The economic value of children in Asia and Africa: comparative perspectives. Papers of the East-West Population Institute No. 50. Honolulu: East-West Population Institute.
Weinberg, Daniela
  1972   Cutting the pie in the Swiss Alps. *Anthropological Quarterly* 45(3): 125–31.
Weiss, Kenneth
  1972   A general measure of human population growth regulation. *American Journal of Physical Anthropology* 37: 337–44.
  1973   *Demographic Models for Anthropology*. Memoirs of the Society for American Archaeology No. 27.
  1975   The application of demographic models to anthropological data. *Human Ecology* 3(2): 87–103.
  1976   Demographic theory and anthropological inference. *Annual Review of Anthropology* 5: 351–81.
Weiss, Kenneth and Peter E. Smouse
  1976   The demographic stability of small populations. In R. H. Ward and K. M. Weiss (eds.), *The Demographic Evolution of Human Populations*. New York: Academic Press, pp. 59–73.
White, Benjamin N. F.
  1976   Production and reproduction in a Javanese village. Ph.D. dissertation in Anthropology. Columbia University.

1980 Rural household studies in anthropological perspective. In Hans P. Binswanger (ed.), *Rural Household Studies in Asia.* Singapore: Singapore University Press, pp. 3-25.

White, Leslie A.
1949 *The Science of Culture: A Study of Man and Civilization.* New York: Grove Press.

Wiegandt, Ellen
1977 Inheritance and demography in the Swiss Alps. *Ethnohistory* 24(2): 133-47.

Wilk, Richard R. and Robert McC. Netting
1984 Households: changing forms and functions. In R. Netting, R. Wilk, and E. Arnould (eds.), *Households: Comparative and Historical Studies of the Domestic Group.* Berkeley: University of California Press, pp. 1-28.

Wood, James W., Patricia L. Johnson, and Kenneth Campbell
1985 Demographic and endocrinological aspects of low natural fertility in Highland New Guinea. *Journal of Biosocial Science* 7(1): 57-79.

World Bank
1979 *Nepal: Development Performance and Prospects.* Washington, D. C.: The World Bank.

Worth, Robert M. and Narayan K. Shah
1969 *Nepal Health Survey, 1965-1966.* Honolulu: University of Hawaii Press.

Wright, Daniel
1972 *History of Nepal.* Kathmandu: Nepal Antiquated Book Publishers. [Original 1877]

Wrigley, Edward Anthony
1969 *Population and History.* New York: McGraw Hill.

Yanagisako, Sylvia Junko
1979 Family and household: the analysis of domestic groups. *Annual Review of Anthropology* 8: 161-205.

Yon, Bernard
1976 Le Nepal central: contribution a l'étude ecologiques de l'étage alpin. Ph.D. dissertation, Université Scientifique et Medicale de Grenoble.

Index

Adaptation: and population, 19–20, 194–95; and social change, 187–88; and variation, 18; as a perspective, 20; economic, 188–91; spatial, 188–91
Adaptive process, 18–19; in Timling, 192–95
Adaptive strategies, 18–19
Administration: in Timling area, 44–48
Adultery, 144–45
Age at marriage, 137–39
Age-sex pyramid, 48–51
Age-specific fertility: all women, 97; regiona comparisons for Nepal, 89; women of completed fertility, 89
Agriculture: agricultural cycle, 74, 78–79; intensification in, 194; labor requirements, 80; reducing risk in, 80; slash and burn, 193–94. *See also* Land; Work: agricultural
Agro-pastoral economy, 61–62, 74–77
Alirol, Philippe, 62–63, 65
Alps, 159, 162
Andes. *See* Brush, Stephen B.; Uchucmarca
Angsa, 139. *See also* Inheritance; Property transmission
Ankhu Khola, 32
Annual cycle and long-term process, 191–92
Anthropological demography. *See* Demographic anthropology
Anthropology: holism in, 9; pre-paradigmatic status of, 15
Arable land, 67–68: available, 69; crop acreage, 68–69; measurement of, 68. *See also* Land
Arranged marriage and wealth, 137–39

Barlett, Peggy, 18, 20, 170
Barley, 79
Barth, Fredrik, 18
Bastards (*pro*), 144
Bennett, John W.: model of cultural ecology, 191, 196; on adaptation and process, 18, 188

Berkner, Lutz, 23–24
Bhabil Khola, 32, 37
Birth: becoming human after, 133; rituals of, 132–33. *See also* Childbirth
Blake, Judith, 16, 22
Bompo, 31, 44
Bongaarts, John, 193; measures in, 98–102; modification of Davis and Blake framework, 22
Borang, 44, 46
Boserup, Ester, 17, 194
Breastfeeding, 109
Brush, Stephen B., 20–21, 158; on adaptation, 18; on household labor, 170; on levels of analysis, 62
Buchanan, Francis, 29, 32

Cain, Mead, 13; 197
Caldwell, John C., 197; and wealth flows, 198–99; critique of demographic transition theory, 11–12; reaction to, 12–14; theory and method of, 11–12, 53
Caplan, Lionel, 68, 172
Carroll, Vern, 85
Cash, 168; and social change, 179–81
Census, 48–50, 56
Chayanov, A.V., 170–73, 183–84
Chewar, 134
Childbirth: and household fortunes, 184; mean age at, 97; social conceptions of, 132–33
Childcare, 133
Childhood, 133
Children: and networks, 190–91; desire for, 182–83; economic contributions and costs of, 134, 198–99
Clan distribution, 41
Climate, 63
Clothing, 71, 78
Cohabitation effects on fertility, 103
Consumer/worker ratio, 183–84

224   Index

Consumption: household developmental cycle and, 154–56
Cooking: labor requirements of, 77–78
Cooperative labor, 165–68
Crop rotation, 78–80. *See also* Agriculture
Cultural ecology: adaptive context, 17–20; analytic program of, 20; and process, 17–20, 197; and social change, 191; equilibrium models in, 17–18. *See also* Adaptation; Bennett, John W.: model of cultural ecology; Brush, Stephen B.; Orlove, Benjamin

Damrong (clan), 41, 177–82
Data collection: census, 56; economic survey, 57–58; field conditions, 55–56; formal survey, 55–59; informal methods, 59; language used, 55; life history matrix, 58–59; marriage and fertility, 56–57; mortality, 57
Data quality: economic, 58; event timing, 53–55; fertility, 93–95; inheritance, 141–43; public interviews and, 57
Davis, Kingsley, 16, 22
Death: causes of, 114–15; significance of, 113, 146–47
Decision-making, 191, 192
Deforestation, 67
Demographic anthropology: and cultural ecology, 16–17; and social change, 196–97; early trends in, 15–16; examples of, 8–9; theoretical sophistication in, 16, 195–96. *See also* Data collection
Demographic transition theory, 9–11
Dhingaba: age structure, 50; mortality, 114
Distribution of wealth, 158–65
Diversification: ecological and economic, 184, 188–89
Divorce: consequences of, 136
Domestic economy: and expansion, 194–96; and household developmental cycle, 169–73
Domestic mode of production, 131–32, 165
Doubling time, 193

Easterlin, Richard, 10
Economic change, 194
Economic survey, 57–58
Economy and kinship, 190–91
Egalitarianism, 158, 197–98
Elevation: Ankhu Khola Valley 32; Timling 32. *See also* Vertical zones
           ated to, 159
Ethos of abundance, 198
Event timing, 53–55
Exchange, 168–69

Expectation of life at birth: female, 127; male, 128

Family composition, 169–70. *See also* Household developmental cycle
Family size and wealth, 170–72
Fecund period, 90
Feeney, Griffith, 85
Fertility: all women, 97–101; cohort, 93–96; period rates, 93–96; potential, 109, 193; proximate determinants of, 21–22, 97–110; psychological supports for, 14–15; sources of data, 85
Fertility analysis: issues in, 85–86
Field methods. *See* Data collection: field methods
First birth: average age at, 89–90
Fix, Alan, 86
Forest resources, 64–67
Fortes, Meyer, 23, 132
Foster, Brian, 23, 24, 147
Fuel consumption, 66–67
Fürer-Haimendorf, Christoph von, 31, 37

Ganesh Himal, 32
Ghale, 41–42; lineage expansion among, 174–77, 185–86
Ghewa, 146
Gini index, 159–65
Goldman, Noreen, 93
Goldstein, Melvyn C., 21
Gompo, 38
Gomtsa (clan), 41
Gorer, Geoffrey, 56, 172
Greenfield, Sidney, 18
Greenwood, Davydd, 22
Grel, 146
Guillet, David, 21
Gurkha service, 83, 182
Gurung: age at marriage among, 208; age structure, 50–51; household, 129; stratification, 199–200. *See also* Macfarlane, Alan: on Gurung household; Messerschmidt, Donald A.; Thak

Hajnal, John, 199
Halperin, Rhoda, 22
Hareven, Tamara, 23
Harvests, timing of, 76
Health conditions, 113–14
Hearth, 131
Herbs: medicinal, 64
Herding: cooperative, 80–82
High fertility: as rational behavior, 11; institutional supports for, 13–14. *See also* Fertility
High pastures, 65

Hitchcock, John T., 1, 20-21, 25; on land acquisition, 172, 176; on Magar households, 129; on stratification, 199-200
Hodgson, Brian, 29, 193
Höfer, András, 32, 39, 159
Hoffpauir, Robert, 199
Holmberg, David, 31
House: construction costs: 73; value in Timling, 72-73
Household: as a unit of analysis, 23, 62, 129; deaths in, 146-47; decline, 181-82; definitions, 130; importance of, 144-45, 190-91; internal hierarchy in, 189-90; labor, 166-67; production and consumption, 131; variation, 131-32
Household capital, 69-73; clothing, 71-73; land, 67-69; livestock, 70
Household developmental cycle, 23-24; 132; 147-56; and demography, 24; and economic expansion, 152, 154-56, 184-85; and subsistence, 191-92; model of, 148-54; variations in, 152-54, 157-58
Household economy: diversification in, 154
Household fission. *See* Inheritance
Household formation systems, 199
Household production: variations in, 157-58
Household size, 65, 170-72
Household status: determinants of, 192
Household time, 169
Household work, 77-78
Howell, Nancy, 16, 86, 111-12, 115
Hull, Terence H., 56
Hull, Valerie C., 56
Hunt, Diana, 170

Illegitimacy, 144
Infant mortality: Nepal, 117; Timling, 117-19
Infertile women, 56
Informants, principle, 59. *See also* Data collection
Inheritance, 137-43; age at, 139, 141-43; and siblings, 141; case history, 139-41; consequences of, 143, 185
Investment, 159

Jajmani relations, 168

Kami, 32, 168
Kham Magar, 114. *See also* Molnar, Augusta
Kinship: domestic mode of production and, 168; network expansion, 170; terminology, 39-41
Kulgi lha, 39-41, 131
Kunstadter, Peter, 188
Kyerong, 61, 186

Labor: household, 77-78, 82, 131-32; intensity, 173
Lactational infecundability: index of, 109
Land: acquisition, 172, 174-76; and social equality, 25, 158; expansion and contraction of holdings, 173; per household, 68; value of, 159
Lapdung, 35
Lauro, Donald, 59, 86
Lee, Richard B., 8
Lepcha. *See* Gorer, Geoffrey
Leridon, Henri, 21, 85, 99
Lho calendrical system, 53
Life history matrix, 59
Life table: basis for, 111-12; model comparisons with Timling, 123-28; varieties of, 112, 123
Lifecourse: birth and childhood, 132-34; death, 145-47; having children, 143-4; inheritance, 139-43; marriage, 134-39
Lifecycle and household, 147
Lineage expansion: case history of, 174-
Lingjyo, 37
Livestock, 70; herds, 82; kinds of, 70-71; l requirements, 82; value of, 71, 159
Lorenz curve, 159-60
Lorimer, Frank, 15
Lotka, Alfred, 111

Macfarlane, Alan, 21; on class, 199; on demographic anthropology, 8; on Guru household, 129; on land acquisition, 17 on peasantry, 22-23. *See also* Gurung; Thak
McGuire, Randall, 21
McNicoll, Geoffrey, 10, 14, 197
Magar: family life, 129; land acquisition among, 176; stratification, 199-200. *See also* Hitchcock, John T.: on Magar households
Maize, 79
Malnutrition: absence of, 69
Mamba (clan), 37, 41
Mamdani, Mahmood, 9, 16
Mani, 31, 44
March, Kathryn, 31
Marital dissolution, 137-39
Marriage: age at, 137-39, 199; and household fission, 139-41; arranged, 135; daughter's participation in, 135-37; effects on fertility, 101-3; property transfers at, 135; strategies of, 135-36, 137, 176-77
Marriage and fertility histories, 56-57
Mayr, Ernst, 17-18
Menstruation, 134
Mepa (clan), 37, 41
Messerschmidt, Donald A., 21

Index

Micro-demography, 53–55. *See also* Data collection; Demographic anthropology
Millet, 79
Miscarriage, 132–33
Mode of production: transition in, 12
Molnar, Augusta, 114, 119
Monsoon, 63
Mortality: age specific, 117; infant, 115–19; Nepal, 113; sex differentials, 119
Mountain ecology, 20–21, 62
Murmi. *See* Tamang

Nag, Moni, 16
Nardi, Bonnie Ann, 21
Natural fertility, 21, 85, 193
Natural increase: intrinsic rate of, 123, 128, 193
Natural vegetation, 64
Neighborhoods in Timling, 37–38, 174–77, 189
Nepal: crisis in, 188; fertility, 89; marriage age, 137; mortality, 117
Netting, Robert McC., 21, 130
Nisbet, Robert A., 18
Nuclear family, 152

Organization: levels of, 195–96
Orlove, Benjamin, 19, 23

Pang Sang La, 35
Parity: of women of completed fertility, 86
Partible inheritance, 173
Pastoral economy, 70–71
Pastoral work: labor requirements, 82; prestige of, 78
Pastures: forest zone, 66; high pasture acreage, 65; summer, 65–66; temperatures in, 63–64
Paternity: disputed, 145; social significance of, 143–45
Peasantry: characteristics of, 22–23, 196–97
Pewa, 135
Phyang, 37
Polygyny, 135
Population: adaptive processes and, 24–25; as a dependent variable, 21–22; as a determining variable, 24–25; density, 65
Population anthropology. *See* Demographic anthropology
Population growth, 8, 25, 128, 188, 193
Population studies, 9–10, 197–99; anthropological contributions, 8–9, 15–17; community level, 11, 85; historical treatments, 8. *See also* Demographic anthropology
Portering, 83
Potatoes, 79, 194
Pradhan panch, 44
Pregnancy: premarital, 143–44

Premarital sex: attitudes toward, 56, 102
Pre-transition society, 11–12, 110, 198
Production, 69; household developmental cycle and, 154
Productive resources and social equality, 24–25, 197–98, 199–200
Property transmission, 131. *See also* Inheritance
Proportion married: index of, 101–2, 103
Provisioning society, 20, 197
Proximate determinants of fertility, 101. *See also* Bongaarts, John

Rappaport, Roy, 8, 17
Rationality: defined, 19–20
Reproductive physiology: components of, 21
Reproductive span, 89–93; 97–101
Resource crisis, 188
Resource frontiers, 25, 194
Resources: forest, 66; land, 65, 67–68; natural, 64–69; relative wealth in, 46
Richerson, Peter J., 18
Ritual calendar, 76–77
Rituals: death, 145–46
Ross, James L. *See* Dhingaba

Sahlins, Marshall, 131, 165, 174, 193
Salt trade, 61, 186
Scott, James C., 22
Sertang, 32, 46–48
Sex: premarital, 56–57, 102, 143–44
Sex preference and mortality, 117–19
Shanin, Teodor, 22
Social change: and primary causes, 18–19; in Timling, 192–95; teleological fallacy, 18
Spouse: death of, 147
Stable population models, 111–12
Stem family, 152
Steward, Julian, 16, 20
Stratification, 24–25, 162–65, 198–200
Strickon, Arnold, 18
Subsistence economy, 189–90
Surplus, 158
Survivorship: female, 123; male, 119, 123, 128

Tamang: agriculture, 300; clans (*rui*), 31; conceptions of full life, 132; history, 29–30; household, 130; in Ankhu Khola region, 32; relations with neighboring groups, 30–32; religion, 30–31; variations among, 30–31
Thadani, Veena, 13
Thak: infant mortality, 117; jewelry, 69; land, 68; livestock, 70–71; wealth distribution, 162–65; wood consumption, 66–67. *See also* Gurung; Macfarlane, Alan
Thouret, J.C., 63

Timling: administration in, 44–48; and theory, 20–23, 187–88, 195–99; daughter settlements, 35–37; external relations, 46–48, 189–90; health conditions, 113–14; house design, 38–39; its future, 199–200; population, 24–25, 48–51; religious life, 42–44; setting, 32–37, 64; tradition of settlement, 41–42
Total fertility: marital, 105–9; women of completed fertility, 93
Transitions, individual, 132
Trisuli Bazaar, 61

Uchucmarca, 69

Value of children: East-West Population Institute, 14–15; economic diversification, 24; insurance 13, 198–99
Vertical zones, 62–64
Village lands: administration of, 46–48
Village selection criteria, 55

Wealth: concentration of, 159–62; intergenerational transfers, 177–80; variation in, 158–59
Wealth flows: household, 166–67; in John Caldwell's theory, 11–12
Weinberg, Daniela, 21
Weiss, Kenneth, 16, 112
Wheat, 69
White, Benjamin, 16
Widowhood, 147; effects on fertility, 103
Wiegandt, Ellen, 21
Wife-givers and wife-receivers, 135–36
Wilk, Richard, 130
Women: high status of, 31, 119
Wood, James W., 86
Wood production and consumption, 66, 77
Work: agricultural, 78–80; household, 76–78, organization of, 74–77, 165–69; pastoral, 80–82; types of, 73–74; value of, 167–68; wages, 83

Yambu, 30
Yanagisako, Sylvia Junko, 23, 130
Yon, Bernard, 64